# FINDERS Keepers

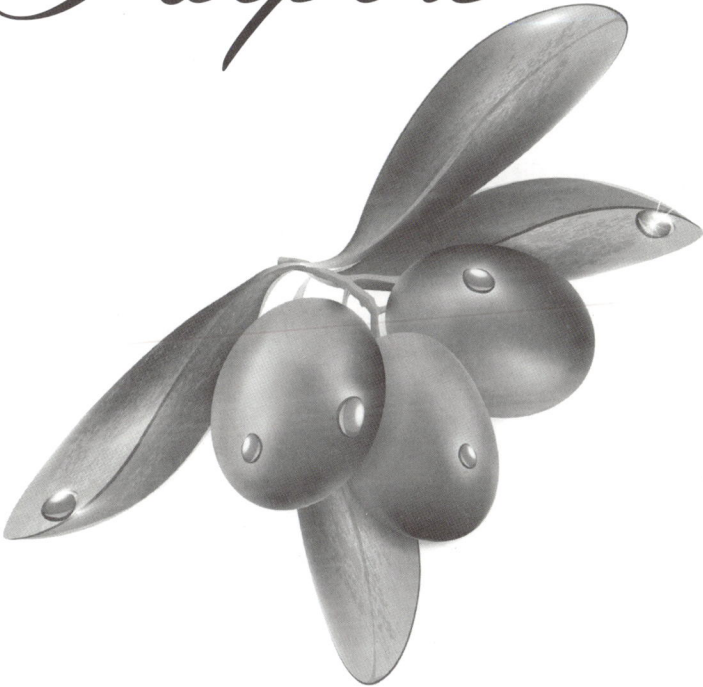

FOUND AND FUN RECIPES FROM A FABULOUSLY FULL LIFE

## JO DUNBAR SNOW

*FINDERS*
*Keepers*

Page Six
Thursday August 1, 1963

JO REID

"KOZY KITCHEN"

by

JO REID

Production by

b o o k s  *à la carte*
p u b l i s h i n g   r e s o u r c e s

www.booksalacarte.com

Printed in South Korea

ISBN: 978-0-692-00833-1

# FINDERS Keepers

## FOUND AND FUN RECIPES FROM A FABULOUSLY FULL LIFE

This line says it all—wonderful loves, wonderful family, wonderful friends and the wonder of being alive and happy. It has been six years since *Keepers* was published, three years since *Even More Keepers* arrived and now we have *Finders Keepers*. Life continues to be exciting—there are many delightful days of entertaining, being entertained, developing new recipes, exchanging recipes, dissecting recipes, discussing recipes ad infinitum! Included here are recipes from my children, friends and several recipes that follow me wherever I go! Some are long-time favorites that have been tweaked one day and then tweaked differently another day. I cannot portray perfection but my heart and tummy have awarded them a place herewith!

Interspersed in this collection are a few inserts of my newspaper columns that go back to 1963—fifty years ago! There was no such thing as the Food Network in those days and the only food magazine was *Gourmet*. Alas! So much has changed over the years. I now hide in shame when I read how easily I used some of those "now-out-of-favor" ingredients, but that was then and this is now! Many of the "oldies" continue to be favorites these many years later.

The newspaper columns came about when I was contacted by a gentleman who was starting a local newspaper and asked if I would like to write a food column. He had heard about my love of entertaining and cooking. Coincidentally I had been a writer for the US. Forest Service so it all seemed a natural. The column was a success and soon after I was contacted by several newspaper editors in the Wine Country who were interested in the column and the rest is history. I have been told I was ahead of the times—I was in my early 30s and thought it was a lark.

And these many years later, it IS a lark!

# Jo Reid joins Times staff

Jo Reid, Fairfax housewife, is the Times' answer to "What's cooking?"

Jo will conduct the Kozy Kitchen column which starts in this issue. All her recipes are her own, tested in her own kitchen. Her ambition is to get away from the "hamburger and yam" dishes on one hand, and the exotic ones on the other.

She was in Sebastopol last week, making arrangements for the weekly column. She was born and educated in San Francisco. She and her husband, John, a food broker representative, have two daughters, 14 and 3. Jo has been writing short stories since she was in school. Along the way she got interested in cookery, and has quite a reputation among friends for her cooking and hostessing.

Constant requests for recipes and menus led to her writing this column on cookery. Questions from readers for Jo's attention should be addressed in care of the Sebastopol Times. Too, arrangements may be made at a later date for her to appear at a limited number of women's club meetings in the area.

Mrs. Reid's enthusiasm and zest for living is reflected in her recipes. That's one reason why our women readers will find this column refreshing, and never dull.

4

FINDERS
*Keepers*

# TABLE OF CONTENTS

# Thank you, Loved Ones...

I am thrilled to acknowledge friends and family who
contributed recipes and love to *Finders Keepers*...

Irene Angelo
Carole Beebe
Fran Billington
Gloria Coates
Sue Coleman
Amy Cubre
Lauren Cubre
Bill Dunbar
Nancy Dunbar
Janice Emerzian
Marilyn Franzia
Candy Heer
Patti Houlihan
Martha Jones
Dennis Lanigan
Libbie Lanigan
Jean Lowell
Vita McSherry
Melinda Mendelson
Cindy Murray
Julia Nelson
Joann Nunes
John Pearson
Kathy Pearson
Carole Phillips
Shellie Phippin
Claudia Platt
Marilyn Porges
Judi Rackley
Elvera Rollins
Renee Rollins
Chris Reed
Nanci Reid
Barbara West
Jennie Zeff

# The Famous Dunbar Margarita

*Happy Days in Tahoe!*

### LIMEAIDE

**Fresh limes**

**Water**

Half and juice as many limes as needed. Add an equal amount of water to lime juice.

### THE MARGARITA

**1 part limeade**

**1 part Silver or Reposado tequila**

**½ part Cointreau, Grand Marnier or Citronage (Petron)**

**Ice, as needed to chill mixture**

Shake, pour and enjoy!

# Negroni

*So Italian. So right.*

**1 ounce Compari**

**1 ounce sweet vermouth**

**1 ounce dry gin**

Put ice in a cocktail shaker and add ingredients. Stir with ice and strain over fresh ice or serve "up" in a cocktail glass. Garnish with an orange twist.

*Another option is to serve this in a tall glass with a generous splash of seltzer water.*

# Orange Julia

SERVES 4

*The secret is out of the bag!*

1 (6-ounce) can frozen orange juice concentrate, thawed

1 cup water

1 cup whole milk

1 teaspoon vanilla

¼ cup confectioner's sugar

¼ cup granulated sugar

Place all ingredients in blender and blend until smooth and frothy.

# Sangria Blanca

*Make everyone happy with Joann's creation!*

**SANGRIA**

1 bottle chilled dry white wine

½ cup Cointreau

¼ cup sugar

Ice cubes

1 (10-ounce) bottle club soda

**GARNISHES**

1 unpeeled orange, sliced

1 unpeeled lemon, sliced

2 limes cut in wedges

4 fresh pineapple sticks

1 unpeeled green apple cut in wedges

Small bunches of green grapes

Combine wine, Cointreau and sugar in a large clear-glass pitcher. When ready to serve, stir in ice cubes and club soda. Garnish pitcher with fruit.

*Great at lunch served with a yummy quiche.*

# Libation Creations

*A holiday celebration starts out on the right note when Nancy's specialties are poured!*

## PUMPKIN FRENCH 75

(Fun at Halloween!)    Serves 4

**Gin Mixture:**

**1 ounce gin**

**1 ounce pumpkin butter**

**1 ½ ounces lemon juice**

**1 ½ ounces simple syrup**

**Champagne**

**2 tablespoons sugar**

**¼ teaspoon ground cinnamon**

**⅛ teaspoon nutmeg**

Combine gin, pumpkin butter, lemon juice and simple syrup. On a small plate, combine sugar, cinnamon and nutmeg. Rim champagne glasses with sugar mixture. Fill glass partially with Gin Mixture and top with champagne.

## CRANBERRY DAIQUIRI

(Great at Thanksgiving or Christmas)    Serves 4

Dissolve ½ cup sugar in ½ cup water with 1 cinnamon stick. Bring to a boil and mix in ½ cup fresh cranberries. Cook until berries pop. Add ½ cup light rum and chill.

Strain into a pitcher, reserving cranberries. Add 6 tablespoons each of dark rum, light rum, cranberry juice and lemon juice. Chill again before serving over ice with the reserved cranberries.

## ORANGE SATIN COSMO

Makes a pitcher

**8 cups vodka**

**2 ½ cups mango juice**

**2 ½ cups Cointreau**

**1 ¼ cups fresh lime juice**

**7 tablespoons superfine sugar**

Shake all ingredients with ice. Pour and serve with a black licorice straw.

## SPIKED WATERMELON

(Perfect for 4th of July or any summer party)

Combine 1 cup fresh lemon juice, ⅔ cup sugar, ½ cup vodka, 6 tablespoons crème de cassis and ¼ cup chopped fresh mint. Pour over 1-inch cubes of watermelon. Chill.

## WHISKEY SOUR

(Grandma's standard Christmas drink)     Serves 4

¾ **cup bourbon**

½ **cup fresh lemon juice**

½ **cup fresh lime juice**

⅔ **cup simple syrup**

Mix all ingredients and serve over ice, garnished with a stemmed maraschino cherry.

## KITCHEN KAPERS

### Kitchen-Tested Recipes from the Kitchen of JO REID

Every egg has been hidden with care, the baskets filled, egg coloring hopefully removed from the living room rug, the carrot sticks set out for Mr. Easter Bunny, and long past midnight, mother finally sets her head down to rest.

But dawn breaks through only too soon, and the little images are up and about with the steely-eyed gleam of Great White Hunters! EVERY egg is unearthed. Can they have multiplied through the night? But just about then, dad hands mother a Golden Glory and makes it all worthwhile!

1 can undiluted frozen orange juice (any size can be used, depending upon the quantity desired) Pour into electric blender. Fill empty can with gin or vodka

### GOLDEN GLORY

Empty into blender
Fill can with ½ & ½ cream.
Empty into blender
Add ½ cup crushed ice
Whirl in blender 30 seconds
Serve in champagne glasses.
This is smooth!

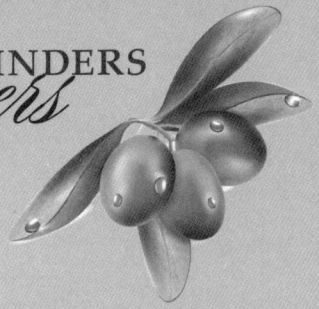

# Brie with Pesto

*One of the easiest crowd-pleasers.*

1 (2-pound) Brie round
1 cup basil pesto

Preheat oven to 350 degrees.

Cut shallow circle in the center of Brie, leaving a 1-inch edge. Cut just deep enough to hold pesto. Place Brie on a foil-lined baking sheet.

Bake 5 to 7 minutes or until Brie becomes soft and a bit "runny". Serve with toasted baguette rounds or crackers.

# Wasabi Shrimp on Cucumbers

*A delicious wallop!*

1-2 English cucumbers
1 (8-ounce) package cream cheese, softened
4 teaspoons wasabi paste
30 medium prawns, cooked
1 scallion, thinly sliced

Cut cucumbers into 30 thin slices.

Puree cream cheese with wasabi. Mound 1 teaspoon onto each cucumber slice. Top with one prawn and sprinkle with scallion.

*Be sure cucumber slices have enough "bulk" to hold the toppings. You don't want them paper thin.*

# Melted Rosemary Brie on Apples

*This is such an easy treat—and it sinless!*

1 large Granny Smith apple

1 large red apple

1 (10-ounce) round of Brie, trimmed and thinly sliced

Chopped fresh rosemary

Pepper

Core apples and cut into ½-inch wedges and arrange on a baking sheet. Top each with a slice of Brie. Sprinkle with rosemary and pepper.

Preheat broiler. Broil apple wedges, uncovered, until cheese melts. Move sheet for even cooking, about 1 minute. Serve hot.

*Alternate colors of apple on an oblong platter (about 14x4-inches). Proceed with the recipe. Platter should be safe since cooking time is short.*

*Also, this dish may be made an hour ahead of baking time. Simply prep it and cover with plastic wrap, letting it stand at room temperature. Preheat the broiler, uncover and bake as directed.*

# Shrimp Butter

*Nanci reminds us the magic of this recipe is to use it only on Ritz crackers, to leave the baby shrimp whole and to serve it with a glass of chilled Pinot Grigio.*

1 (8-ounce) package cream cheese at room temperature

6 tablespoons mayonnaise

1 tablespoon lemon juice

8 ounces baby shrimp

1 stick butter, softened

½ cup finely chopped parsley

½ cup finely minced green onion

Combine all ingredients; mix well and chill. Bring to room temperature at least 30 minutes before serving.

# Chicken Liver Pâté

*An updated version—fantastic depth of flavor.*

1 pound chicken livers

2 tablespoons unsalted butter

¼ cup extra virgin olive oil, divided

1 white onion, finely chopped

2 sage sprigs

1 rosemary sprig

1 anchovy fillet, minced

1 tablespoon capers, drained

Salt and pepper

¼ cup cognac or brandy

1 large baguette, thinly sliced

Trim chicken livers of any sinews and veins. Set on paper towels to dry for 20 minutes.

Preheat oven to 350 degrees.

In a large skillet, melt butter in 1 tablespoon olive oil. Add onion, sage and rosemary and cook over moderately high heat until onion is softened—about 5 minutes. Stir in anchovy and capers and cook over low heat until onion is lightly browned. Scrape mixture into a medium bowl.

Add remaining 3 tablespoons of olive oil to the skillet. Season chicken livers with salt and pepper. Cook over high heat until browned, about 2 minutes. Toss and cook for 1 minute longer; stir in onion mixture. Add the cognac and carefully ignite with a long match. Cook livers until flames subside.

Discard herb sprigs and place the mixture in a food processor. Let cool slightly, and then pulse until chunky. Adjust seasonings as needed.

Pate mixture may be left somewhat chunky or processed until silky, depending on taste. Spoon pate into ramekins and top with a thin layer of rendered chicken fat.

Serve with baguette slices.

# Curried Crab Dip

*Serve sweet potato chips alongside this deeply flavored and colorful dip.*

2 tablespoons butter

2 scallions, finely chopped

2 tablespoons minced fresh ginger

2 teaspoons Madras curry powder

3 tablespoons mango chutney, chopped

1 (8-ounce) package cream cheese at room temperature

1 cup mayonnaise

2 tablespoons lime juice

1 (16-ounce) can crabmeat

Salt and pepper

Blend all ingredients except crabmeat, salt and pepper. Mix well and gently fold in crabmeat, being careful to not break it up too much. Season to taste with salt and pepper.

# Hummus

*Much better than "store bought".*

1 (15-ounce) can garbanzo beans, rinsed and drained

1 small clove garlic, minced

6 tablespoons olive oil, divided

3 tablespoons lemon juice

½ teaspoon sugar

¼ teaspoon cumin

Salt and pepper

In food processor, puree beans with garlic and 3 tablespoons olive oil. Add remaining olive oil, lemon juice, sugar and cumin. Puree until very smooth—about 1 ½ minutes. Season with salt and pepper.

Chill at least 1 hour before serving.

# Olive Pesto

*Not only a zesty appetizer spread but an easy substitute for basil pesto. Try a spoonful over meat or fish or stir into hot pasta. It is beloved by Italians.*

1 clove garlic, minced

3 tablespoons olive oil, divided

2 cups pitted black and green Italian olives

2 teaspoons lemon zest

1 teaspoon lemon juice

Freshly ground black pepper

2 large red peppers, roasted and coarsely chopped

Heat garlic in 1 tablespoon olive oil for about 30 seconds. Place garlic, olives, lemon zest and juice in a food processor and pulse until mixture forms a coarse paste.

Add remaining 2 tablespoons olive oil, black pepper and red peppers and process until mixture is blended. Transfer to a bowl, cover and refrigerate to allow flavors to meld.

To serve, bring to room temperature and spread on slices of baguettes or rounds of pumpernickel.

# Radish and Anchovy Butter on Sliced Baguette

*We all need a little pizzazz in our lives. Shall we start with a glass of wine and Kathy's knockout hors d'oeuvre?*

1 stick unsalted butter at room temperature

2-3 anchovy fillets, finely chopped

2 tablespoons finely chopped chives

Freshly ground black pepper

1 baguette cut diagonally into ½-inch slices

10 radishes, thinly sliced diagonally

Chopped chives for garnish

Mix butter, anchovy and 2 tablespoons chives in a small bowl. Season with black pepper. Spread over one side of each baguette slice.

Top with radish slices, overlapping slightly to cover bread. Garnish with additional chopped chives

# Kim Chee

*John P. is an aficionado when it comes to Kim Chee. This is an excellent accompaniment to many dishes other than Korean food (a couple of big spoonsful in ramen soup is terrific!). Not for everyone but definitely for those who are willing to venture into the uncommon.*

2-3 heads Napa cabbage

½ cup kosher salt

1 cup sliced daikon or radishes

2 bunches scallions, thinly sliced

½ cup minced garlic (about 40 cloves)

4 tablespoons minced fresh ginger

3 teaspoons fermented shrimp, finely chopped

2 small fresh hot peppers, finely chopped

1 cup Korean chile powder

½ cup fish sauce

¼ cup low sodium soy sauce

¼ cup sugar

Cut cabbage into quarters and then into 1-inch strips. Place in large bowl, add kosher salt and mix well. Allow to rest 2 to 4 hours. Rinse thoroughly and dry cabbage by pressing it gently in a dish towel. Set aside.

Mix remaining ingredients. Add mixture to the cabbage and blend well. Cover and leave at room temperature for several days, tasting often. When it reaches desired taste, spoon into smaller glass jars, cover and refrigerate.

*This will last indefinitely...unless you eat it all! By the way, the fermented shrimp and Korean chile powder are always available at Asian markets.*

# Endive Caesar Leaves

SERVES 6-8

*You can skip the salad course when serving these as an appetizer!*

White bread, cut into ¼-inch dice

4 tablespoons olive oil, divided

4 anchovy fillets, mashed

2 cloves garlic, mashed

½ cup mayonnaise

Zest of 1 lemon

2 tablespoons lemon juice

½ cup grated Parmesan Reggiano, divided

8 Belgian endive, leaves separated

Preheat oven to 350 degrees. Toss bread cubes with 2 tablespoons oil and spread on a baking sheet. Bake 10 minutes, watching carefully and tossing as needed.

Mash anchovies with garlic. Whisk in mayonnaise, lemon zest and juice and remaining 2 tablespoons olive oil. Stir in half of the Parmesan Reggiano.

Spoon mixture into endive leaves and arrange on a large platter. Top with croutons and remaining cheese immediately before serving.

# Shrimp Puffs

MAKES 20

1 (7.5-ounce) can refrigerated biscuits

1 cup shredded Monterrey Jack cheese

1 scallion, chopped

½ cup mayonnaise

8 ounces baby shrimp, patted dry in paper towels

Preheat oven to 350 degrees. Use cooking spray to coat a muffin tin.

Split each biscuit in half and place each half into muffin cups, pressing into bottom and up the sides.

In medium bowl, mix cheese, scallion, mayonnaise and shrimp. Place 1 tablespoon of mixture into each biscuit-lined cup.

Bake 20 minutes or until puffs are golden and bubbling. Repeat all steps with second batch of puffs.

# Mushroom Turnovers

## MAKES 24

*We ladies from the "olden days" passed this recipe around from household to household. It continues to be a favorite.*

### PASTRY

3 (3-ounce) packages cream cheese

1 stick butter

1 ½ cups all-purpose flour

Bring cream cheese and butter to room temperature. Mix thoroughly. Add flour and work with fingers until smooth. Wrap in plastic wrap and chill at least 30 minutes.

Preheat oven to 450 degrees.

On a floured surface, roll dough to ⅛-inch thickness and cut into 3-inch rounds. Place a teaspoon of Mushroom Filling on each and fold dough over the filling. Press the edges together with a fork. Prick top crust to allow steam to escape. Place on ungreased baking sheet and bake until lightly browned, about 15 minutes.

### MUSHROOM FILLING

3 tablespoons butter

1 large onion, finely chopped

½ pound mushrooms, finely chopped

½ teaspoon thyme

½ teaspoon salt

Freshly ground black pepper to taste

2 tablespoons all-purpose flour

¼ cup cream, sweet or sour

In a skillet over medium heat, melt butter; add onion and brown lightly. Add mushrooms and cook, stirring often, about 3 minutes. Add thyme, salt and pepper. Sprinkle with flour. Mix well and stir in cream; cook gently until thickened.

*This crust works beautifully with any kind of filling...try it with chicken or meat.*

# Smoked Salmon on Cocktail Rye

*A favorite, always!*

1 (8-ounce) tub whipped cream cheese

2 tablespoons prepared horseradish

2 tablespoons capers, drained

24 slices cocktail rye, toasted

8 ounces smoked salmon, chopped

Sprigs of dill weed for garnish

Combine cheese, horseradish and capers in a medium bowl and mix well. Spread cheese mixture on toasted rye slices. Arrange on a serving platter and top each with bits of smoked salmon.

Garnish with sprigs of dill.

# Smoked Salmon with Mascarpone

SERVES 4

*Easy, delicious and oh, so pretty! Can be eaten in one luscious bite!*

16 potato chips

1 (4-ounce) package thinly sliced smoked salmon, cut into 16 pieces

¼ cup mascarpone

Chopped chives

Capers, rinsed and drained

Seek unbroken potato chips from the bag. Arrange them on a long platter.

Top each potato chip with a piece of smoked salmon, a dollop of mascarpone, a sprinkling of chive and a few capers.

*These are addictive, so doubling the recipe is always a good idea. Also, the thicker cut chips work especially well for this.*

# Swiss Chard Frittata

MAKES 20 PIECES

*This is Italian soul food.*

1 pound Swiss chard, cooked, drained and chopped

1 tablespoon olive oil

1 onion, chopped

½ pound mild Italian sausage

8 eggs

¼ cup whipping cream

Salt and pepper

1 cup Parmesan

Chopped Italian parsley for garnish

Preheat oven to 325 degrees. Grease an 8x8x2-inch baking dish with olive oil and set aside.

Sauté onion in oil 4 or 5 minutes. Add sausage and cook until golden and crumbly, stirring often.

In a large bowl, whisk eggs with cream, salt and pepper. Stir in chard, sausage and cheese. Pour mixture into prepared dish.

Bake 40 to 45 minutes. Remove from oven and cool. Cut into small pieces to serve as an appetizer.

# Tahoe Pizza

*This is a hit! It was thrown together last minute but now it is painstakingly made since it is our favorite pizza, bar none. The trick is using the Ciabatta bread.*

2 Ciabatta loaves split in half

Olive oil

1 (16-ounce) jar marinara sauce with basil

1 small can petite-diced tomatoes with jalapeno, drained

4 green onions thinly sliced

2 cans anchovies, drained and chopped

Pinch of crushed red pepper

Oregano

Grated Fontina cheese

Preheat oven to 350 degrees.

Drizzle olive oil on Ciabatta halves. Combine marinara sauce, diced tomatoes, green onion and anchovies. Spread mixture on bread halves and sprinkle with generous amount of oregano and top with cheese. Drizzle with additional olive oil.

Bake 30 minutes and allow to rest for 10 minutes. Cut as desired into hearty slices.

*If you are unable to find the petite tomatoes with jalapeno, simply add a small amount of canned jalapeno to a can of plain tomatoes.*

# KITCHEN KAPERS

Kitchen-tested recipes from the kitchen of
**JO REID**

Do you buy fresh mushrooms often? Or better still, go mushroom-hunting in the meadows? The first thing one must know, of course, is how to differentiate the common edible meadow mushroom from the highly poisonous toadstools. Whatever way you come by "champignons" is a good way for there is something special about nature's little umbrella that changes an ordinary meal into a gourmet's delight.

## APPETIZER MUSHROOMS

12 large fresh mushrooms
½ cup drained canned crab
    meat
1 tablespoon butter
¼ cup finely chopped celery
2 tablespoons mayonnaise

1 teaspoon lemon juice
Dash of salt
2 tablespoons fine dry bread
    crumbs
1 teaspoon melted butter

Wash mushrooms and trim off tips of stems. Remove caps. (If the mushrooms are extra large, pour boiling water over caps and let stand 1 minute. Drain.) Chop stems very fine, and cook in 1 tablespoon butter till tender but not brown. Add crab, celery, mayonnaise, lemon juice and salt. Stuff caps with this mixture. Mix bread crumbs with 1 teaspoon melted butter and sprinkle over tops. Broil 10 minutes, watching carefully. Offer forks and plates for this appetizer.

## MUSHROOMS WITH ONIONS

2 medium-size yellow onions,
    sliced and separated into
    rings

3 tablespoons butter
½ lb. fresh mushrooms,
    cleaned and sliced

Saute onion rings in butter until golden. Add mushrooms and saute 5 minutes. Spoon over sliced roast beef on serving plate for a garnish. Canned mushrooms may be substituted.

## MUSHROOMS ON TOAST

1 pound mushrooms
3 tablespoons olive oil
1 clove garlic
3 green onions
1 tablespoon olive oil
1 tablespoon flour

1 cup dry white wine
1 tablespoon chopped parsley
½ teaspoon thyme
Salt and pepper to taste
Buttered toast

Wash mushrooms and cut off the stems close to the caps. In a skillet saute the caps in olive oil. Remove caps and keep warm. To juice in skillet add finely chopped mushroom stems, garlic, onions, and additional tablespoon of olive oil. Saute 3 or 4 minutes. Stir in flour, gradually add wine and cook until the sauce is thickened. Add herbs and seasonings and cook, stirring occasionally for 10 minutes.

Reheat the mushroom caps in this sauce and serve on hot buttered toast. So good!

Have a nice day!

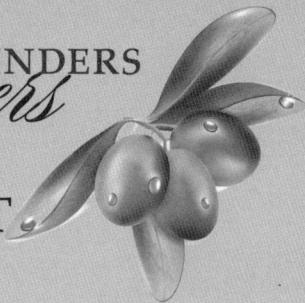

# Nanci's Famous Muffins

*This is a gift! Although the ingredients do not seem unusual, the result is outstanding. Nanci tells us the recipe began as a basic coffee cake recipe which she found in the 1960s. She has embellished it over the years and now—the perfect muffin!*

## MUFFINS

2 ½ cups sifted all-purpose flour

1 cup brown sugar, packed

¾ cup granulated sugar

1 teaspoon salt

1 teaspoon cinnamon

¼ teaspoon allspice

¼ teaspoon ginger

¼ teaspoon ground cloves

¾ cup canola oil

1 unbeaten egg

1 cup buttermilk

1 scant teaspoon baking soda

1 teaspoon baking powder

½ cup chopped almonds

## TOPPING

1 cup confectioner's sugar

¼ teaspoon almond extract

Water, as needed to blend

Preheat oven to 350 degrees. Grease muffin tins and set aside.

Combine flour, brown sugar, granulated sugar, salt and spices. Add canola oil and mix together until crumbly. Remove 1 cup of mixture and set aside.

To the remaining dry ingredients, add egg, buttermilk, baking soda and baking powder. Beat until smooth. Pour into prepared muffin tins. Top each muffin with reserved mixture and sprinkle with chopped almonds.

Bake 25 to 30 minutes or until middle is firm. While muffins bake, mix confectioner's sugar and almond extract; stir in enough water to make a thin glaze.

After muffins have cooled about 2 minutes, drizzle tops with glaze and serve warm.

## OF INTEREST TO WOMEN

### SOUR-CREAM OMELET

5 eggs
1 cup commercial sour cream
1 teasp. salt
2 tablesp. butter or margarine
Strawberry preserves or cranberry jelly

Start oven at moderate 325 degrees.

Beat egg yolks until thick and lemon-colored. Beat ½ cup sour cream into yolks with salt. Beat egg whites stiff. Fold yolks into whites. Heat butter or margarine in 10-inch skillet. Pour in omelet mixture, leveling gently. Cook over low heat about 5 minutes, until fluffy and lightly browned on bottom. Set pan in oven about 12 to 15 minutes or until top is golden. Loosen and slide onto warmed plate. Cut in wedges quickly with 2 forks. Serve at once with dab of remaining sour cream and either strawberries or cranberry jelly. Makes 3 or 4 servings.

### KOZY KITCHEN
#### KITCHEN-TESTED RECIPES
#### x   JO REID   x

What's for breakfast, Mom? Serving some of the old standbys in a different way can make this the most interesting meal of the day, and certainly, the most beneficial.

When reading through the following recipe for buttermilk pancakes, do not immediately plan to cut the recipe in half since it uses a quart of buttermilk. They are so light and delicious you will find everyone having three times as many as usual.

They are not eaten -- they are simply inhaled.

#### BUTTERMILK PANCAKES

1 quart buttermilk
2 cups flour
1 tesp. baking powder
1 tsp. baking soda
Pinch of salt
½ teasp. vanilla
4 eggs

Put quart of buttermilk in bowl. Separate eggs. Beat yolks until light and creamy. Beat egg whites until stiff. Sift dry ingredients. Add beaten egg yolks to buttermilk in bowl. Add dry ingredients. Fold in egg whites, add vanilla.

Isn't the word "brunch" a cheery word? It sounds relaxed and carefree with time to prepare and eat a good breakfast-lunch on the weekend. A sour cream omelet with plenty of hot rolls and coffee is a meal fit for a king.

On another day try this French Toast with a juicy grilled ham steak.

#### RAISIN CUSTARD FRENCH TOAST

2 eggs, separated
½ tsp. salt
1 tablesp. sugar
2 tsp. Sherry or 1 tsp. vanilla
¼ cup light or heavy cream
6 slices raisin bread
Butter or margarine

Beat egg yolks well with salt, sugar and sherry. Stir in cream. Beat egg whites until stiff but not dry. Gently fold into first mixture. Turn into shallow pan or dish; quickly dip raisin bread slices on both sides in fluffy custard batter. Saute in a little butter over moderate heat until golden brown on both sides, turning just once.

Serve immediately on heated plates with a sprinkling of powdered sugar and desired toppings. Makes 6 servings.

Impress the family with whipped butter. Just put a cube or more in the electric mixer and whip until light and fluffy (7-10 minutes).

Try heating maple syrup before serving.

See you next week!

# The Supreme Carrot Muffin

MAKES 16-20

*One of these with a cup of coffee in the morning is the perfect start to the day!*

2 ½ cups sugar

4 cups all-purpose flour

4 teaspoons cinnamon

4 teaspoons baking soda

1 teaspoon salt

1 cup raisins, plumped in brandy and drained

1 cup shredded coconut

4 cups shredded carrot

2 apples, peeled and shredded

1 cup chopped walnuts

6 eggs, lightly beaten

2 cups canola oil

1 teaspoon vanilla

Preheat oven to 375 degrees. Grease muffin tins and set aside.

Sift dry ingredients into a large bowl. Lightly dust raisins with flour. Add coconut, carrot, apples and walnuts. Stir well. Add eggs, oil and vanilla, stirring just until combined.

Spoon batter into prepared tins and bake for 20 minutes.

Store cooled muffins in a covered container and "ripen" for 24 hours to maximize flavor.

# Oven French Toast

Serves 4-6

*Heaven on Sunday! Freshly brewed coffee, fresh fruit, sautéed sausages—Yum!*

1 loaf French bread

1 stick butter, softened

4 eggs

½ cup maple syrup

¼ cup sugar

3 cups milk

Confectioner's sugar

Let bread sit on counter overnight, allowing it to dry slightly.

When ready to prepare, preheat oven to 350 degrees.

Slice bread into thick slices and spread butter on both sides. Place in a 9x13-inch glass baking dish and set aside.

In a large mixing bowl, beat eggs. Add maple syrup, sugar and milk and blend well. Pour mixture over bread, turning the slices to moisten. Bake approximately 35 to 40 minutes. The top should be slightly golden and the edges crispy.

Sprinkle lightly with confectioner's sugar before serving.

# Blueberry Pancakes

*Another beautiful weekend breakfast!*

**2 cups all-purpose flour**

**1 ¼ teaspoons sugar**

**½ teaspoon salt**

**1 cup plain yogurt**

**2 tablespoons baking soda**

**¼ cup club soda**

**2 eggs, lightly beaten**

**Butter**

**Blueberries**

**Confectioner's sugar**

**Maple syrup**

Combine flour, sugar and salt and set aside. In a separate bowl, combine yogurt with baking soda and let sit 10 minutes.

Add yogurt to flour mixture; stir in club soda and eggs, whisking gently. Let batter rest 10 minutes.

In a large electric skillet or griddle, heat butter, 1 tablespoon at a time. Dip pancake mixture using a ¼-cup measure or scoop. Gently spread batter with the back of a spoon. Cook about 2 minutes. Sprinkle with blueberries, turn and finish cooking.

To serve, dust lightly with confectioner's sugar and offer butter and syrup.

## KITCHEN KAPERS

Kitchen-Tested Recipes by JO REID

At last! A cold breakfast cereal so pure and chuck full vitamins it's guaranteed to bring roses to your cheeks after the first mouthful!

It's delicious with fruit and milk or cream and is also a wonderful snack, just by the handful. You will be doing the best for your family with this one and even though the recipe seems large and you may want to half it the first time you won't the second.

### POWERHOUSE CEREAL

14 cups rolled oats (not Quick)
2 teaspoons salt
2 cups wheat germ
1 cup brown sugar
2 cups coconut
3 tsp. vanilla

1 cup corn oil (do not use soya or safflower which has a tendency to become rancid when heated as this recipe requires)
1 cup water

Mix dry ingredients together. Add last 3 ingredients and mix thoroughly. Place in large ungreased pans and bake in slow 225 degree oven, stirring occasionally until dry and golden brown. Makes 1 gallon.

Speaking of cereals, there are many, many recipes for Cereal Appetizer Snacks but this combination of cereal, nuts and spices seems to bring extra raves.

### SCRAMBLE

3 tablespoons butter
4 tsp. Worcestershire sauce
½ teaspoon garlic salt
½ tsp. onion salt

2 cups wheat Chex
2 cups rice Chex
2 cups corn Chex
2 cups mixed nuts (no peanuts)

Melt butter, add worcestershire sauce, garlic and onion salts and place in large roasterpan. Add cereal and nuts and coat well with butter mixture. Cook slowly, mixing every 15 minutes in 250 degree oven for 1 hour and 15 minutes.

(Thank you each and everyone for the wonderful response to this column.—jr.)

Jo Reid, Food Editor
St. Helena Star
St. Helena, Californi

Dear Miss Reid,

Every time we sit down to a breakfast of Powerhouse Cereal I remember that I want to thank you for the recipe. Ever since I saw it in the Shopper last summer, I've been making it by the gallon at least every two weeks. I've tried a few substitutions, but it's best just as it is.

# Wonderful Waffles

*Such a treat!*

1 ½ cups all-purpose flour
½ cup cornstarch
¾ teaspoon baking soda
2 ½ teaspoons baking powder
½ teaspoon salt
1 tablespoon sugar
4 eggs, separated
1 cup sour cream
1 ½ cups milk
1 ½ sticks butter, melted
Sugar, for beating egg whites

Combine all dry ingredients. Beat egg yolks with sour cream, milk and melted butter.

In a separate bowl, beat egg whites until stiff, adding sugar as needed for volume. Gently fold egg whites into first mixture.

Follow waffle iron instructions and proceed to happiness.

# Blue Cheese and Scallion Bread

*Wonderful!*

4 ounces crumbled blue cheese
6 ounces butter, room temperature
4 scallions, chopped
2 cloves garlic, chopped
1 (1-pound) loaf Ciabatta

Preheat oven to 400 degrees. Cut Ciabatta in half, horizontally.

In food processor, combine all remaining ingredients and pulse until well combined. Spread mixture on the cut sides of the bread.

Place buttered loaves on a baking sheet and bake 10 to 12 minutes. Watch carefully to prevent over-browning.

Cut into 1-inch thick slices and serve immediately.

*Use Cheddar or any other cheese as desired.*

# KITCHEN KAPERS

## Kitchen-Tested Recipes from the Kitchen of
### JO REID

HEADLINE: The kitchen moves into the house! This was a noteworthy news item circa 1850 when great, great grandmother's kitchen was usually in the basement or attached to the main house. Finally, a wise wife or practical husband realized the kitchen shouldn't be hidden but given its rightful place of honour in the home. And in 1964, we can boast outdoor barbecues, hibachis, outdoor kitchens, outdoor electric outlets for plugging in the electric frying pans and percolators. And nothing thrills the kids more than a Sunday morn cookout when Dad fixes sausage, eggs and hotcakes on the outdoor grill.

We've come a long way in the last 100 years!

## BRUNCH BREAD
### (Better than Grandmothers)

1 cup milk
4 cups unsifted flour
1 tsp. salt
¼ cup sugar
1 cup soft butter
¼ cup warm water, not hot

1 pkg active dry yeast
Mixture of ½ cup granulated sugar and 1½ tsp. cinnamon
Melted butter
3 egg yolks, beaten

Measure flour and level off with straight-edged spatula. Scald milk; cool. Stir flour, salt and sugar into large bowl. Cut in butter until mixture looks like meal. Dissolve yeast in warm water and add to flour mixture along with egg yolks and cooled milk; beat well. Chill in refrigerator overnight. This recipe makes 2 loaves. Dough will keep in refrigerator for at least 3 days half could be saved for later use. To make loaves: Grease two 9x5x3 in. loaf pans. Roll ½ dough into a rectangle about 13x8". Brush with melted butter, sprinkle ½ sugar-cinnamon mixture. Roll up as for jelly roll. Place in pan, cover and allow to rise about 2 hours in warm place (85 degrees). Do the same with the remaining dough. Heat oven to 375 degrees. Bake loaves about 1 hour. Check after 40 minutes and if loaf looks sufficiently brown, cover with brown paper during last of baking. Carefully remove from pan while hot and frost with Creamy Glaze. Cool before cutting.

Creamy Glaze: Mix 1½ cups sifted confectioners sugar, 2 tbsp. soft butter, 1½ tsp. vanilla and 1 or 2 tbsp. hot water to make medium thick frosting.

# Gloria's Sourdough Rolls

*We love it when our Book Club (aka Book/Food Club) meets at Gloria's. She serves these warm from the oven… such a treat!*

**1 tablespoon yeast**
**3 tablespoons sugar**
**1 ½ cups warm water**
**1 cup sourdough starter**
**1 tablespoon salt**
**2 tablespoons olive oil**
**3-4 cups bread flour**
**Melted butter**

Lightly oil a cookie sheet or cover it with parchment paper and set aside. In a small bowl combine yeast, sugar and warm water. Allow it to set a few minutes until mixture begins to bubble slightly.

In a large mixing bowl combine starter, salt and oil. Stir in yeast mixture, mixing well. Stir in flour, ½ cup at a time, until dough becomes manageable. Turn out on a floured surface and knead well.

Place dough in a large bowl and cover. Set it in a warm place and let it rise until it doubles in size. Punch dough down with lightly floured hands. Form into rolls.

Place rolls on prepared cookie sheet and allow to rise once more until doubled. Preheat oven to 375 degrees and bake rolls for 15 to 20 minutes. Brush tops with melted butter before serving.

*Sourdough starter packets are readily available at grocery stores and specialty markets.*

## KOZY KITCHEN

**Kitchen-Tested Recipes From The Kitchen Of**

x JO REID x

Let's get down to basics! What could be better than warm, just out-of-the-oven bread and butter? There are many meals that can be changed from "everyday" to "feasts" by just adding a home baked bread. But many times there just isn't time to go through the many steps required. These are quickies and easy to prepare.

How long has it been since you've served Spoon Bread?

Best Spoon Bread
1 cup boiling water
1/2 cup yellow corn meal
1/2 tsp. salt
1/2 tablespoon butter
1 cup milk
2 eggs
Add cornmeal slowly to boiling water stirring constantly. Cook until thick. Remove from fire, add salt and butter. Now add milk and beaten egg yolks. Lastly, fold in beaten egg whites. Place in small greased baking dish. Bake 50 minutes at 375 degrees. Serves 4.

Onion Batter Bread
2 large yellow onions
3 tablespoons butter
2 cups biscuit mix
Milk
1 egg
1/2 pt. sour cream
1/2 tsp. salt

Poppy seeds

Saute sliced onions in butter for 10 minutes or until soft. While onions cook, prepare 2 cups biscuit mix with milk (following directions for drop biscuit). Spread in greased baking pan 9x5x3. Spoon cooked onions over. Beat the egg into the sour cream and add salt. Spread on top of onion mixture. Sprinkle with poppy seeds. Bake at 375 30 minutes or until topping is set.

Mushroom Batter Bread
1 can condensed cream of mushroom soup
2 eggs well beaten
2 tablespoons cooking oil
2 cups Bisquick
1 tsp. minced onion (instant)
1/4 cup butter
1/4 cup shredded Parmesan cheese
Celery or Sesame seed.
Blend soup, egg, oil together. Stir instant onion into biscuit mix, mix in bowl and make well in center of mixture. Add soup, stir until blended. Heat butter in 8" skillet with heat risistent handle. Spoon the batter into the skillet and sprinkle with cheese and celery or sesame seed. Bake 400 degrees about 25 minutes. Serve hot.

Honey Oatmeal Casserole Bread
1 package yeast, compressed or dry
1/4 cup water (lukewarm for compressed yeast, warm for dry)
1 cup hot water
1/2 cup softened butter or margarine
1/4 cup honey
1 teaspoon salt
3-1/4 cups sifted flour
2 eggs
1 cup old-fashioned rolled oats
Melted butter or margarine
Soften yeast in 1/4 cup water. Blend 1 cup hot water, butter, honey and salt in large bowl. Cool to lukewarm. Stir in about 1-1/3 cups flour and beat until smooth and elastic, about 1 minute (the electric mixer can do this). Blend in softened yeast, eggs, and rolled oats. Stir in enough more flour to make a very thick batter and beat until smooth and elastic about 1 minute. Cover and let rise in warm place (80 degrees) until bubbly, about 1 hour. Stir down and turn into well-greased 2 quart round casserole dish. Bake at once in 375 degree oven 55 to 60 minutes or until top is golden brown and bread begins to shrink from sides of dish. Allow to stand 10 minutes in casserole before removing. Brush with

# Chicken Salad Sandwiches

MAKES 3 SANDWICHES

*Our favorite luncheon spot went out of business and along with it went their Chicken Salad Sandwich. How could we live without it? This might be even better!*

2 cups finely diced poached chicken breast

1 medium Gala apple, peeled and finely diced

2 celery sticks, finely diced

½ cup raisins

½ cup walnuts, finely chopped

Mayonnaise

Salt and pepper

6 slices 12-grain or sprouted wheat berry bread

Mango Chutney

Lettuce leaves

Combine chicken, apple, celery, raisins and walnuts. Stir in just enough mayonnaise to bind ingredients and season to taste.

Lightly spread additional mayonnaise onto each slice of bread. Spread small amount of chutney on three of the slices; pile on chicken salad. Top with several lettuce leaves and a second slice of bread.

Cut diagonally to serve.

# Open-Faced Tuna Sandwiches

## SERVES 4

*A grey and wintry day is the perfect time to gather with good friends for a game of Dominos or Bridge. Martha brightened our day when she served these sandwiches accompanied by a creamy tomato bisque.*

2 cans solid white tuna, packed in water

⅓ cup mayonnaise

4 teaspoons capers, rinsed and dried

1 tablespoon fresh lemon juice

Salt and pepper to taste

¼ teaspoon dried oregano, crumbled between fingers

¼ cup finely chopped green onion

4 slices crusty bread, toasted on one side

Additional mayonnaise for assembling sandwiches

8 thin slices tomato

4 slices provolone

Preheat broiler with rack in high position.

Drain tuna and combine with mayonnaise, capers, lemon juice, salt, pepper, oregano and onion.

Arrange toasted side of bread on a baking sheet. Spread each untoasted side with a little mayonnaise. Divide tuna mixture evenly over each slice and top each with two slices of tomato and one slice of provolone.

Broil until golden brown, watching carefully, for 3 to 4 minutes.

```
x x x x x x x x x x x x x x x x x x x x x x x x x x x x x x x x x
x
x    KOZY KITCHEN                              x
x    Kitchen-Tested Recipes From The Kitchen Of   x
x              x   JO  REID   x               x
x                                             x
x x x x x x x x x x x x x x x x x x x x x x x x x x x x x x x x x
```

A whoop and a holler for
Mother today,
As she proudly presents her
first souffle'.
She sets it down on the table
with care,
There's hardly a whisper —
who would dare?
As she gently serves the
golden mass,
What torture to wait
as the dishes are passed.
This one is made with eggs,
bread and cheese,
Seconds anyone? Thonk you,
please!

cheese. Cover with a heavy
plate and keep in refrigerator
overnight.

Just before baking, mix
together 1 egg and 1 cup
milk and pour over the top.
Serve immediately.

Your interest in this column is so gratifying. Many
thanks. See you next week
with a simple way of making
soup!

## TURID'S CHEESE SOUFFLE'
(Bake 1½ hours at 300
degrees. Serves 6)

1 loaf round sour-dough
French bread
1 lb. sharp cheddar cheese
7 eggs
1 quart ½ & ½
1 cup milk
1 tablesp. Worcestershire
sauce
1 tsp. Tabasco
Salt and pepper to taste.

The night before:

Cut the bread in slices ¾
inch thick. Cut off crusts
and cut slices into 3 or 4
pieces and cover the bottom
of a 3-quart souffle' dish
(or large-sized Pyrex casserole). Grate cheese and
make three layers of bread
and cheese. Blend the quart
of ½ & ½, 6 eggs, worcest-
shire, tabasco, salt and pepper, and pour over bread and

# Chiles Relleno Bake

*This is a hit!*

1 (27-ounce) can whole green chiles

1 (16-ounce) bag Colby Jack shredded cheese mixture

6 eggs, beaten

½ cup all-purpose flour

2 cups half-and-half

½ teaspoon salt

Pinch of cayenne

1 (16-ounce) jar mild salsa

Preheat oven to 375 degrees. Grease a 9x13-inch baking dish and set aside.

Rinse and dry chiles; remove all seeds. Place chiles in prepared dish and top with cheese.

In a medium mixing bowl, combine eggs, flour, half-and-half, salt and cayenne. Pour over chiles and cheese. Bake for 30 to 35 minutes or until set. Do not over bake.

Remove dish from oven and spread salsa over top; return to oven for additional 5 minutes.

Remove from oven and allow to rest 20 minutes before serving.

# Southwestern Quiche

½ package refrigerated piecrust dough

¾ cup grated Cheddar cheese

½ cup grated Monterey Jack cheese

3 large eggs, lightly beaten

1 teaspoon salt

¼ teaspoon pepper

1 ½ cups half-and-half

1 (4-oz) can diced green chiles, drained

1 (2 ¼-oz) can sliced ripe olives

2 tablespoons chopped green onion

Preheat oven to 350 degrees.

Unroll piecrust and press into a 9 ½-inch pie plate. Mix cheeses and sprinkle into bottom of crust.

Mix eggs, salt, pepper, cream, chiles, olives and green onion. Pour over cheese-covered pastry. Bake 40 to 45 minutes or until knife inserted in center comes out clean.

# Sausage and Mushroom Quiche

*Joann's specialty—absolutely the best; and the Southwestern Quiche on the previous page is another one of her treasures!*

½ pound mushrooms, sliced

1 tablespoon butter

1 pound bulk sausage

4 eggs, lightly beaten

1 ½ cups half-and-half

¼ teaspoon salt

1 ½ cups grated Cheddar cheese

1 tablespoon all-purpose flour

1 (9-inch) unbaked pastry shell

2 tablespoons finely chopped parsley

Preheat oven to 375 degrees.

Sauté mushrooms in butter until golden. Set aside. Brown sausage and set aside. Combine eggs with half-and-half and salt. In separate bowl, combine cheese and flour.

Into the pie shell, layer sausage, cheese mixture, then mushrooms. Pour egg mixture over all and sprinkle with parsley.

Bake for 35 minutes. Allow to rest briefly and cut into wedges to serve.

## KITCHEN KAPERS

Kitchen-Tested Recipes from the Kitchen of
**JO REID**

A cocktail party—the fourth meal! This is the simplest way to introduce a new neighbor, honor a visiting fireman, or bid adieu to Tom, Dick, or Lou. Lots of ice with spirits, dips and chips, and a few interesting hot hors doevres and we help perpetuate an ole' American custom!

### TOASTED MUSHROOM SANDWICHES:

Everyone loves these hot savory rolled sandwiches.

½ lb. mushrooms, chopped fine
¼ cup butter
3 tablespoons flour
¾ teaspoon salt
1 cup light cream
2 teaspoons minced chives
1 teaspoon lemon juice
25 slices sandwich bread

Clean mushrooms and chop fine. Saute in butter for 5 minutes. Blend in flour, salt, _____. Stir in cream and cook until thickened, stirring constantly. Add chives and lemon juice. Cool. Trim crust from bread and spread with mushroom mixture and roll up each sandwich, jelly-roll fashion. Pack in boxes or pans, cut edge down, cover with aluminum foil and freeze. Before serving, cut each roll in half and place under the broiler. Toast each sandwich on all sides and serve very hot. This makes 50 sandwiches.

### QUICKIE PIZZAS

1 tube refrigerator rolls
Catsup
Stuffed green olives, sliced
Parmesan cheese

Cut each refrigerator roll in half or thirds and place on ungreased cookie sheet. Make an indentation in each roll. Fill with catsup, add a slice of olive and sprinkle with cheese. Bake in 425° oven until golden (5 to 7 minutes).

### REFRIGERATOR CHEESE COOKIES:

It's all done ahead of time.

½ lb. grated sharp cheddar cheese
½ pound butter
½ tsp. salt
2 tsps. chili powder
3 cups flour

Combine cheese and butter. Add salt, chili powder and flour. Work together with your hands until smooth. Form into roll. Wrap in foil. Chill. Slice as you would for icebox cookies. Bake at 350° until lightly browned.

### LIVER PATE RING MOLD:

A delicious, inexpensive pate.

1 lb. chicken livers
1 can consomme
1 can water
2 pkgs. gelatin
2 pkgs. cream cheese
¼ cup sherry
¼ cup brandy
1 tsp. Worcestershire
2 tbs. chopped parsley
Salt and pepper

Boil soup and water with several pieces celery, onion, and parsley. Strain. Add gelatin which has been dissolved in water. Add sherry and brandy. Cover bottom of ring mold with half of this liquid. Cool until fairly well set. Boil livers. Chop very fine or sieve. Add all other ingredients to this. Mix well. Fill ring and chill. Unmold and serve with melba toast.
Cheers!

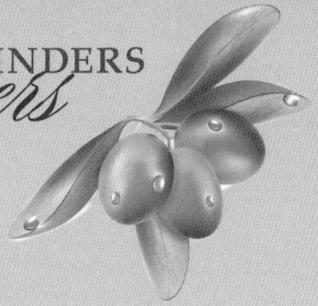

# *Dump Soup*

*Patti suggests burying the cans deep in the recycling bin before your guests arrive!*

1 (14-ounce) can black beans

1 (14-ounce) can white beans

1 (14-ounce) kidney beans

1 (14-ounce) can pinquito beans

2 (16-ounce) jars prepared salsa

½ pound smoked sausage, diced

Handful of fresh cilantro, chopped

### TOPPINGS

Sour cream

Shredded cheese

Tortilla strips

Diced avocado

Chopped onions

Chopped olives

Chopped jalapenos

Dump all beans (do not drain), salsa and sausage in a large soup pot. Bring to a boil, and then simmer for at least 15 to 20 minutes. Add cilantro during the last few minutes of simmering.

Garnish with any or all toppings. There are no official Dump Soup rules.

*The heat factor of the salsa is the cook's choice.*

*Once the mixture has been brought to a boil it can be transferred to a slow cooker. Set on low and enjoy it later. As with most soups, this is even better the second day. And, finally, if pinquito beans are not available in your area you may substitute pinto beans.*

# "KOZY KITCHEN"

## by

## JO REID

Soup! A boiled dinner — what else on a chilly night? There is nothing like it! The soup mother used to make usually necessitated her hovering over the kettle most of the day and putting up with a steamy kitchen and spilled-over range. The modern gal finds it a lot easier to open a can and who is to say she is wrong. There are usually so many other needs that require her time.

But we've come up with an idea that is not only time-saving but does away with the unacceptable aspects of making soup. Make it in the OVEN, and automatically! Of course, if you haven't an automatic timer, it can still be made in the oven. Try it, and we are pretty sure that you won't make your soup any other way in the future!

## SCOTCH BROTH — 1964

Preheat oven 325° with automatic timer.

Set oven temperature to 325° with automatic timer.

6 lamb shanks
¾ cup pearl barley
1 large onion
2 tsp. salt
½ tsp. pepper
2 bay leaves
2 tbsp. finely-chopped parsley
8 carrots, large pieces
4 stalks celery, large pieces
4 quarts water or enough to cover meat

Use large roaster pan with cover. Place meat, onions, salt, pepper, bay leaves, parsley in pan. Cover with water. Put on lid. Place in oven and set timer, for soup to cook 3 hours. An hour before soup is ready, add carrots and celery. Correct seasoning if necessary.

Try this method with any of your favorite soup recipes and for corned beef and cabbage, it is perfect! The usual cabbage aroma that permeates the entire house is eliminated and the flavor seems to be twice as good.

## SPICE CORNED BEEF

Oven temperature 325° 1 hour per pound of meat.

4 pound corned-beef brisket
1 orange, sliced
1 large onion, quartered
2 stalks celery, cut in half
2 cloves garlic, quartered
½ teaspoon dill seed
½ teaspoon rosemary
6 whole cloves
3 inches stick cinnamon
1 bay leaf

Cover corned beef with water, using roasting pan. Add remaining ingredients. Cover and place in oven and cook until tender. One half hour before meat is ready, remove 1 quart of water from the corned beef, place in a saucepan, quarter a large cabbage and cook until just tender. Remove meat from liquid while hot, brush with light corn syrup to glaze. Serve at once or chill. Serves 6. You can even cook this the day ahead — nice for entertaining. Delicious plain or sandwiched!

## HAM AND SPLIT PEA SOUP

Set oven temperature 325° and cook 2½ to 3 hours.

1 smoked boneless ham butt (about 2½ pounds)
1 pound split peas, washed
2 quarts water
1 onion, chopped
3 stalks celery, chopped
1 carrot, chopped
1 bay leaf
6 whole black peppers
Salt and pepper
Croutons.

Put all ingredients in roaster pan, except salt, pepper and croutons. Simmer in over 3 hours, or until meat is tender and peas mushy. Season to taste. Remove meat; cut half into bite-size pieces. Put meat into soup bowls, fill with soup and sprinkle with croutons. Serves 6.

Good day!

# California Clam Chowder

SERVES 8 GENEROUSLY

*Intensive study can produce superior results—hence, this delicious Clam Chowder. I pursued at least 20 recipes, gleaned suggestions from each, started chopping and adlibbing. This is as good as it gets!*

**6 cups clam broth**

**6 medium red potatoes, large dice**

**8 (6 ½-ounce) cans chopped clams, drained, juices reserved**

**3 ounces pancetta, finely diced**

**4 tablespoons butter**

**1 large onion, chopped**

**3 stalks celery, large dice**

**1 tablespoon chopped fresh thyme, or ½ teaspoon dried**

**1 bay leaf**

**¼ cup all-purpose flour**

**2 cups half-and- half**

**1 tablespoon Worcestershire sauce**

**Tabasco sauce to taste**

Combine clam broth with potatoes and simmer until potatoes are barely tender, about 10 minutes. Strain broth into a large bowl and set potatoes aside. Also, open and drain clams, reserving that liquid as well.

In a large stock pot, sauté pancetta slowly until lightly crisped. Add butter, onion, celery, thyme and bay leaf. Cook slowly until onion is soft, about 15 minutes. Add flour, stirring with wooden spoon for 3 minutes. (Do not allow flour to brown.) Whisk in reserved clam broth and reserved clam liquid. Simmer on low heat for 5 minutes.

Add potatoes, half-and-half, clams, Worcestershire sauce and Tabasco. Simmer 5 minutes to blend flavors, stirring frequently.

For best results, using an old-fashioned potato masher, press into chowder several times in order to mash a small amount of the potatoes. Chowder consistency is a personal preference. Additional clam broth or half-and-half may be added according to taste.

Chowder may be made ahead, refrigerated and reheated gently (do not boil). Serve with saltines.

*Better Than Bouillon Clam Base is a wonderful product and available at most major food markets*

# Filet Mignon Soup

*The Aston-Martin of soups by way of Shellie!*

**1 ½ pounds trimmed beef tenderloin**

**2 tablespoons olive oil**

**1 pound mushrooms, coarsely chopped**

**2 tablespoons butter**

**1 large onion, chopped**

**2 medium carrots, coarsely chopped**

**2 cloves garlic, minced**

**½ teaspoon freshly ground black pepper**

**1 tablespoon all-purpose flour**

**4 cups beef broth**

**2 beef bouillon cubes**

**4 cups water**

**1 ½ cups small dried pasta shells**

**6 tablespoons minced fresh chives**

Cut beef into ¼-inch thick slices, and then cut into 2-inch strips.

In a medium flameproof Dutch oven, heat olive oil over high heat for 1 minute. Add half the beef strips and cook until well seared, about 5 minutes. Using tongs, transfer the strips to a platter. Repeat with remaining strips. Set aside.

Add mushrooms to the pot and cook, stirring often, until browned and dry. Reduce heat to low and stir in butter. Add onion and carrots and cook about 10 minutes. Stir in garlic and pepper and cook 3 minutes. Add flour and cook 1 minute.

Gradually stir in beef stock, water and bouillon cubes and bring to a boil. Reduce heat and cook for 5 minutes. Skim fat from surface and discard. Stir in pasta, increase heat to high and cook 8 to 10 minutes. Do not overcook pasta. Reduce heat, add beef strips and cook 5 minutes. Ladle soup into shallow bowls and sprinkle with chives.

Serve with crusty French bread.

*Placing the beef in the freezer for a short time before preparation makes slicing it easier.*

# Zucchini Soup and Tomatoes on English Muffins

SERVES 4

*Jean's summer lunch at the lake and yours—anywhere!*

## SOUP

**4 zucchini, chopped**
**1 cup chicken broth**
**½ yellow onion, chopped**
**4 tablespoons butter**
**¼ cup all-purpose flour**
**2 cups half-and-half**
**Grated Parmesan**

Simmer zucchini in chicken broth until tender.

Saute onion in butter until softened but not browned, 6 to 8 minutes. Add flour and stir several minutes to eliminate raw taste of flour. Gradually add half-and-half and cook for 5 minutes or until the sauce is thickened, stirring often. Fold in cooked zucchini. Pour mixture into blender and blend, in batches if necessary, until smooth. Refrigerate. Serve chilled with a sprinkling of Parmesan.

## TOMATOES ON ENGLISH MUFFINS

**4 English muffins, split**
**2 tablespoons olive oil**
**Finely crushed fresh tomatoes, drained**
**Chopped fresh basil**
**Shaved Asiago or Parmesan**

Brush muffins with olive oil and lightly broil. Top with tomatoes, basil and cheese and return to broiler to melt cheese, watching closely to prevent burning.

# Watermelon & Tomato Gazpacho

*It is not your classic gazpacho but this adaptation sings!*

4 cups seedless watermelon pieces
(about 1 ¼-inch dice)

2 large heirloom tomatoes cut into
1 ¼-inch dice

2 cups vegetable juice

1 tablespoon olive oil

1 tablespoon balsamic vinegar

1 tablespoon chopped fresh basil

1 tablespoon chopped fresh thyme

1 tablespoon chopped fresh parsley

½ cup Italian-seasoned bread
crumbs

2 tablespoons Parmesan

½ teaspoon paprika

1 teaspoon onion powder

½ teaspoon fleur de sel or any good
sea salt

1 tablespoon finely chopped almonds

Combine all ingredients in food processor and pulse carefully, taking care to not emulsify. Add more vegetable juice if a thinner soup is preferred. Adjust seasoning as necessary.

Refrigerate at least 4 hours before serving in individual bowls. To use as a main course for lunch pass several toppings.

## Suggested Toppings

Chopped cucumber

Diced avocado

Baby shrimp

Finely-diced red onion

Sour cream

*Always select the best balsamic vinegar you feel you can afford. I buy the large size Trader Joe's Balsamic Vinegar. Pour some into a saucepan and simmer to reduce and thicken. Watch carefully—it may take an hour or so. Not quite a 50-year-old balsamic but a fine substitute.*

# White Peach Gazpacho

MAKES 1 QUART

*Chef David in Lake Tahoe shares this with us. Smo-o-o-th.*

¼ cup slivered almonds
2 pounds white peaches
1 small clove garlic, peeled
½ cup extra virgin olive oil
¼ cup sherry vinegar
½ cup fine dry bread crumbs
Kosher salt and freshly ground
   white pepper

Preheat oven to 350 degrees and toast almonds until golden browned. Split peaches, remove pit and cut into 1-inch chunks.

Place almonds, garlic, olive oil, vinegar, pinch of salt and a couple grinds of white pepper in a blender. Blend on high speed until smooth.

Add peaches and bread crumbs, season with salt and pepper. If the peaches are very ripe, a bit more of the bread crumbs might be needed for proper consistency.

Blend until smooth and pass through a fine mesh strainer. Adjust seasoning and chill until ready to serve. When serving, offer some or all of the Suggested Toppings.

## SUGGESTED TOPPINGS

Diced peaches

Toasted almonds

Small croutons

Chopped chives

Extra virgin olive oil

**Kitchen-Tested Recipes from the Kitchen of**

### JO REID

Two weeks vacation with pay! Sweet music. Pack the car, pack the children, pack the pocketbook! Sunburn, sand, surfers. Three square meals. Five pounds. Rise and shine 5 a.m. Fish running. No fish in sight 'til Sunday. Who wants fish on Sunday? Pack the car, pack the children, pack the dirty laundry. Home. Sweet music.

### WELCOME HOME BARBECUE

Roquefort Romaine                    Crisp Stringbeans
CHUCK ROAST BBQ                  Foil-Baked Potatoes

### ROQUEFORT ROMAINE

Combine ½ cup olive oil, the juice of ½ lemon, and enough wine vinegar to measure ¾ cup in all. Add 1 clove garlic and ¼ tsp. sugar, ½ tsp. salt. Let stand. Remove and discard garlic. Use 2 heads romaine lettuce, discarding large outer leaves. Break into small pieces. Add 1 cup croutons and a 3 oz. package Roquefort cheese, grated. Toss with dressing and sprinkle with freshly-ground pepper. This salad will become a "specialty of the house"!

### CHUCK ROAST BBQ

Select a good-sized chuck roast. The night before the BBQ: Sprinkle meat generously with tenderizer, salt and pepper. Combine 2 cups red wine, ½ cup wine vinegar, 1 tsp. ground ginger, 2 cloves crushed garlic and pour over meat. Cover and refrigerate. Turn meat several times the next day. Broil over hot coals. Tender, juicy, delicious!

### CRISP STRINGBEANS

1 lb. green beans                     1 tsp. salt
4 slices bacon                          ¼ tsp. pepper
6 green onions including tops

Snip off ends and slice green beans into thin slivers. Now dice the bacon and fry until crisp. Scoop out the bacon bits and set aside. Brown chopped green onions in the bacon fat, add the beans and cook over moderate heat for about a minute. Now add 1 tbsp. water, cover tightly and cook 5 minutes. Remove cover and cook until beans are tender but still crisp. Sprinkle with bacon and season with salt and pepper to taste.

# Cucumber Salad

*Such a refreshing side dish. Easily assembled, easily consumed.*

**2 English cucumbers**
**¼ cup light soy sauce**
**¼ cup rice vinegar**
**1 ½ teaspoons sesame oil**
**2 scallions, sliced**
**Pepper to taste**

Cut cucumbers in half lengthwise, then crosswise into ½-inch half-moons.

Combine remaining ingredients and pour over cucumbers. Refrigerate and serve chilled.

# Melon with Prosciutto

*An artful presentation of this classic first course.*

**1 ripe cantaloupe or honeydew melon**
**¼ pound prosciutto, julienned**
**¼ cup shaved Parmigiano Reggiano**
**2 cups arugula**
**2 tablespoons olive oil**
**Juice of 2 limes**
**Cracked black pepper**

Thinly slice melon and arrange on plate. Sprinkle with prosciutto. Add Parmigiano Reggiano. Cover entire dish with arugula and drizzle with a combination of olive oil and lime juice. Top with cracked pepper.

# Elegant Endive

*If it is sinless you land in heaven! This is the right path.*

Endive leaves

Crumbled blue cheese

Chopped candied pecans or other spiced nuts

Honey

Separate endive leaves and place on a decorative tray or serving platter. Fill the base of each one with a rounded teaspoon of blue cheese. Sprinkle with chopped nuts and drizzle lightly with honey.

# Endive Pear Salad

4 Belgian endive, leaves separated

2 small heads romaine lettuce, torn into small pieces

2 Bosc pears, thinly sliced

4 ounces crumbled gorgonzola

½ cup chopped walnuts

Freshly ground black pepper

4 tablespoons seedless raspberry jam

4 tablespoons balsamic vinegar

Arrange endive leaves around outer edge of a large platter. Fill center of platter with romaine. Scatter pears, gorgonzola and walnuts over all.

In a small bowl, mix raspberry jam and balsamic and microwave for several seconds to soften jam. Stir with whisk and drizzle over the salad.

# Orange, Avocado and Onion Salad

*A refreshing salad that fills the bill for many meals. It is eye-catching, mouth-watering and simple to prepare. Use your own judgment as to how many oranges and avocados to use, depending on how many servings you want to prepare.*

**Oranges, peeled and sliced**

**Avocados, peeled and sliced**

**Amy's Red Onions**

**Freshly ground black pepper**

Symmetrically layer slices of oranges and avocado on a serving platter. Top with Amy's Red Onions and sprinkle with black pepper.

## AMY'S RED ONIONS

**1 red onion, thinly sliced into rings**

**Water**

**2 tablespoons red wine vinegar**

**1 tablespoon olive oil**

**½ teaspoon garlic powder**

**¼ teaspoon salt**

Place onion slices in a small glass bowl. Cover with water and add remaining ingredients. Microwave about 5 minutes. Remove, drain and refrigerate.

*These onions are a great garnish for salads and are delicious piled on roast beef sandwiches.*

# Basil Caesar Salad

*A new twist on the classic. It is possible you will never go back to the old!*

1 egg

2 tablespoons fresh lemon juice

1 tablespoon anchovy paste

½ teaspoon pepper

6 tablespoons olive oil

1 cup loosely-packed basil leaves

½ cup flat leaf parsley

4-6 cups torn romaine leaves

1 cup Parmigiano Reggiano, divided

Croutons

1 baguette, cut into cubes

Olive oil

Salt and pepper

Blend egg, lemon juice, anchovy paste, pepper, olive oil, basil and parsley. Toss with romaine, croutons and half the cheese. Sprinkle remaining cheese over top when ready to serve.

Combine all ingredients and toast in 375 degree oven for 12 minutes.

*Since it is not cooked, the egg may be omitted if you are concerned about including the raw ingredient.*

# B. W.'s Salad

*The "inner circle" knows and loves this salad and now Barbara shares her much-coveted recipe with us. It is a palate refresher and great at a holiday dinner.*

½ cup canola oil

¼ cup seasoned rice vinegar

1 clove garlic, minced

1 teaspoon Dijon mustard

1 Granny Smith apple, peeled and finely diced

⅓ cup roasted slivered almonds

¼ cup feta cheese crumbles

½ teaspoon kosher salt

½ teaspoon pepper

Romaine, butter and red leaf lettuces

Mix oil, vinegar, garlic, mustard, salt and pepper in a jar with a tight-fitting lid. Before serving, shake the jar vigorously and mix 2 teaspoons of the dressing with the diced apple. Place lettuces in a bowl; add apple, roasted almonds and feta. Pour in remaining dressing and toss.

## JO REID'S KITCHEN-TESTED RECIPES

### MENU OF THE WEEK

Melon Ball Compote*
Baked Ham with Barbecue Sauce**
Applesauce
Succotash
Scalloped Potatoes
Angel Food Cake
Coffee

### RECIPES OF THE WEEK

#### Melon Ball Compote*

1 cup sugar
1 cup water
¼ teaspoon salt
3 sprigs fresh mint

1 cup watermelon balls
1 cup cantaloupe balls
1 cup honeydew balls

Combine sugar, water, salt and mint in saucepan and boil 15 min. Let cool. Remove mint, pour syrup over melon balls and cover bowl. Chill 2 or 3 hours. Serve in stemmed fruit cup with garnish of fresh mint leaf. Serves 4.

# Mexican Chopped Salad

SERVES 12 GENEROUSLY

*The perfect touch for that colorful Mexican feast!*

## SALAD

8 hearts romaine, chopped

2 (15-ounce) cans black beans, rinsed and drained

8 tomatoes, coarsely chopped and drained

2 (16-ounce) packages frozen corn, thawed

2 English cucumbers, peeled, large dice

1 cup thinly sliced radish

3 large Haas avocados, large dice

8 ounces crumbled feta cheese

## LIME DRESSING

1 cup fresh lime juice

1 cup olive oil

8 tablespoons honey

3 cloves garlic, minced

Combine all salad ingredients in a large bowl and toss with Lime Dressing.

Add all dressing ingredients to a small mixing bowl and whisk well to blend.

# Asian Chicken Salad in Lettuce Cups

SERVES 6

*It takes but minutes to arrive at this tasty salad.*

½ cup mayonnaise

2 teaspoons sambal oelek or Chinese chile-garlic sauce

1 teaspoon Dijon mustard

½ teaspoon sesame oil

1 rotisserie chicken, skinned and boned, meat pulled into bite-size pieces

⅓ cup coarsely chopped water chestnuts

2 whole green onions, thinly sliced

Salt and pepper to taste

12 Bibb lettuce leaves

1 avocado, peeled and cut into 12 slices

Lime wedges

Mix mayonnaise, sambal oelek, mustard and sesame oil. Stir in chicken, water chestnuts and green onion. Season with salt and pepper. Spoon salad into lettuce leaves, top each with two slices of avocado and serve with lime wedges.

*Any time you use a rotisserie chicken, save the skin and bones in a zip top bag in the freezer. When you have a full bag, add some cold water, celery tops and a quartered onion and boil gently for an excellent homemade chicken stock.*

# Day-Ahead Chicken Salad

SERVES 6-8

*How easy to entertain when the main course is prepared 24 hours in advance! There are many variations to the overnight salad—this one is particularly refreshing with the use of bean sprouts and water chestnuts.*

6 cups shredded iceberg lettuce

¼ pound bean sprouts

1 can water chestnuts, drained and sliced

½ cup thinly sliced green onion

1 English cucumber, thinly sliced

4-6 cups cooked chicken, cut into strips

1 package frozen petite peas, thawed (can use strips of pea pods)

2 cups mayonnaise

3 teaspoons curry powder

½ teaspoon ground ginger

½ cup Spanish-style peanuts or sliced almonds

Cherry tomatoes, halved

Mango Chutney

In a shallow 4-quart serving dish, evenly distribute shredded lettuce. Top with bean sprouts, water chestnuts, green onion, cucumber and chicken. Sprinkle peas over top.

In a small bowl, stir together mayonnaise, curry powder and ginger. Spread mayonnaise mixture evenly over peas. Cover dish and refrigerate as long as 24 hours.

To serve, garnish salad with peanuts or almonds and cherry tomato halves. Remind guests to scoop down to the bottom of the dish to lift out a portion of all the layers. Pass a bowl of chutney as a condiment.

# Composed Spinach Salad with Chicken

SERVES 12

*The colors and textures in this salad make it one of the best. Be prepared for compliments.*

## SALAD

4 bags baby spinach

2 cups grapes, halved

6 pears, peeled and sliced

2 cups crumbled blue cheese

2 cups chopped walnuts

1 cup dried cranberries

8 cups large dice cooked chicken breasts

Line a very large platter with spinach. Creatively arrange all ingredients in "composed" style. Pour Dressing over salad to serve.

## DRESSING

1 cup olive oil

⅔ cup balsamic (the older the better)

2 tablespoons honey

1 tablespoon Dijon mustard

2 tablespoons chopped green onion

1 teaspoon salt

½ teaspoon pepper

Combine all ingredients in a mixing bowl and whisk to blend thoroughly.

# Chicken Chopped Salad

SERVES 4-6

*This salad covers all the bases!*

## SALAD

3 cups diced cooked chicken

2 hearts of romaine, coarsely chopped

1 pint grape tomatoes, halved

1 English cucumber cut in ½-inch dice

2 scallions, thinly sliced

1 cup corn kernels

1 cup green grapes, halved

3 ounces crumbled feta cheese

## DRESSING

6 tablespoons olive oil

2 tablespoons finely chopped mint

2 tablespoons finely chopped fresh basil

4 tablespoons red wine vinegar

1 tablespoon lime juice

1 teaspoon sugar

Salt and pepper to taste

Combine all ingredients and gently toss with the desired amount of Dressing.

Add all dressing ingredients to a jar with a tight-fitting lid and shake vigorously to blend.

# Composed Salad with Crabmeat Louis Dressing

SERVES 6

*Choose a variety of any of the following vegetables. Arrange creatively on a large lettuce-lined platter. Allow space in the center of the platter to accommodate a chilled bowl of the Crabmeat Louis Dressing. This is a luncheon entrée fit for royalty!*

## SALAD

**Butter lettuce leaves**

**Asparagus spears, steamed**

**Green beans, blanched**

**Beets, sliced**

**Tomatoes, diced**

**Carrots, grated**

**Avocado, large dice**

**Scallions, chopped**

**Radishes, sliced**

**Artichoke hearts**

Combine mayonnaise, pickle relish, Tabasco, egg and whipped cream. Gently fold in crabmeat. Spoon mixture into a decorative bowl and place in center of the salad.

Guests help themselves to vegetables and top with the Crabmeat Louis Dressing.

## CRABMEAT LOUIS DRESSING

**1 cup mayonnaise**

**¾ cup pickle relish**

**Dash of Tabasco**

**1 hard-cooked egg, chopped**

**1 cup heavy cream, whipped**

**1 pound crabmeat**

# Tuna & Green Bean Potato Salad

*Time to beautify the almighty potato salad—this is a great meal.*

2 pounds small Yukon Gold potatoes

½ pound French green beans

2 cans oil-packed tuna, drained

16 cherry tomatoes, halved

¼ cup olive oil

2 tablespoons red wine vinegar

2 tablespoons Dijon mustard

2 tablespoons capers, drained

1 tablespoon dried oregano

4 cups assorted field greens

Cook potatoes until tender. Drain, cool and cut into quarters. Cook green beans until tender; plunge into ice bath to stop the cooking. Drain well and combine tuna, potatoes, green beans and tomatoes.

Pour olive oil into a small bowl and whisk in vinegar, mustard, capers and oregano. Pour dressing over salad and gently toss. Serve over field greens.

# Italian Tuna & White Bean Salad

*A plate of this salad, slices of crusty Ciabatta, a glass of Pinot Grigio and in Italy you have landed!*

### DRESSING

1 clove garlic

½ cup Italian parsley

¼ cup fresh basil leaves

1 ½ tablespoons chopped fresh oregano, or 1 teaspoon dried

¼ cup capers

2 tablespoons pine nuts

¼ cup olive oil

1 tablespoon fresh lemon juice

Salt and pepper to taste

### SALAD

3 (7-ounce) jars or cans oil-packed Italian tuna, drained

2 cans cannelloni beans, drained and rinsed

3 Belgian endives, thinly sliced crosswise

Combine dressing ingredients in a food processor and pulse to blend. Gently toss with tuna, beans and endive.

# Wild Rice Salad with Prawns

SERVES 4                    *Quickly assembled with knock-out results.*

2 cups cooked wild rice

1 can Niblet corn, drained

3 scallions, white part only, thinly
  sliced

½ cup chopped fresh mint

1 pound medium-size prawns,
  cooked

½ cup olive oil

½ cup vegetable oil

½ cup fresh lemon juice

Salt and pepper

In a large serving bowl, add rice, corn, scallions, mint and prawns. Season with salt and pepper to taste.

In a small mixing bowl, blend oils and lemon juice well. Adjust seasoning as needed and pour over rice mixture. Toss lightly before serving.

# Shrimp Rice Salad

*This is Sue's original salad and then some!*

4 cups cooked rice, cooled

1 large bunch parsley, chopped

8 green onions, chopped

2 cups mayonnaise

1 (16-ounce) bag frozen petite peas,
  thawed

2 pounds medium prawns, cooked
  and halved

1 cup slivered almonds

Combine parsley, onion and mayonnaise. Stir into rice. Fold in peas, prawns and almonds. Add additional mayonnaise if needed to bring salad to proper consistency.

# January Salad

SERVES 6

*Lauren created a winner when she started combining ingredients. We were cooking together and decided the New Year was here and we wanted to experiment with health-conscious recipes. A beautiful, colorful result.*

## SALAD

½ head red cabbage, chopped into bite-size pieces

6 green onions, finely chopped

1 cup frozen green peas, thawed

## DRESSING

⅓ cup rice vinegar

1 tablespoon sesame oil

1 tablespoon canola oil

1 ½ teaspoons sugar

1 tablespoon soy sauce

½ teaspoon ground ginger

½ teaspoon dry mustard

Combine cabbage, onion and peas and set aside while making Dressing.

Add all dressing ingredients to a mixing bowl and blend well. Pour over reserved salad and toss well.

*Leftovers, if any, are delicious.*

## KOZY KITCHEN
### KITCHEN TESTED RECIPES
### FROM THE KITCHEN OF
### JO REID

Happy New Year! It is just Midnight and we start 1963 with new hope and promise and resolve. The hugs and kisses have been exchanged, a group in the corner are singing "Auld Lang Syne" and with a smile, our hostess announces the buffet supper is ready.

There is Baked Ham, Potatoe Salad, Shrimp-Tomato Aspic, Rye Bread piled high, a pretty dish of relishes, a carafe of steaming coffee, and tiny pieces of English Fruitcake.

### BAKED HAM

Have butcher slice and tie a canned ham and bake in a slow oven at least two hours or according to the directions on the can. Baste with gingerale every 15 minutes. Three-quarters of an hour before ham is done cover with marmalade and continue baking. Place on serving platter, remove string, garnish with parsley and kumquats.

### POTATO SALAD

Boil 8 to 10 medium potatoes. Add salt, 2 tablesp. wine vinegar and 1 tablesp. pickling spice to boiling water. Peel and cube the potatoes while they are still warm, allowing the potatoes to crumble a little. Immediately add:

½ onion, grated (try putting the onion in your electric blender with a little mayonnaise and blend until smooth).
½ cup sweet pickle relish
1 small can chopped olives
1 small can pimento, finely chopped
2 chopped hardboiled eggs.
Mayonaise, according to taste.

The ingredients are all added while the potatoes are warm. Firmly pack in a bowl. Refrigerate. Unmold on dish, sprinkle with paprika and garnish with pitted black olives, strips of pimento, and parsley.

### TOMATO-SHRIMP ASPIC

1 package lemon-flavored gelatin
1½ cups hot water
1 can tomato sauce
1½ tablesp. vinegar
¾ tablesp. Worchestershire sauce

Dash of pepper
1 can drained shrimp
Dissolve gelatin in hot water. Add tomato sauce and other ingredients. Blend. Pour into mold. Chill until firm. Place on crisp greens with mayonnaise. Serves four to six. (This recipe should be doubled for the buffet). Have fun!

See you next week — we'll glamorize meatballs.

# Green Bean Salad Provençale

*Janice serves this with Grandma Annie's Chicken—the perfect accompaniment.*

Fresh green beans, trimmed

2 cloves garlic, crushed with 1 teaspoon salt

¼ cup red wine vinegar

1 teaspoon Dijon mustard

1 cup olive oil

1 teaspoon dried basil

Freshly ground black pepper

¾ cup toasted walnut halves

2 (5-ounce) cans sliced black olives, drained

Blanch green beans in boiling water for 7 minutes. Refresh by rinsing with cold water. Dry thoroughly.

In a small mixing bowl, combine garlic, vinegar, mustard, oil, basil and pepper and blend well. Place beans in salad bowl and add walnuts and olives. Pour dressing over all and toss gently.

# White Bean and Tomato Salad

*A zesty salad to serve alongside any barbecued main course.*

2 (15-ounce) cans cannellini beans, drained and rinsed

2 ½ cups cherry tomatoes

1 small red onion, finely diced

½ cup chopped Italian parsley

¼ cup olive oil

3 tablespoons lemon juice

1 tablespoon balsamic vinegar

2 cloves garlic, minced

Salt and pepper to taste

Combine all ingredients and marinate at room temperature for 1 hour.

# Spicy Bean Salad

*The perfect buffet salad—it will not wilt.*

## SALAD

1 (15-ounce) can red kidney beans

1 (15-ounce) can pinto beans

1 (15-ounce) can garbanzo beans

1 can whole kernel corn

3 green onions, thinly sliced

½ cup chopped parsley

4 stalks celery, thinly sliced

1 (4-ounce) can diced green chiles

Pour beans and corn into a large colander. Rinse and drain well. Add all salad ingredients to a large salad bowl. Pour on Chili Dressing. Cover and chill, stirring several times. When ready to serve, spoon salad on lettuce-lined plates.

## CHILI DRESSING

¾ cup olive oil

¼ cup wine vinegar

1 clove garlic, minced

1 teaspoon salt

½ teaspoon chili powder

1 teaspoon dried oregano

¼ teaspoon cumin

Dash of Tabasco

Combine all ingredients in a screw-top jar and shake well to blend.

# Tomato and Burrata Salad

*We have such a great Book Club—good friends, good books, good conversation, good food. Veta's salad was a sensational hit!*

½ loaf Ciabatta bread, crusts removed

8 tablespoons olive oil, divided

1 clove garlic

1 tablespoon fresh oregano

1 tablespoon kosher salt

1 tablespoon red wine vinegar

1 tablespoon balsamic vinegar

1 pint cherry tomatoes, halved

3 pounds heirloom tomatoes, half cut into wedges and half into thick slices

1 tablespoon sea salt

Freshly ground black pepper to taste

1 pound burrata cheese, cut into 12 slices

1 shallot, thinly sliced

3 tablespoons chopped fresh basil

Tear bread into small pieces and toss with 2 tablespoons olive oil, making sure bread is saturated. Toast in oven for 12 to 15 minutes until golden. Watch carefully.

Make a paste of garlic, oregano and salt. Add the vinegars and whisk in the remaining 6 tablespoons olive oil, blending well.

Layer sliced tomatoes on a large platter. Top with burrata cheese and drizzle with some of the vinaigrette. Combine tomato wedges and cherry tomatoes with the remaining vinaigrette. Add salt and toasted croutons and toss gently. Spoon mixture over the tomato slices and burrata. Sprinkle chopped basil over the top.

# Watermelon and Tomato Salad

SERVES 8-10          *A beauty on the buffet table—loved by one and all.*

**8 cups large bite-size pieces seedless watermelon**

**3 large ripe tomatoes cut into bite-size pieces**

**4 tablespoons olive oil**

**3 tablespoons chopped fresh herbs**

**1 ½ tablespoons balsamic vinegar**

**Sprinkling of pepper**

**1 teaspoon fleur de sel or kosher salt**

**1 cup feta**

**½ cup sliced toasted almonds**

Combine watermelon and tomatoes. Let stand 15 minutes (or refrigerate if made earlier). Drain well.

In a separate bowl combine oil, herbs, vinegar and pepper. Add to watermelon and tomatoes and toss gently.

Spoon into a large decorative bowl. Sprinkle with salt, feta and almonds.

*Any fresh tomatoes are fine for this salad but if can get yellow heirlooms they work the best. Also, including fresh basil in the herb blend makes is especially tasty!*

# Basil Caesar Salad Dressing

*Create a summer salad extravaganza with flavors that sing in this dressing. Another time you may want to use it as a dip for raw vegetables.*

1 cup mayonnaise

½ cup sour cream

1 can anchovies, drained

½ cup fresh basil leaves

½ cup chopped Italian parsley

3 green onions, chopped

3 tablespoons vinegar

½ teaspoon dried tarragon

1 teaspoon Worcestershire sauce

½ teaspoon dry mustard

1 clove garlic

Place all ingredients in a food processor and pulse to blend. Store tightly covered in the refrigerator.

# Ginger Sesame Dressing

*Wonderful over baby spinach or shredded cabbage or shrimp with greens— your imagination will create a strikingly unusual salad.*

¾ cup rice vinegar

¼ cup soy sauce

1 tablespoon ground ginger

1 tablespoon dry mustard

1 tablespoon sesame oil

1 tablespoon sesame seeds

Blend all ingredients well and refrigerate.

# Baked Penne and Cheese

*The vote is unanimous—this IS the luscious pasta and cheese recipe!*

1 (16-ounce) package penne

1 quart half-and-half

1 tablespoon all-purpose flour

½ teaspoon salt

¼ teaspoon pepper

2 cups grated Fontina, divided

¾ cup grated Reggiano Parmesan, divided

¾ cup mozzarella, divided

2 tablespoons finely chopped Italian parsley

Preheat oven to 450 degrees.

Butter a 9x13-inch baking dish and set aside. Cook pasta in boiling salted water until just tender—about 5 minutes. Drain well.

Combine half-and-half, flour, salt and pepper in a large bowl. Add 1 cup of the Fontina, ½ cup Reggiano, ½ cup mozzarella and parsley. Add penne and mix well.

Transfer to prepared baking dish. Combine the remaining 1 cup Fontina, ¼ cup Reggiano and ¼ cup mozzarella in a small bowl. Sprinkle mixture over the pasta.

Bake 20 minutes and let stand 20 minutes before serving.

# Tortellini with Cream Sauce

*Sinful…but worth it!*

3 cups whipping cream

⅛ teaspoon ground nutmeg

2 packages tortellini, cooked and drained

1 cup grated Reggiano Parmesan

In a large skillet, add whipping cream and nutmeg. Cook over medium heat until bubbles form and the sauce is reduced by about a third, stirring constantly.

Add to the cooked tortellini and gently stir in Parmesan.

# Spicy Peanut Noodles

*Plate-lickin' delicious.*

1 (16-ounce) package spaghetti

¾ cup creamy peanut butter

6 tablespoons unseasoned rice vinegar

3 tablespoons sugar

6 tablespoons low sodium soy sauce

¼ cup water

1 teaspoon sesame oil

1 teaspoon crushed red pepper

1 clove garlic, mashed

1 (2-inch) piece fresh ginger, coarsely chopped

Cook pasta in salted water until tender. Drain under cold water and set aside.

Meanwhile, thoroughly combine remaining ingredients. Blend half with spaghetti. Transfer to a serving bowl and drizzle remaining peanut mixture over all.

# Turkey Cheese Alfredo

*Libbie created this sublime dish with leftover Thanksgiving turkey. It is delicious—makes you feel very happy.*

2 tablespoons butter

4 tablespoons Wondra

1 can chicken broth

2 cups fat-free half-and-half

1 teaspoon garlic powder

Salt and pepper

¾ cup turkey gravy

1 (8-ounce) package grated Colby Cheddar cheese

1 ¼ cups shredded Parmesan, divided

3 cups chopped turkey breast

2 (10-ounce) packages wide egg noodles, cooked al dente

Preheat oven to 350 degrees. In a medium saucepan, melt butter and stir in Wondra. Make a roux by adding broth and half-and-half gradually to make a smooth sauce. Add garlic powder, salt and pepper to taste; stir in gravy. Mix well. Blend in Colby and 1 cup Parmesan.

Add mixture to the cooked noodles. Spoon into a large casserole dish and sprinkle with remaining Parmesan. Bake 10 to 15 minutes or until hot through.

*If you are making this after a holiday, it is a good way to use both your leftover turkey and gravy. If you didn't have gravy left from the big day, you may use a good jarred chicken or turkey gravy instead.*

# KITCHEN KAPERS

Kitchen-Tested Recipes from the Kitchen of

## JO REID

Don't you just adore Verdi, Michelangelo, Dante, and Tetrazzini?

We're all artists in our own kitchens when we plan a meal for taste, color, and texture. We are called upon to create masterpieces every day and it's very nice, indeed, to receive an excellent review from the critics!

### SPECIAL SHOWING

Tomato Aspic Abstract
with Avocado Slices
Tetrazzini at Sundown

Vegetable Still-life
Summer Snow
Oriental Interlude

### TETRAZZINI AT SUNDOWN

1 pkg. (8 oz.) noodles
1 cup fresh mushrooms or 1 can
3 oz. sliced
¼ cup butter or margarine
1 medium onion
3 tablespoons flour
2 teaspoons salt

Dash pepper
Dash cayenne pepper
2½ cups milk
2 cups cooked pork, chicken
or turkey
2 tablespoons grated
Parmesan cheese

Start your oven at 400 degrees. Cook noodles until tender, according to package directions. Drain thoroughly. Cut fresh mushrooms in slices (drain canned ones) and cook in butter or margarine along with chopped onion for several minutes or until onions look limp. Stir in the flour as smoothly as possible, season with salt and both kinds of pepper and add milk gradually. Cook, stirring constantly until sauce bubbles. Toss in the cubed meat or poultry and cheese. Cook again until mixture is heated through. Put noodles in the bottom of a greased casserole or baking dish, making a cavity in the center and banking noodles around the sides. Pour meat sauce in center and bake 15 minutes. Serves 6.

### VEGETABLE STILL-LIFE

1 medium-size head of cauliflower (about 2 pounds)
8 medium-size carrots, scraped

4 tablespoons butter
(½ stick), melted
2 tablespoons chopped parsley
¼ teaspoon nutmeg.

Trim green leaves from cauliflower, but leave head whole. Cook covered in boiling salted water 25 minutes or until crispy tender. Lift out carefully with 2 large spoons, drain. Slice carrots thin. Cook, covered in boiling salted water 15 minutes, or until crispy tender, drain. Season carrots with 2 tablespoons of melted butter. Spoon half into a heated serving bowl; place cauliflower on top; spoon remaining carrots in a ring around edge; keep hot. Stir parsley and nutmeg into remaining melted butter; spoon over both vegetables.

# Heavenly Cauliflower Pasta

*And in the pasta category, the winner is….Heavenly Cauliflower Pasta! The applause is deafening. Try this and learn what all the fuss is about!*

**1 large head cauliflower**
**½ teaspoon salt**
**4 tablespoons butter**

Separate cauliflower into flowerets. Steam until tender. Heat 4 tablespoons butter in a large skillet and sauté cauliflower until golden and broken in small pieces. Remove and set aside. Do not rinse skillet.

Preheat oven to 350 degrees. Lightly butter a large casserole dish and set aside.

## SAUCE

**4 tablespoons butter**
**4 tablespoons all-purpose flour**
**1 ½ cups half-and-half, warmed**
**1 ½ cups milk, warmed**
**Pepper to taste**
**¾ cup grated Parmesan**
**1 (16-ounce) package penne, cooked al dente and drained**

In the same frying pan, melt 4 tablespoons butter. Add flour and whisk until smooth. Gradually add half-and-half and milk and continue to whisk over medium heat until smooth and bubbling. Remove from heat and immediately add Parmesan.

Combine cauliflower, Sauce and penne.

Spoon into prepared casserole and bake for 30 minutes.

# Asian Pasta

*A Shellie specialty—she suggests doubling the sauce for an extra "Yum" factor!*

1 (16-ounce) package thin spaghetti
4 tablespoons sesame oil, divided
1 bunch green onions, sliced
2 cloves garlic, minced
½ teaspoon red pepper flakes
2 tablespoons rice vinegar
1 teaspoon sugar or agave
2 tablespoons soy sauce
½ cup chopped dry roasted peanuts
⅓ cup chopped cilantro

Cook pasta al dente. Drain and toss with 2 tablespoons sesame oil. In a large saucepan combine remaining sesame oil, green onion, garlic, red pepper flakes, rice vinegar, sugar and soy sauce. Heat until hot through but do not boil. Toss mixture with cooked pasta. Sprinkle with peanuts and cilantro.

Serve hot or at room temperature.

# Pesto with Linguini

*Amy's is the best! It is a good idea to quadruple the ingredients and freeze in individual containers for future happiness!*

2 cups fresh basil leaves, packed
4-6 cloves garlic, blanched for 5 minutes
⅓ cup pine nuts
¼ teaspoon salt
Freshly ground black pepper
½ cup Reggiano Parmesan
½ cup olive oil
1 (16-ounce) package linguini
1 stick butter, softened
Additional cheese, for topping

In food processor, process basil, garlic, pine nuts, slat and a generous amount of ground black pepper. Add cheese and oil. Process until smooth and set aside.

Boil linguini to al dente in heavily salted water. Drain, reserving ½ cup of the pasta water. Toss linguini with pesto and reserved pasta water. Remove from heat and incorporate softened butter. Serve topped with additional cheese.

# PASTA

## KITCHEN KAPERS

SEBASTOPOL TIMES
THURSDAY          JUNE 6, 1963

Kitchen-tested recipes from the kitchen of
### JO REID

There's a Swiss-Dutch girl we know who makes the best spaghetti with green sauce, and an Irish-American girl who does wonders with mock ravioli, and then there's that little Italian gal who concocts a mean lasagna, so here we are with pasta recipes!

These are the kind of dishes that cannot be surpassed for buffet suppers, and the spaghetti with green sauce is a winner for a Friday night dinner. With a salad, French bread and wine, a party we have!

## SPAGHETTINI WITH GREEN SAUCE

2 tablespoons dried basil
2 tablespoons dried parsley
¼ cup butter
1 8-oz. cream cheese
⅓ cup Parmesan cheese

¼ cup olive oil
1 clove garlic
½ teaspoon pepper
2/3 cups boiling water

Mix above ingredients thoroughly. The electric blender is ideal for this. Boil spaghettini according to directions and add sauce.

## LASAGNA

½ pound monterey jack, grated or shredded
½ pound sharp cheddar cheese, grated or shredded
1 cup grated Parmesan cheese
Meaty Italian spaghetti sauce (use at least a pound of chuck ground when making the sauce and have a generous amount of sauce since the lasagna seems to absorb more gravy than plain spaghetti)
1 package lasagna (boil according to directions on box)

In a 10x12 glass baking dish, arrange a layer of lasagna, a generous sprinkling of monterey jack, cheddar and Parmesan cheese, Italian sauce to cover. Repeat layers until all ingredients are used, and sprinkle finally with Parmesan cheese. Bake in 350 degree oven 30 to 40 minutes.

## MOCK RAVIOLI

2 lb. ground chuck
2 cans tomato paste
2 cans water
1 pkg. dried mushrooms
2 large chopped onions

Sauce
1 tsp. poultry seasoning
Dash rosemary
¼ cube butter
2 tablesp. oil

Saute onions in butter and oil, then add meat and brown. Add tomato paste and mushrooms. Add seasonings and 2 paste cans water. Cook slowly 2 hours.

1 cup bread crumbs
1 pkg. frozen chopped spinach
¼ cup oil

Filling
1 cup sharp cheddar cheese
1 egg

Cook spinach, drain well. Add cheese, oil, egg and bread crumbs.

Now cook 1 package wide noodles or butterfly noodles. Place in greased pan and alternate noodles with filling and meat sauce. Alternate until all ingredients have been used. Bake 300 degrees for 1 hour.

Good day!

73

# Pasta with Roasted Tomatoes

*No need to wait for summer tomatoes to prepare this simply wonderful pasta dish since baking tomatoes intensifies the flavor and texture.*

10-12 small sweet tomatoes, halved

Salt and pepper

1 cup fine dry bread crumbs

Olive oil

1 (16-ounce) package linguini

¼ cup olive oil

6 cloves garlic, halved

1 cup whole basil leaves

1 ladle pasta water

½ cup Reggiano Parmesan

Ricotta salata

Preheat oven to 300 degrees.

Season tomatoes with salt and pepper. Place on a parchment-lined baking sheet. Sprinkle with bread crumbs and lightly splash with olive oil. Bake about 30 minutes.

Cook pasta and drain, reserving water.

In a large fry pan, heat oil and add garlic, cooking until garlic is soft, about 2 minutes. Watch carefully to avoid burning. Add basil leaves and combine. Add a ladle of pasta water and cook several minutes. (The starch in the water thickens the mixture and makes a sauce.)

Add drained pasta to cooked tomatoes. Combine all gently and fold in Parmesan. Serve in deep dish pasta bowl and top with grated ricotta salata.

*Add a pinch of crushed red pepper if you like a bite to your pasta dishes.*

# Linguini with Seafood & Pinot Grigio

**SERVES 4-6**

*The result belies the simplicity in preparing one of the world's best and showiest seafood dishes.*

1 (16-ounce) package linguini, cooked al dente and drained

¼ cup olive oil

3 shallots, chopped

5 cloves garlic, minced

¾ cup chopped sun-dried tomatoes

½ teaspoon red pepper flakes

Several sprigs fresh thyme

2 cups Pinot Grigio

2 pounds clams, washed

1 pound large prawns, peeled and deveined

1 teaspoon kosher salt

¼ teaspoon black pepper

4 tablespoons butter

1 cup arugula, sliced into chiffonade

Zest of 1 lemon

1 cup shaved or grated Parmesan

Heat olive oil in a large heavy skillet. Add shallots and cook 3 minutes; add garlic and cook 30 seconds longer (do not brown). Stir in sun-dried tomatoes and cook for another minute. Sprinkle in red pepper flakes and thyme.

Add wine and bring to a boil. Reduce liquid by one quarter the original amount (the wine flavor should remain and alcohol will evaporate). Add clams, cover and simmer until clams open. Remove clams from pan, discarding any that failed to open properly, and set aside.

Add prawns to pan, cover and simmer just until they are pink, taking care not to overcook. Return clams to pan and adjust seasonings to taste.

Pour onto warm serving platter. Mix in cooked linguini and butter. Add arugula and stir gently. Sprinkle with lemon zest and Parmesan to serve.

# Seafood with Saffron & Linguini

SERVES 6-8

*It is impossible to prepare a seafood dish that can come close to this in creativity, taste or style. It can only be described as supreme—definitely company fare. Much of the prep can be done early in the day.*

3 tablespoons olive oil

1 large onion, chopped

1 shallot, chopped

6 cloves garlic, finely minced

3 cups white wine

1 cup dry vermouth

3 cups clam juice

1 cup heavy cream

1 teaspoon crumbled saffron threads

1 ½ pounds linguini

3 pounds mussels

1 ½ pounds medium prawns, peeled

1 pound salmon or halibut, cut into 1 ½-inch pieces

4 Roma tomatoes, diced

Grated Parmesan

Early in the day, sauté onion and shallot in olive oil until tender— about 5 minutes. Add the garlic and mix well. Add wine and vermouth and boil, uncovered until liquid is reduced to about 1 cup. Add clam juice, cream and saffron and bring to a boil. Turn off heat, cover and allow to sit several hours.

When ready to serve, cook linguini al dente. Drain linguini and put it on an extra-large decorative dish.

While linguini is cooking, uncover sauce and bring it to a gentle boil. Turn heat down to medium and add mussels, prawns, salmon or halibut and the tomatoes. Cook until mussels are open and the prawns have turned pink—about 5 minutes.

Transfer seafood with a slotted spoon into a large bowl. Boil cooking liquid, uncovered, until reduced by half, about 5 minutes. Return seafood to cooking liquid and heat over moderate heat until just heated through.

Pour seafood and sauce over linguini and serve. Pass Parmesan.

# Linguini with Clams

*A feast in minutes.*

1 (16-ounce) package linguini, cooked al dente and drained

4 tablespoons butter

1 clove garlic, finely chopped

2 tablespoons all-purpose flour

2 cups clam juice

¼ cup chopped parsley

Salt and pepper to taste

1 tablespoon dried thyme

2 cups minced clams

In a medium saucepan, melt butter and add garlic. Cook 1 minute. Whisk in flour and clam juice, stirring constantly, until slightly thickened.

Add parsley, salt, pepper and thyme. Simmer 20 minutes. Add clams and heat gently.

Serve over prepared linguini.

# Orzo Pilaf with Cheese

*Competes with classic risotto for customer satisfaction!*

5 cups chicken broth

4 tablespoons butter

5 green onions, thinly sliced

1 (16-ounce) package orzo

1 cup Reggiano Parmesan

Salt and pepper to taste

Zest of 1 lemon

Chopped Italian parsley

Bring broth to boil. Set aside.

In a large frying pan, melt butter and sauté onions for a few minutes. Remove onions from pan and set aside. Sauté orzo in the same pan until light golden. Add orzo to hot broth and simmer about 8 minutes or until orzo is tender. Remove from heat. Add reserved onion and cheese and stir to blend. Season to taste with salt and pepper. Mix in lemon zest. Transfer to a large bowl to serve. If made ahead, rewarm over low heat and mix in more broth by ¼ cup increments as needed to moisten.

# Pastitsio

SERVES 15 -20

*This is a hearty Greek classic, much like the Italian lasagna. Can be served as a main course or as a side for that special party.*

6 tablespoons olive oil

2 large yellow onions, chopped

2 pounds lean ground beef

4 cloves garlic, chopped

2 tablespoons dried oregano

Salt and pepper to taste

2 (14.5-ounce) cans petite diced tomatoes

1 cup beef consommé

6 tablespoons tomato paste

1 ½ teaspoons ground cinnamon

¼ teaspoon ground allspice

1 teaspoon ground nutmeg

¼ teaspoon ground cloves

3 large eggs, well-beaten

1 ½ pounds long tube pasta (Greek or Italian)

3 tablespoons olive oil

3 ½ cups grated Parmesan, divided

Heat oil in large heavy skillet and brown onions about 8 minutes. Add beef and sauté until beef begins to brown, breaking up pieces. Add garlic and cook 1 minute longer. Mix in oregano, salt and pepper. Add tomatoes, consommé and tomato paste. Stir to blend well. Simmer 20 minutes. Mix in cinnamon, allspice, nutmeg and cloves and simmer 1 minute longer. Cool completely and stir in eggs.

*Pastitsio (continued)*

## BÉCHAMEL SAUCE

4 cups milk, divided

4 large egg yolks

1 stick butter

½ cup all-purpose flour

1 teaspoon salt

½ teaspoon black pepper

⅛ teaspoon nutmeg

⅛ teaspoon allspice

1 ½ cups grated Parmesan

Whisk ½ cup milk and egg yolks in a small bowl. Melt butter in a large saucepan. Add flour and whisk about 1 minute. Gradually whisk in remaining milk, salt, pepper, nutmeg and allspice. Simmer until sauce is thick, whisking often— about 8 minutes. Whisk yolk mixture and Parmesan into sauce. Continue to simmer 2 minutes whisking constantly.

To assemble, preheat oven to 375 degrees and brush two 9x13-inch baking dishes with oil and set aside.

Cook pasta until tender but still firm to the bite. Drain pasta and add 3 tablespoons olive oil and 1 cup Parmesan; toss gently. In each prepared dish layer half of pasta, half of meat mixture, ½ cup Parmesan and half of lukewarm Béchamel Sauce. Sprinkle each with ¾ cup Parmesan.

Cover each dish with foil and bake for 25 minutes. Uncover and return to oven for an additional 25 minutes. Allow to stand for 15 minutes before cutting to serve.

# Prawn Pasta Bill D

*Uncensored, unaltered, verbatim recipe from Bill (emailed immediately to me upon completion!)*

## STEP 1

Roast 8-12 cloves garlic (roll with me here...I know it's a painful additional step but...yummm...)

## STEP 2

In ¼ cup olive oil, fry/sauté one pound pancetta cubed into small pieces

Cook down until meat begins to get crispy

Skim half the fat and add one finely diced sweet onion to pancetta

Cook onion down thoroughly until all bits are completely translucent

Add two quarts cherry tomatoes

Add reserved 8-12 cloves roasted garlic

Add one + cup white wine

Cook sauce down for 40 minutes over low heat, stirring frequently

## STEP 3

(10 minutes before serving time)

In a large frying pan heat 4 T olive oil

Add 20 large prawns with shells ON

Add healthy dash of cayenne and healthy dash chili powder

Add 6-8 cloves SLICED garlic

Sauté for 3 minutes over medium heat

Add 3 T butter, sauté for another minute to allow butter to absorb

Add ¼ cup sweet vermouth—allow to flame if you like...fun!

Turn heat on high and let liquid evaporate until it starts to get a bit syrupy

Turn heat off

## STEP 4

(5 minutes before serving)

Add one container small fresh mozzarella balls (cut 'em in half) to tomato sauce

Add 3-4 T julienned basil

Add 1 T dried oregano or 2 T fresh

Allow to simmer for 3-5 minutes, stirring constantly to ensure cheese is incorporated thoroughly into sauce

FINALE   Plate two pounds of cooked linguini

Pour the sauce over the pasta

Pour prawns and all of their goo/sauce over the tomato sauce

Garnish with a little Reggiano

*FREAK OUT at how good this is.*

## KITCHEN KAPERS

### By JO REID

First of all, buy two yards of red and white check gingham. Then make six man-sized bibs. Now go through your list of friends and choose six gourmets. Give them a buzz and an invitation to dinner next Saturday. Greet them with a smile, CIOPPINO, beer, French bread, a salad, and the bibs.

It will be an evening long to remember. Don't you agree?

### CIOPPINO

½ cup olive oil
3 cloves garlic, chopped
1½ cups chopped onion
¾ cup chopped green onion
¾ cup chopped green pepper
1 jar whole clams
1 No. 2½ can whole tomatoes
1 can tomato paste
1¾ cups Burgundy

⅓ cup chopped parsley
2 teaspoons dried oregano
1 teaspoon diced basil
2 teaspoons salt
¼ teaspoon pepper
1½ lb. halibut steak
½ lb. raw shrimp, shelled
    and deveined
3 cans king crab meat, drained

In hot oil in large kettle, saute onions, green pepper 10 minutes. Stirring occasionally. Add garlic. Add liquid from drained clams. (Set clams aside.) Add undrained tomatoes, tomato paste, Burgundy, spices, herbs an dseasonings, ¾ cup water. Mix well. Bring to boil; reduce heat and simmer uncovered for 10 minutes. Cut halibut in 1-inch pieces. Discard skin and bones. Add to tomato mixture with shrimp, crab and clams. Simmer covered 15 minutes. Uncover and simmer 15 minutes longer. Serves 8. (This may be made in the morning or the day before and gently heated just before serving.)

Black, black coffee, cheese and fruit would top this dinner nicely, but a scrumptious dessert would be hard to resist.

### FRESH PEACH MELBA

1 pkg. frozen raspberries
¼ cup brandy
4 medium-size fresh ripe

peaches
1 qt. vanilla ice cream

Thaw raspberres. Press with juice through sieve or blend in blender to make a sauce. Add brandy, mixing well. Wash peaches; peel. Cut in half. Pit. Place peaches in bowl. Pour raspberry sauce over peaches and refrigerate covered for several hours or overnight. To serve: Remove the peach halves to individual serving dishes. Place a scoop of vanilla ice cream in center of each peach and spoon raspberry sauce over the top.

Have a good time!

Dear Jo: Read your column all the time + have tried many of the good things you have printed. Liked them all! Will look thru my files + see what I can dig up. So you may hear from me later. Bring so many Italian folks in St. Helena may be one will be kind enough to give a recipe for real Italian Cioppino. How to get that good gravy they get from it. My loved it. Keep your column

# Spicy Shrimp with Spaghetti

*For those with a "spicy tooth" among us.*

2 pounds jumbo shrimp, peeled and deveined

Juice of 1 lemon

¼ cup chopped Italian parsley

½ teaspoon crushed red pepper flakes, divided

12 cloves garlic, minced, divided

¼ cup plus 2 tablespoons olive oil

1 tin anchovy fillets

1 (16-ounce) package spaghetti, cooked al dente and drained

Chopped parsley

In a large skillet combine shrimp, lemon juice, ¼ cup chopped parsley, ¼ teaspoon red pepper flakes, 4 cloves minced garlic and 2 tablespoons olive oil. Cook over high heat for 3 minutes or until shrimp are pink and just firm. Remove mixture to a warm dish and set aside.

Return skillet to heat and reduce to low. Add ¼ cup olive oil, anchovies, 8 cloves minced garlic and ¼ teaspoon red pepper flakes. Break up anchovies with a wooden spoon until they melt away into the oil and garlic.

Combine pasta and all other ingredients. Sprinkle with additional chopped parsley before serving.

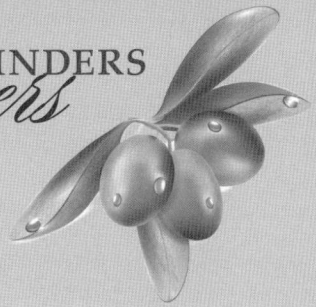

# Couscous with Currants and Almonds

*Good company for Noni's Chicken Curry.*

**2 tablespoons butter**

**2 tablespoons olive oil**

**4 shallots, chopped**

**3 cups rich chicken broth**

**Salt and pepper to taste**

**1 ½ cups couscous**

**½ cup toasted sliced almonds**

**½ cups currants**

Melt butter with olive oil in a large sauté pan. Add shallots and cook 3 minutes. Add stock and salt and pepper to taste. Bring to boil.

Remove from heat and add couscous. Cover pan and let sit 10 minutes.

Stir in almonds and currants before serving.

# Risotto with Leeks, Shiitake Mushrooms and Truffles

*The ultimate risotto recipe follows!*

## LEEKS

2 large leeks, white and pale green parts only, halved and thinly sliced crosswise

¾ cup whipping cream

Bring leeks and cream to a boil in a heavy saucepan. Reduce heat to medium and simmer until leeks are tender and cream is thick. Stir often for about 15 minutes. Season with salt and pepper. This may be prepared a day ahead of serving. Cover and chill leeks then rewarm before continuing with recipe.

## MUSHROOMS

1 pound shiitake mushrooms, stemmed, cut into ¼-inch slices

½ onion, thinly sliced lengthwise

2 tablespoons butter

1 tablespoon truffle oil

1 teaspoon minced fresh thyme

Preheat oven to 400 degrees. Toss all ingredients on rimmed baking sheet. Sprinkle with salt and pepper. Roast until mushrooms are tender and light brown around edges, stirring occasionally for about 25 minutes. Mushrooms may be made 2 hours ahead. Let stand at room temperature.

# *Risotto with Leeks* *(continued)*

## RISOTTO

2 tablespoons olive oil

4 tablespoons butter, divided

½ onion, chopped

1 ½ cups Arborio rice

½ cup white wine

4-5 cups hot vegetable or chicken broth

½ cup grated Parmesan

2 teaspoons shaved or chopped black truffle

Chopped fresh parsley

Place oil and 2 tablespoons butter in heavy large saucepan. Add onion and cook until beginning to soften, about 5 minutes. Add rice and stir 1 minute. Add wine and stir until almost all liquid is absorbed. Add 1 cup hot broth. Simmer, stirring often for about 4 minutes. Add more broth, 1 cup at a time, stirring constantly until rice is tender and mixture is creamy. Stir in leek and mushroom mixtures. Add remaining 2 tablespoons of butter, cheese and truffle. Transfer to large bowl, sprinkle with parsley and serve.

*Both the truffle oil and shaved truffle may be omitted from the recipe but they really add such a nice touch! White truffle oil is sold at some supermarkets. Black truffles are available from igourmet.com. A flavorful substitute for the shaved truffles is the Truffle Gatherers Sauce ($19) which can be ordered from fungusamongus.com.*

# Baked Vegetable Risotto

SERVES 6-8

*Everyone knows that Risotto is Italian soul food. Change the veggies as your refrigerator dictates. This is the most recent creation—four stars!*

3 tablespoons olive oil

½ pound shiitake mushrooms, thinly sliced

¾ cup dried porcinis, reconstituted; liquid drained and reserved

1 ½ cups shredded carrot (or small dice)

¾ cup broccolini, large dice

Salt and pepper

2 tablespoons butter

2 shallots, minced

1 ½ cups Arborio rice

3 cups chicken stock

1 cup Parmesan

1 cup panko

Heat olive oil in large oven-proof skillet. Sauté shiitake and porcini mushrooms, carrots and broccolini for 4 minutes. Remove from skillet and set aside.

In the same pan, add butter and sauté shallots until soft. Add rice and cook, stirring constantly until golden. Add chicken stock and reserved porcini liquid and bring to a boil. Reduce heat and add Parmesan. Cover and cook undisturbed for 15 minutes.

Meanwhile, preheat oven to 350 degrees.

Add reserved vegetables and panko and mix gently. Correct seasoning if necessary. Cover and bake for 30 minutes.

Place mixture in buttered baking dish if skillet is not oven-proof.

*The large size All-Clad Braising Pan is a great investment—a favorite for a lot of dishes and perfect for this one!*

# Baked Rice Medley with Spinach

*A recipe from yesteryear which changes from year to year depending upon the type of rice medley available but which never fails to bring over-the-top compliments.*

2 cups rice medley (brown rice, wild rice, etc.)

2 cans beef broth

2 (10-ounce) packages frozen chopped spinach

½ teaspoon garlic powder

½ teaspoon salt

¼ teaspoon pepper

1 (8-ounce) package cream cheese, softened and cubed

1 pound crimini mushrooms, sliced

3 tablespoons butter

Cook rice according to directions on package, using canned beef broth as part of the liquid required. Check often as it may take additional water. Cooking time will vary between 30 to 60 minutes, depending on the rice medley used. (It takes a little patience!)

Preheat oven to 350 degrees.

Cook spinach and drain well. Season with salt, pepper and garlic powder. Immediately add cream cheese and mix well. Set aside.

Sauté mushrooms in butter until golden.

In a 2 or 3-quart casserole, layer half of rice and half of spinach. Repeat layers and spread mushrooms over top. Cover and bake 40 minutes.

# Saffron Parsley Rice

*The success of this dish lies in following each step precisely. A perfect side.*

4 cups chicken broth

Saffron, several threads

2 cups uncooked long-grain rice

4 tablespoons butter, cut into pieces

1 ½ cups finely chopped Italian parsley

Bring chicken broth to boil in heavy saucepan. Add saffron. Stir in rice and return to boil. Reduce heat to low and cover tightly. Let rice cook, undisturbed, for approximately 25 minutes.

Uncover and add butter and parsley but do not stir. Cover. Remove from heat and let stand 5 minutes.

Uncover and toss with a fork. Serve immediately.

# Ginger Rice

1 ½ tablespoons minced fresh ginger

1 ½ cups water

1 cup jasmine rice, rinsed and drained

1 tablespoon butter

1 teaspoon salt

Place ginger in saucepan. Add water, rice, butter and salt. Bring to a boil over high heat. Immediately reduce heat to low and cook, covered, until rice is tender—about 15 minutes. Remove from heat and let sit 10 minutes.

Uncover and fluff with a fork before serving.

*If you are lucky enough to have any left over, heat and add a bit of sugar and milk for a delicious treat.*

## KOZY KITCHEN
### KITCHEN-TESTED RECIPES
### JO REID

January 31, 1963

Rice is an annual cereal grass which is widely cultivated in warm climates for its seed and used for human food.

It is rich in starch, but low in fat and protein. Brown rice has a much greater food value than white since the brown coatings and germ are rich in vitamins of the B-complex group and in minerals.

Neither the dictionary nor the encyclopedia "glowingly" describe rice, but there is no other food which is as versatile in meat and seafood dishes, desserts, and salads.

The following rice casserole will become a favorite and can be assembled early in the day. You'll use it often when serving barbecued chicken.

### RICE-MUSHROOM DELIGHT

4 tblsp. butter
¾ cup raw rice
1 can 4 oz. mushrooms
2 tblsp. chopped onion
1 can chicken gumbo soup
1 can chicken with rice soup

Melt butter, stir in rice. Combine mushrooms, including liquid, onion, soups. Heat. Pour over rice and stir. Pour into small casserole. Cover and bake 45 minutes at 350 degrees. Serves 4.

Another Friday night offering, using rice.

### RISOTTO WITH CLAMS

¼ cup oil
1 onion, finely chopped
1 clove garlic, minced
2 cups tomatoes (or half tomatoes and half clam broth)
2 tbs. chopped parsley
Pinch dried sweet basil
Pinch of saffron (optional),
1 cup raw rice

¾ tsp. salt
2 cans minced clams or 2 pounds fresh clams in shell.

Heat oil in heavy pan with tightfitting lid. Add onions. Saute' lightly, watching carefully. Add garlic. Stir in tomatoes or clam broth, parsley, sweet basil, rice, salt, saffron, and juice from canned clams. Cover. Steam until rice is tender (15 to 20 min). Stir clams into mixture and cover. Heat until flavors are blended. When fresh clams are available, lay well-scrubbed clams on top of cooked rice mixture. Cover and steam until clams are open. Makes 4 servings.

Rice pudding is a dessert we all remember from childhood and perhaps your children will remember this Butterscotch Rice Pudding.

### FRUIT BUTTERSCOTCH RICE PUDDING

1 cup dried apricots
2 tblsp. butter or margarine, melted
½ cup brown sugar, firmly packed
1½ cups hot cooked rice
2 eggs
½ cup granulated sugar
½ teasp. salt
1 tsp. vanilla extract
2 cups milk, scalded
1/8 teasp. nutmeg
1/4 teasp. cinnamon
1 cup whipped cream

Heat oven to 350 degrees. Cook apricots until tender. Drain. Pour melted butter into 2-quart casserole; sprinkle brown sugar over this. Arrange apricots, rounded side down, in a single layer over this mixture. Spoon on rice.

Beat eggs until light and fluffy; stir in granulated sugar, salt, and vanilla. Then slowly stir in scalded milk. Pour milk mixture over rice and apricots; sprinkle with nutmeg and cinnamon. Set casserole in pan of hot water and bake for 50 minutes or until knife inserted in center comes out clean. Cool.

Serve with dollops of whipped cream. 6 servings.

Next week we will continue the rice story with a marvellous recipe for "Paella" — an adventure in cooking.

# Polenta with Mascarpone

*A side dish that is simple to prepare but challenges the main dish for supremacy! A natural with stews, delicious topped with a tasty marinara, even great for a hearty breakfast with a side of sausages.*

1 (16-ounce) roll ready-made polenta

4 ounces mascarpone

¾ cup Parmigianino Reggiano

Pepper to taste.

Preheat oven to 450 degrees. Generously grease a 9x13-inch glass baking pan with olive oil and set aside.

Pat polenta roll dry. Cut crosswise into ½-inch slices. Arrange slices in the baking dish overlapping slightly and covering the bottom of the dish completely.

Stir mascarpone in a small bowl to loosen and then spread it over polenta, holding slices down as necessary.

Sprinkle Parmesan evenly over all. Bake 18 minutes and allow to rest 5 minutes to become firm. Season with pepper as desired.

# Southern Grits

6 cups water

1 ½ cup grits

1 ½ sticks butter

1 pound grated cheese of choice

Salt and pepper to taste

Dash of Tabasco

3 eggs, beaten

In a large saucepan, bring water to boil and slowly stir in grits. Cook for 20 minutes, stirring often. Stir in butter, cheese, salt and pepper to taste and a dash of Tabasco. Slowly add eggs to the mixture and combine thoroughly.

Pour into a buttered casserole dish; cover and bake in 350 degree oven until center is done.

*Clean-up will be much easier if you fill your saucepan with cold water immediately after transferring grits to the baking dish.*

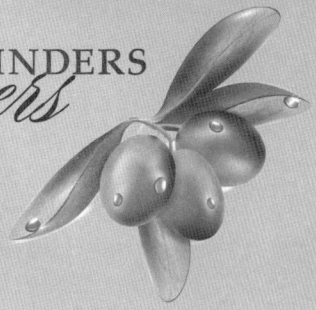

# Colcannon

*Delicious on St. Patrick's Day and any other "Saints' Days" throughout the year!*

## POTATOES

10 medium-size russet potatoes
1 stick butter
1 cup half-and-half
½ cup crème fraiche or sour cream
Salt and pepper to taste

Peel and cut potatoes into 1-inch pieces. In a saucepan, cover potatoes with salted water and simmer for 15 minutes or until they are tender. Drain; add the butter, half-and-half and crème fraiche. Add salt and pepper to taste. Mash until smooth and fluffy; set aside to complete dish.

## CABBAGE AND LEEK MIXTURE

4 tablespoons butter
4 leeks, slices
1 head green cabbage, cored and thinly shredded
½ teaspoon garlic powder
1 teaspoon salt
¼ teaspoon pepper

Melt butter in a large skillet. Add leeks and cook until tender, stirring often. Add cabbage and cook until cabbage is cooked through, about 10 minutes. The skillet may be covered during part of the cooking time. Stir in garlic powder, salt and pepper. Add to reserved potato mixture and stir well to blend.

*Potato mixture may be made ahead. Keep warm in a slow cooker or cover with foil and place in a 200 degree oven.*

# Accordion Potatoes

SERVES 6

*The standard accompaniment to our Steak au Poivre—this is one potato that "makes a statement"!*

**6 baking potatoes, approximately 4x2-inches**

**4 tablespoons butter, melted**

**1 ¼ teaspoons salt**

**⅛ teaspoon pepper**

**2 cloves garlic, minced**

**Olive oil**

**2 tablespoons grated Parmesan**

**1 tablespoon fresh rosemary, chopped**

Preheat oven to 425 degrees. Peel potatoes and drop into cold water to prevent darkening.

Insert a skewer lengthwise into potato ¾-inch from the bottom. Beginning about ½-inch from one end of potato, slice down to the skewer at intervals of ¼-inch. Carefully remove potato from skewer and drop back into the cold water. When ready to bake, drain potatoes and pat dry with paper towels, handling potatoes carefully to prevent breaking.

Combine butter, salt, pepper and garlic. Generously oil a 9x13-inch baking dish and arrange potatoes, sliced side up. Brush tops with half of butter mixture and bake 35 to 45 minutes.

Pour remaining butter mixture over potatoes and baste occasionally. Dust with Parmesan and rosemary and continue to roast another 20 to 25 minutes or until golden browned and done.

Potatoes should have opened like the folds of an accordion into a fan shape.

# KITCHEN KAPERS

## JO REID

It's that time of year again when we pay homage to that very, very special man—dear ole' Dad! This is one day when he shouldn't have to shave, mow the lawn, or empty the garbage! And won't he know he's loved if you serve him this kind of a meal?

## FATHER'S DAY DINNER

Artichokes Gourmet
Prime rib roast
Scalloped potatoes with mushrooms
Fresh spinach
Chocolate angel pie

## ARTICHOKES GOURMET

Tie string around each artichoke. Place in steamer above boiling salted water or a mixture of white wine and water. Cover steamer tightly and steam 45 minutes to 1 hour, or until leaves are tender. Remove and drain; cool. Now mix 2 tbsp. finely chopped ripe olives into garlic-flavored French dressing. Combine with equal amount dry white wine. Marinate drained, steamed artichokes in this dressing several hours in refrigerator. Serve on lettuce leaves, garnished with sliced tomatoes, and additional dressing.

## SCALLOPED POTATOES WITH MUSHROOMS

8 medium sized boiled potatoes    1 large onion
1 lb. fresh mushrooms
1 tsp. onion salt                 1 tsp. salad herbs
1 tbsp. finely chopped parsley    1½ pints sour cream
                                  Ground pepper

Saute onion in melted butter. In a separate pan saute sliced mushrooms in butter. In a large casserole place sliced boiled potatoes alternately with onions, mushrooms, and seasonings. Then cover with sour cream and bake in a 350 degree oven for 20 minutes. Serves 8.

## FRESH SPINACH

Wash fresh spinach thoroughly through many waters. Drain. Remove thick stems. Pile into large saucepan. Cover and cook in its own moisture over medium heat 5 minutes. Drain well and chop very fine. Now melt 3 tbsp. butter in a saucepan. Add 1 clove of garlic and cook for 2 or 3 minutes. Remove garlic and discard. Now add the chopped spinach, correct seasoning, and heat and serve! Tasty.

## CHOCOLATE ANGEL PIE

2 egg whites                  ½ cup sugar
⅛ tsp. salt                   ½ cup chopped nuts
⅛ tsp. cream of tartar        ½ tsp. vanilla

Beat egg whites with cream of tartar until foamy. Add sugar gradually and keep beating until they form stiff peaks. Fold in the nuts and vanilla. Spread in well greased 9-inch pie plate and bake in 300 degree oven 50 to 55 minutes. Cool.

1 large bar sweet chocolate   FILLING:
3 tbsp. water                 1 tsp. vanilla
                              1 cup whipping cream

Melt chocolate in water over low heat. Cool. Add vanilla and fold in whipping cream. Fill the pie shell and chill at least 2 hours. Serves 6 to 8.

Happy Father's Day!

# Perfect Mashed Potatoes

*Everyone loves mashed potatoes but very often last minute prep can be difficult. Problem solved. These can be made early in the day and popped into the oven just 30 minutes before serving. Perfect!*

4 pounds red potatoes

4 cloves garlic

1 (8-ounce) package cream cheese, softened

½ cup sour cream

½ cup half-and-half

¾ cup chopped fresh chives

Salt and pepper

4 tablespoons butter, cut into small pieces

Shredded Parmesan

Cut potatoes in even chunks. Start with cold salted water and bring to a boil along with garlic cloves. The potatoes should be tender in about 12 minutes. Drain and return to same pot.

Add cream cheese and mash well. Mix in sour cream, half-and-half and chives. Correct seasoning as needed.

Spoon potato mixture into a buttered 9x13-inch baking dish. Dot with butter and sprinkle with cheese. Cover with foil and let stand at room temperature, several hours ahead of serving.

When ready to serve, preheat oven to 375 degrees. Remove foil and bake until potatoes are heated through and golden browned on top, about 30 minutes.

# Mashed Potatoes with Cheese

*Last minute timesaver—choose your flavor.*

**1 recipe of favorite mashed potatoes**

**1 cup heavy cream, whipped**

**1 cup shredded cheese of choice
(Parmesan, Cheddar or Fontina)**

Spoon mashed potatoes in a large, lightly buttered baking dish. Top with whipped cream and sprinkle with shredded cheese.

Bake until warm throughout and browned on top.

# Mashed Potatoes with Green Onions

*Adding glamour to the almighty spud!*

**4 pounds red potatoes, peeled and
cut into 1-inch pieces**

**1 cup whipping cream**

**1 stick butter**

**1 bunch green onions, chopped**

**Salt and pepper**

Cook potatoes in salted water until tender. Drain and return to the same pot and mash.

While potatoes are cooking, combine the cream and butter. Simmer for several minutes, watching carefully. Add onions and remove from heat. Cover and steep for 15 minutes.

Add cream mixture to mashed potatoes and adjust seasoning. Serve immediately or cover and set aside. Rewarm over low heat, stirring.

# Crusty Potatoes

*Show-off potatoes.*

3 pounds small unpeeled red potatoes

⅓ cup olive oil

3 cloves garlic, chopped

4 shallots, chopped

½ cup chopped parsley

½ teaspoon salt

⅛ teaspoon pepper

1 stick butter, melted

Early in the day you are planning
to serve the dish, parboil the potatoes until just tender, taking care
not to overcook. Drain and refrigerate several hours.

In a food processor, blend olive
oil, garlic, shallot, parsley, salt and
pepper. Pour into a small bowl and
add melted butter. Set aside.

About two and one half hours prior
to serving, preheat oven to 350
degrees. Cut chilled potatoes into
quarters and place in a 9x13-inch
baking dish. Add reserved butter
mixture, covering potatoes on all
sides.

Bake for 2 hours or until potatoes
are crispy. Stir occasionally.

# Squashed Potatoes

*How can something this easy be so outstanding???*

6 medium potatoes, unpeeled

Sea salt

Olive oil

Preheat oven to 400 degrees.

Place potatoes in a baking dish.
Add water to reach one quarter up
the side of the dish. Cover tightly
with foil. Bake 40 to 50 minutes or
until tender. Drain potatoes and
dry well.

Return potatoes to pan and, using
a smaller pan over the potatoes,
press it down to "squash" the potatoes, still keeping them somewhat
intact, but flattened. Hence, they are
squashed!

Sprinkle with sea salt and olive oil.
Increase oven temperature to 500
degrees and bake for 30 minutes.

*Potatoes may be steamed until tender
then follow the same directions.*

April 18,

# KOZY KITCHEN

**Kitchen-Tested Recipes From The Kitchen Of**

x JO REID x

The topic today will be Italian foods. All in favor, signify by saying Aye.

And I Aye by sighing -- "Oh, for a good frittata!" Granted, pasta is great, but oh, those Italian Fritatta's. What is it?

It's an omelet, chuck full of imagination, conjured up by a little signora while her signor grabbed a wink under the shade of the old olive tree.

There's where it all started, you know -- the way to a man's heart, et. etc. No sandwiches in sunny Italy for the Master's lunch.

Our American male is seldom home for lunch, however, and what's more, he's more calorie-conscious at his noonday meal. But why not find the way to his heart at dinnertime by serving a Frittata along with a broiled steak? See?

"Si".

## PATATA FRITTATA

(Preheat oven to 375 degrees)

6 large potatoes, peeled and diced
1 large onion, chopped fine
Salt and pepper
4 large eggs
Oil

Heat skillet. Add oil to cover bottom generously. Add potatoes and onions, frying until golden brown and turning often. Cool.

Beat eggs in large bowl. Add potatoe mixture, blending quickly.

Add little more oil to skillet if necessary. Add fritatta and bake in oven 20 to 25 minutes. Brown under broiler the last minute, or so, to desired goldness.

## VEGE-FRITTATA

(Preheat oven to 375 degrees)

8 artichokes (the tiny ones)
6 zucchini, sliced
1 bunch swiss chard
1 large onion, chopped
1 cup cooked rice
1 cup grated Parmesan cheese
6 large eggs
½ teasp. rosemary
½ teasp. sage
Salt and pepper
Oil

Boil artichokes until tender using hearts only. Slice. Set aside. Boil swiss chard until cooked. Drain thoroughly. Chop. Set aside.

Put enough oil in skillet to cover bottom. Cook onion until golden, stirring constantly. Add sliced raw zucchini and saute slowly. Now add artichokes and swiss chard mixing well. Beat eggs in large bowl. Add cheese, cooked rice, seasonings, and vegetable mixture. Mix thoroughly. Heat more oil in black iron skillet and put in the frittata. Place in oven and bake 20 to 25 minutes. If the top is not browned enough, it may be placed under the broiler for a minute or so, watching carefully.

Have a wonderful day! Polish the chopsticks.

# Potato Gratin with Boursin

*Carol accompanies this with Grilled Flank Steak. Perfect partners.*

2 cups whipping cream

1 (5-ounce) package Boursin cheese with herbs

3 pounds Yukon Gold potatoes, unpeeled and thinly sliced

Salt and pepper

1 ½ tablespoons chopped fresh parsley

Preheat oven to 400 degrees. Butter a 9x13-inch baking dish and set aside.

Stir whipping cream with Boursin in a heavy saucepan over low heat only until cheese melts and mixture is smooth.

Arrange half the sliced potatoes in prepared baking dish, slightly overlapping. Season potatoes with salt and pepper. Pour half of cheese mixture over potatoes. Arrange remaining potatoes in a second layer and season with salt and pepper. Pour remaining cheese over potatoes.

Bake about 1 hour or until top is golden browned and potatoes are tender. Sprinkle with chopped parsley to serve.

# Roast Potatoes with Garlic

SERVES 4-6

*This is the perfect roast potato. They may need a little more attention but the result is worth every minute!*

**2 pounds red potatoes**

**3 tablespoons olive oil**

**Salt and pepper**

**2 tablespoons chopped fresh rosemary**

**3 cloves garlic**

**¼ teaspoon salt**

Place rack in the middle of the oven and preheat it to 425 degrees.

Scrub, dry and halve potatoes. Cut into ¾-inch wedges. Toss potatoes with olive oil, salt and pepper. Place potatoes, flat side down, in a baking pan. Cover with foil and bake 20 minutes.

Remove foil but do NOT turn potatoes. Roast an additional 15 minutes. Meanwhile, place garlic and sea salt in a bowl large enough to hold potatoes. Blend to a paste.

Remove pan from oven and carefully turn potatoes over, using a metal spatula. Sprinkle with rosemary and roast 5 to 10 minutes or until golden. Immediately add potatoes to garlic/salt mixture and serve.

# Roasted New Potatoes

*The perfect little roasted potato.*

2 pounds small red potatoes

6 whole cloves garlic

3-4 sprigs rosemary

4 tablespoons unsalted butter, melted

¼ teaspoon fresh cracked black pepper

Preheat oven to 400 degrees.

Combine all ingredients in roasting pan and cover with foil. Place in oven and bake 15 minutes.

Uncover and continue to bake 15 minutes, stirring occasionally, until potatoes are cooked and golden in color.

## JO REID'S KITCHEN-TESTED RECIPES

### Sweet Potato Casserole**
In a frying pan, break apart and brown 1 pound bulk pork sausage along with ¼ cup chopped onions. Pour off the accumulated fat. Cook and mash enough sweet potatoes (yams are just as good) to measure 6 cups. Mix together the sausage and onion mixture, 2 eggs, ⅔ cup milk and the mashed potatoes. Season to taste with salt. Pour mixture into a shallow 2-quart casserole and smooth surface with a spoon. Now blend ¼ cup melted butter with ½ cup firmly packed brown sugar and ¼ cup heavy cream; boil together, stirring occasionally for 3 minutes. Pour sauce evenly over potatoes. Bake in a moderate oven (350°) for 30 to 40 minutes or until hot. Makes 8 to 10 servings.

# Brussels Sprouts with Parmesan

SERVES 6-8

*This is one of Libbie's most requested recipes—they are in competition, always, with the main course.*

**2 pounds Brussels sprouts**

**2 tablespoons olive oil**

**2 tablespoons butter**

**3 cloves garlic, minced**

**Pinch of red pepper flakes**

**Salt and pepper to taste**

**½ cup grated Parmesan**

Trim ends off sprouts, remove outer leaves and cut in half. Place in a large sauté pan and cover with water. Steam for 5 minutes—they should be al dente. Drain well.

In sauté pan, heat olive oil with butter. Return sprouts to pan and sauté with garlic, red pepper flakes, salt and pepper until lightly browned. Turn off heat and sprinkle with Parmesan. Allow Parmesan to melt into sprouts before serving.

# Brussels Sprouts with Shallots

*Sprouts with an attitude!*

1 ½ pounds Brussels sprouts, thinly sliced

2 tablespoons butter

3 tablespoons olive oil

12 medium shallots, thinly sliced

6 cloves garlic, thinly sliced

4 tablespoons pine nuts, lightly toasted

Place butter and oil in a large skillet. Add shallots and sauté 5 minutes. Add garlic and sauté for 1 minute. Add sprouts and cook until just tender. Do not overcook. Season with salt and pepper and sprinkle with pine nuts before serving.

# Baked Spinach

3 pounds fresh spinach, blanched in salted water

1 ¾ cups whipping cream

2 eggs

¼ cup Parmesan

½ teaspoon nutmeg

Salt and pepper

After cooking spinach, drain well, chop and set aside. Preheat oven to 375 degrees. Butter a 1 ½-inch deep baking dish and set aside.

Combine whipping cream, eggs, Parmesan, nutmeg, salt and pepper. Mix chopped spinach with egg mixture. Pour into prepared dish.

Bake 30 minutes. The top will be crisp and the underneath slightly creamy.

# Eggplant Parmesan

*A more delicate approach to this time-honored Italian specialty.*

## EGGPLANT

2 eggplants, peeled and cut into
¼-inch slices

Olive oil-flavored cooking spray

Preheat oven to 400 degrees.

Spray eggplant slices on both sides with cooking spray. Place in a single layer on cookie sheets and bake, turning once, until the slices are golden on both sides—about 20 to 30 minutes. Remove from oven and set aside.

## TOMATO SAUCE

2 tablespoons olive oil

1 large onion, chopped

2 cloves garlic, minced

1 (29-ounce) can crushed tomatoes

2 tablespoons tomato paste

1 teaspoon dried basil

1 teaspoon dried oregano

1 teaspoon sugar

Freshly ground pepper

8 ounces mozzarella, sliced

½ cup Parmigianino Reggiano

Heat oil in a nonstick sauté pan and sauté onions until they soften and become golden. Add garlic and cook 30 seconds. Add tomatoes, tomato paste, basil, oregano, sugar and pepper. Mix well and simmer 30 minutes.

Arrange eggplant on the bottom of a 9x13-inch pan. Add a layer of mozzarella and spread sauce over top. Sprinkle with Parmigianino Reggiano.

To serve, preheat oven to 375 degrees and bake 20 to 30 minutes or until it bubbles and browns. Allow to rest 10 minutes before serving.

# Athenian Moussaka

SERVES 10-12

*Many of us were privileged to attend Irene's cooking classes years ago—the recipes were great, the lunch was delicious and many lasting friendships were formed. This is one of our favorites.*

## EGGPLANT

2 medium-sized (1 pound each) egg-plants

½ cup olive oil

Meat Sauce

Custard Topping

½ cup shredded Parmesan

Preheat oven to 425 degrees.

Trim stem ends from eggplant and cut lengthwise into ¼-inch slices. Pour oil into two large baking pans and turn eggplant slices in it, coating both sides. Arrange in a single layer. Bake for 30 minutes, turning occasionally, or until tender. To assemble, arrange half the eggplant in an 11x15-inch baking pan. Spoon on Meat Sauce and top with remaining eggplant. Pour Custard Topping over top and sprinkle with Parmesan.

Reduce heat to 350 degrees and bake, uncovered, for 1 hour.

# Athenian Moussaka (continued)

## MEAT SAUCE

2 medium onions, chopped

2 tablespoons olive oil

2 ½ pounds ground beef or lamb

2 teaspoons salt

2 (6-ounce) cans tomato paste

1 ¼ cups dry red wine

¼ cup finely chopped parsley

1 cinnamon stick, optional

2 cloves garlic, minced

3 tablespoons fine dry bread crumbs

1 cup shredded Parmesan

Sauté onion in oil. Add ground beef or lamb and cook, stirring until crumbly. Add salt, tomato paste, wine, parsley, cinnamon (if using) and minced garlic. Cover and simmer 30 minutes. Remove cinnamon, cover and cook down until liquid is evaporated. Stir in bread crumbs and Parmesan.

## CUSTARD TOPPING

⅓ cup butter, melted

½ cup all-purpose flour

1 quart milk

1 tablespoon nutmeg

½ cup shredded Parmesan

6 eggs, lightly beaten

Melt butter and whisk in flour. Cook 2 minutes. Gradually stir in milk and cook, stirring until mixture thickens. Add nutmeg and Parmesan. Slowly stir a small amount of hot mixture into eggs to temper. Finally, incorporate egg mixture into the rest of the sauce and mix well.

# Spinach Porcini Bake

*A delicious side with roasted chicken.*

½ cup dried porcini mushrooms

1 cup hot water

½ pound ground mild Italian sausage

3 shallots, chopped

3 cloves garlic, chopped

2 cups French bread cubes (crust removed, cut into ½-inch cubes)

1 (10-ounce) package frozen chopped spinach, thawed

1 teaspoon chopped rosemary

2 eggs, lightly beaten

Preheat oven to 350 degrees. Butter a casserole dish and set aside.

Soak porcini in hot water in a small bowl. Let stand until soft. Drain well but reserve soaking liquid. Chop porcini and set aside.

Sauté sausage until brown, breaking into small pieces. Add shallots and garlic. Cover and cook for 5 minutes. Add garlic and cook 1 minute longer. Stir in bread cubes, spinach, rosemary and reserved porcini and soaking liquid.

Season with salt and pepper as needed. Often, the sausage provides sufficient seasoning for the dish. Mix in eggs and blend ingredients well.

Spoon mixture into prepared dish, cover, and bake 30 minutes.

# Spinach Stuffed Zucchini

*Double whammy of deliciousness!*

6 zucchini or patty pan squash, halved lengthwise

2 tablespoons olive oil

Salt and pepper

2 tablespoons butter

½ yellow onion, diced

1 (10-ounce) package chopped frozen spinach, thawed and squeezed dry

½ cup sour cream

1 cup chicken-flavored stuffing mix

1 cup grated Parmesan

Additional Parmesan for topping

Preheat oven to 400 degrees.

Brush squash with oil and sprinkle with salt and pepper. Place, cut side down, on baking sheet and bake 15 minutes until tender.

Scoop out pulp, keeping shells intact. Chop and reserve pulp.

Reduce heat to 350 degrees.

In a skillet melt butter and cook onion until soft. Combine with reserved pulp and all remaining ingredients. Spoon into reserved squash shells. Place shells back on a baking sheet and sprinkle with Parmesan. Bake for 20 minutes.

*Three thinly sliced green onions may be used in place of the chopped yellow onion.*

# Butternut Squash & Red Pepper Casserole

*Always loved!*

3 ½ pounds butternut squash (about 9 cups of 1-inch cubes)

1 large red bell pepper, cut into 1-inch pieces

2 tablespoons olive oil

2 large garlic cloves, minced

3 tablespoons minced fresh parsley leaves

2 tablespoons minced fresh rosemary

Salt and freshly ground black pepper to taste

1 cup freshly grated Parmesan

Preheat oven to 400 degrees.

In a large bowl, stir together squash, red pepper, oil, garlic, herbs, salt and black pepper. Transfer mixture to a shallow baking dish and sprinkle top with Parmesan.

Bake casserole in middle of oven until squash is tender and top is golden, about 1 hour.

# Broccolini with Garlic

SERVES 6

*The perfect side dish for any entrée.*

3 bunches broccolini, coarse ends trimmed

3 tablespoons olive oil

3 cloves garlic, minced

⅛ teaspoon red pepper flakes

Salt and pepper to taste

Cook broccolini in boiling water until tender. Drain well.

Heat oil in a large skillet. Add broccolini, garlic and red pepper flakes. Cook over low heat, stirring occasionally. Season to taste.

# KITCHEN KAPERS

Kitchen-Tested Recipes from the Kitchen of
## JO REID

Remember the good ole' days when it was a real treat to have chicken every Sunday? And it still is a treat, but since chicken is now so plentiful and inexpensive, it is used more often in meal planning.

Volumes have been filled with chicken recipes alone, but one which is especially easy to prepare and delicious is Oven-Fried Chicken. White wine is suggested in the recipe and is very good, but you could experiment with some of the other wines, such as, the rose's, champagne, and even dry or sweet vermouth!

## OVEN-FRIED CHICKEN

1 cup biscuit mix
2 tsp. salt
½ tsp. pepper
2 tsp. paprika
4 tblsp. shortening
4 tblsp. butter
White wine (½ cup or to taste)
1 3-pound frying chicken

Mix dry ingredients. Dip chicken in this mixture and coat well. Melt shortening and butter in baking dish and place chicken, skin side down, in a single layer. Bake in hot oven at 425 degrees for 30 minutes. Add wine and cook an additional 15 minutes.

***Chicken is especially fine-flavored when it has been soaked in evaporated milk overnight.

And what better alliance is there than corn fritters to chicken!. There are two thoughts in corn fritter preparation: one is frying as pancakes and the other is the deep-fry method. The following recipe is adaptable to either way.

## CORN FRITTERS

1 cup flour
¾ teasp. salt
1 teasp. baking powder
2 eggs separated
¼ cup milk
1 pkg. frozen corn, thawed and drained
2 teasp. melted butter or shortening

Sift flour, salt, and baking powder. Mix beaten egg yolks and milk, add to dry ingredients and mix until just smooth. Add corn and shortening. Fold in stiffly beaten egg whites. Drop from tablespoon into deep hot fat (370 degrees) or fry as for pancakes. Drain on paper towel. Serves 4 to 6.

Doesn't a refreshing lemon pie come to mind after a dinner of chicken 'n fritters! This one is different and will become a family favorite.

## LEMON PIE SUPERB
### (Makes 8 in. pie).

Make your favorite pie shell. Bake and set aside.

Filling:
Juice and grated rind of 1 lemon
½ cup granulated sugar
3 eggs, separated

Beat egg whites stiff. Set aside. Mix the juice and rind of lemon with sugar and egg yolks. Cook over low heat, stirring constantly, until just thick. Add the egg whites to the hot lemon mixture. Cool and put in baked pie shell. Make swirl markings with edge of knife and brown pie under broiler but be sure to watch carefully. Serve with dollops of whipped cream.

Have a very nice day, see you next week!

# Corn Fluff

SERVES 4

*You will fall in love with this dish.*

2 cups frozen corn, thawed

2 eggs

½ cup whipping cream

¼ cup milk

1 tablespoon sugar

1 tablespoon all-purpose flour

1 teaspoon baking powder

½ teaspoon salt

2 tablespoons butter, softened

Preheat oven to 350 degrees. Butter a small baking dish and set aside.

Blend all ingredients in processor until almost smooth. Pour batter into prepared dish. Bake until browned and center is just set, about 30 minutes. Cool 10 minutes before serving.

*For a different texture, you may want to process only half the corn kernels and add the remaining ones to the dish before baking.*

# Sauerkraut Up-a-Notch

*The perfect accompaniment for Bratwurst or a Pork Roast or Spareribs or... alone!*

2 tablespoons butter

1 medium onion, sliced

1 (16-ounce) jar sauerkraut, rinsed and drained

1 tart green apple, peeled and grated

1 cup chicken broth, heated

In an oven-proof skillet, melt butter and sauté onion until slightly cooked. Add sauerkraut and sauté for 5 minutes. Stir in apples and heated broth. Preheat oven to 325 degrees.

Cook uncovered on stovetop for 30 minutes. Cover and bake in oven for an additional 30 minutes.

# Green Beans & Zucchini with Sauce Verte

*A very special veggie.*

## SAUCE VERTE

⅓ cup fresh basil

1 green onion

2 tablespoons Italian parsley

2 tablespoons capers, drained

1 tablespoon lemon juice

2 teaspoons Dijon mustard

1 clove garlic, minced

2 tablespoons olive oil

Place all ingredients except oil in food processor. Pulse to blend. Gradually add oil, dripping it slowly through the chute. Process until oil is incorporated. Season with salt and pepper.

## VEGETABLES

1 tablespoon olive oil

1 pound green beans

12 ounces zucchini, cut into strips

½ teaspoon salt

3 tablespoons water

Heat oil, add green beans and zucchini. Sprinkle with salt and stir to coat. Add water. Cover and cook until green beans and zucchini are crisp-tender. Stir in enough of the prepared sauce to coat. Adjust seasoning as needed

# Green Beans with Ginger & Garlic

*This is Asian-inspired but can add a fresh touch to any and all other inspired meals!*

1 pound green beans

3 cloves garlic, minced

1 tablespoon soy sauce

1 tablespoon grated ginger

1 teaspoon rice vinegar

1 tablespoon canola oil

½ teaspoon sesame oil

1 ½ teaspoons toasted sesame seeds

Cook beans in well-salted water, uncovered, until just tender—about 6 or 7 minutes. Drain and plunge into an ice bath to stop cooking. Drain and pat dry.

Mash garlic to a paste with a pinch of salt. Add soy sauce, ginger, vinegar and oils in a large bowl.

Add beans and toss. Serve sprinkled with sesame seeds.

# Snow Peas and Almonds

*Such an easy touch for a special result.*

1 tablespoon butter

½ cup sliced almonds

½ pound snow peas

1 tablespoon minced shallot

Zest of 1 lemon

Salt to taste

Melt butter in skillet. Add almonds and cook until golden, stirring to avoid burning. Add snow peas and shallot and sauté 2 minutes.

Remove from heat. Add lemon zest and salt to taste.

# Sesame Asparagus

*Make ahead and serve at room temperature.*

**2 pounds fresh asparagus**
**1 tablespoon toasted sesame oil**
**1 tablespoon sesame seed**
**1 teaspoon reduced-sodium soy sauce**

Trim tough parts of asparagus and peel the ends. (Takes a little time, but worth it.) Steam asparagus 5 to 7 minutes until tender. Drain and set aside.

In a skillet, heat oil until it is warm. Add sesame seeds and asparagus, stirring to coat. Warm asparagus slightly and stir in soy sauce before serving.

# Lemon Whipped Cream for Asparagus

SERVES 4

*Steamed asparagus does not need much "dolling up" but a dollop of this cream sends it over the top. This is as lavish as Hollandaise but less tricky to prepare.*

**½ cup heavy cream**
**¼ teaspoon salt**
**Juice of ½ lemon**
**Minced chives**

Whip cream until soft peaks form. Whip in salt and lemon juice. Sprinkle with chives. Recipe is easily doubled.

# Tomato Treats

*Is not a tomato sandwich one of the all-time greats? Summertime means tomato time. These recipes will certainly catch your fancy.*

## ROASTED TOMATOES

12 plum tomatoes, halved lengthwise, cored and seeded

4 tablespoons olive oil

1 ½ tablespoons good balsamic vinegar

2 cloves garlic, minced

2 tablespoons sugar, granulated or raw

1 teaspoon salt

½ teaspoon ground pepper

Preheat oven to 450 degrees. Arrange tomatoes on a sheet pan in a single layer. Drizzle with olive oil and vinegar. Sprinkle with garlic, sugar, salt and pepper. Roast 25 to 30 minutes or until tomatoes are concentrated and beginning to caramelize. Serve warm or at room temperature

## SLOW ROASTED TOMATOES

4 pounds plum tomatoes, halved lengthwise

6 cloves garlic, minced

5 tablespoons olive oil

Salt and pepper

Place tomatoes, cut side up, on a large sheet pan. Combine garlic and oil and spoon over tomatoes. Season with salt and pepper. Roast in 200 degree oven for 6 to 8 hours. Cool and store. Use in a spaghetti sauce recipe or as a great pizza topping.

## ROASTED TOMATOES WITH ANCHOVIES, GARLIC & PARSLEY

2 pounds large plum tomatoes, sliced into 6 wedges

1 tin anchovy filets, chopped

½ cup chopped parsley or basil

2 cloves garlic, chopped

¼ teaspoon crushed red pepper

Salt and pepper

½ cup olive oil

Preheat oven to 400 degrees. Arrange tomatoes, rounded side down, in a 9x13-inch glass baking dish. Sprinkle with anchovies, parsley or basil, garlic, red pepper, salt and pepper. Drizzle with olive oil. Bake until tender—between 30 and 40 minutes. Check for doneness.

## Tomato Treats (continued)

### PAN CON TOMATE

1 (6-inch) baguette, halved lengthwise
1 clove garlic
2 tablespoons olive oil
1 large ripe tomato
Coarse sea salt

Heat oven to 500 degrees. Bake bread until golden brown, about 8 minutes. Rub garlic over cut surfaces of bread. Drizzle with oil. Put a box grater into a large bowl and grate tomato over largest holes. Spoon grated tomato onto toast and sprinkle with sea salt.

## Roasted Tomatoes with Anchovies, Garlic & Basil

*Italian ambrosia!*

2 pounds large plum tomatoes
1 tin anchovy fillets
¼ cup chopped basil
4 cloves garlic, chopped
¼ teaspoon red pepper flakes
Salt and pepper to taste
½ cup olive oil

Preheat oven to 400 degrees. Cut tomatoes, lengthwise, into 6 wedges. Arrange tomatoes, rounded side down, in a single layer in a 13x9-inch glass baking dish. Sprinkle with anchovies, basil, garlic and red pepper flakes. Season to taste with salt and pepper.

Drizzle with oil and bake uncovered until tender, wrinkled and starting to brown at the edges— about 40 minutes.

*Great over toasted crostini, pasta, pizza dough, everything!*

# KITCHEN KAPERS

**Kitchen-Tested Recipes from the Kitchen of**
**JO REID**

What's happened to the Sunday Night Supper? It's a great day for visiting with friends informally and the day when our mothers usually had drop-in visitors. The warmth of your welcome and the hospitality of your home, coupled with wholesome food and relaxing conversation are the ingredients for a very pleasant Sunday Night Supper.

## CASSEROLE OF VEAL AND CREAMED PEAS
### (Prepare in the morning)

Cut 3 pounds sliced veal into strips about 2 inches long and ½ inch wide. Roll in flour, then in beaten egg, and last in fine bread crumbs. Saute until crisp and brown. Arrange in a casserole with 1 pound of sliced mushrooms (either canned or fresh) and 1 chopped onion. Sprinkle with salt and pepper. Add enough evaporated milk to cover meat. Cover and bake in 300 degrees 2½ hours. Add 2 packages frozen green peas and continue baking 15 minutes. About half an hour before serving, cover with grated Parmesan cheese and reheat. Serves 6 generously.

## BAKED TOMATOES STUFFED WITH CORN
### (Prepare in the morning)

Cut a lid from the required number of tomatoes and scoop out pulp. Sprinkle inside with salt. Mix the tomato pulp with Mexicorn. Season with grated onion, celery salt, and freshly ground black pepper. Fill the tomato shells, dot with butter and replace lids. Bake in 350 degree oven until the tomato is cooked through. There are so many variations with stuffed tomatoes. Another time, mix the pulp with seasoned bread stuffing or one of our favorites is just scooping out the inside pulp, mixing it with canned pork and beans. Delicious.

## BANANA NUT PIE

For the crust: Grind enough walnuts (Brazil nuts and almonds are equally good) to make 1½ cups powdered nuts. Add 3 tbsp. sugar and press in the bottom and sides of a buttered pie dish. Fill with Banana Cream: Beat 3 egg yolks and add gradually while still beating, 2½ tbsp. cornstarch, 2/3 cup sugar, and ¼ tsp. salt. Melt 1 tbsp. butter in 2 cups scalded milk and pour over the egg mixture. Cook in a double boiler until thick, stirring constantly. Cool. Flavor with 1 tsp. vanilla. Pour mixture into the nut crust and cover with 2 peeled, sliced bananas. Chill for several hours in the refrigerator. Frost with slightly sweetened whipped cream and serve to Sunday guests.

## QUICK RAISED ROLLS

These take only an hour! Heat 1 cup milk to room temperature and add 2 tsp. sugar, 1 egg, 1 tsp. salt, 4 tsp. shortening and 1 pkg. yeast softened with a small amount of warm water. Mix all together, add enough flour to make a soft dough. Roll out and cut in small circles. Let rise until twice their size and bake in 350 oven until golden.

## BAKED CANNED BEANS

So you just have hamburger and canned beans in the house! Try this for a quickie. Chop fine 2 onions and mix with 1 tsp. dry mustard and 1 tbsp. molasses. Place in the bottom of a large glass baking dish and pour in 3 cans of baked small beans. Cover with strips of bacon and bake cover for ½ hour in 300 degree oven. Remove cover and brown the bacon under the broiler. Meanwhile BBQ the hamburgers, mix together a green salad, and discuss last week's world's events!

Have a very nice day.

# Whipped Cauliflower

SERVES 4

*Scrumptious substitute for mashed potatoes! Rich tasting without the calories.*

**1 large head cauliflower**
**½ teaspoon salt**
**2 tablespoons butter**
**Grated Parmesan**

Separate cauliflower into small florets. Sprinkle with salt and place in steamer. Cook until tender throughout.

Carefully place cauliflower in food processor Add butter and process until smooth (to the consistency of mashed potatoes). Adjust seasoning with salt and pepper. Serve with a sprinkling of Parmesan.

If making ahead, place in an oven-proof dish and sprinkle with Parmesan. When ready to serve, heat at 350 degrees for about 12 or 15 minutes.

*Always select snowy white heads of cauliflower. And when preparing it, I prefer using a steamer so the cauliflower will not get water-logged.*

# Baked Mixed Vegetables

*Such a winner! This will become your no-brainer go-to veggie dish.*

**4 medium potatoes cut into wedges**
**2 red peppers, peeled & cut into wedges**
**2 yellow peppers, peeled & cut into wedges**
**3 tomatoes cut in wedges**
**4 red onions, peeled & cut into wedges**
**½ cup olive oil**

Preheat oven to 400 degrees.

Combine all ingredients and spread on a large baking dish taking care not to crowd.

Place baking dish in oven and bake 30 minutes, turning vegetables occasionally. If there is too much liquid at the end of cooking time, increase heat to 450 degrees and cook an additional 5 to 10 minutes.

*The peppers may be peeled very easily with a vegetable peeler.*

# Sicilian Carrots

*Carrots have never been this glamorous. They will liven up the simplest meal.*

2 pounds carrots, thinly sliced on the diagonal

4 tablespoons olive oil, divided

4 tablespoons dried cranberries

3 tablespoons pine nuts

10 basil leaves, cut in julienne strips

Salt and pepper to taste

Preheat oven to 400 degrees. Spray roasting pan with nonstick olive oil spray and arrange carrots in a single layer, mixing with 2 tablespoons olive oil. Bake 30 to 40 minutes, turning occasionally. They should become tender and golden. Remove from oven and cool.

Mix cranberries, pine nuts, basil and remaining olive oil. Stir in carrots. Refrigerate overnight and serve at room temperature.

# *Amy's Salmon*

*This is one of Libbie's most requested recipes—they are in competition, always, with the main course.*

### SALMON

**2 salmon halves (check for bones)**
**Salt and pepper**
**½ cup white wine**

Place salmon halves in a shallow baking dish and add wine. Bake salmon 15 minutes if the pieces are thin or 20 minutes for thicker pieces. Allow to cool.

Place salmon on a large decorative dish and decorate it as you see fit. Amy likes to use kale leaves, lemon slices, bunches of parsley, fresh sunflowers, etc. Serve with Sauce Verte.

### SAUCE VERTE AMY

**Large handful of parsley**
**5 scallions**
**1 clove garlic**
**1 cup mayonnaise**
**Salt and pepper**
**½ teaspoon dried tarragon**
**1 tablespoon lemon juice**

Add all ingredients to food processor and pulse to desired consistency. The recipe is easily doubled.

# KITCHEN KAPERS

### Kitchen-Tested Recipes from the Kitchen of

## JO REID

The working mother—an enigma a few years ago, but she isn't as mysterious in 1963 since more and more women have, for one reason or other, joined the ranks!

Nothing changes in the home when mother leaves it for an outside job. The needs and appetites continue with the family and planning meals very often is the most challenging and difficult duty of all. Try and do something about the dinner before leaving in the morning. Sometimes, starting it after dinner is even more helpful. Preparation dishes and pans can then be washed with the dinner dishes. It's really just a matter of thinking ahead and organization. Let's show them the stuff you're made of, Mom!

## CRAB CASSEROLE

1 cup uncooked rice
1 pkg (lb.) sour cream
1 pkg (lb.) chive cottage cheese
1 can tomato soup
1 tablespoon oil
Salt, pepper
4 green onions, chopped
1 can crab (or a package of frozen crab)
Parmesan cheese

THURSDAY NIGHT: Mix all ingredients. Place in large casserole. Refrigerate.

FRIDAY NIGHT'S DINNER: Preheat oven to 375 degrees. Bake casserole 45 minutes. Remove from oven and sprinkle generously with grated parmesan cheese. Replace for 10 minutes. Add a tossed salad, French bread, ice cream and poundcake.

## TAMALE PIE

2 small onions, chopped
1 clove garlic, chopped
⅓ cup salad oil
1 can whole kernel corn
1 teaspoon celery salt
1 lb. lean ground beef
2 teaspoons chili powder (more or less according to taste)
2 cans (8 oz.) tomato sauce
1 can ripe olives, drained
1½ cups milk
1 cup cornmeal
2 eggs, beaten

TUESDAY NIGHT: Fry onions, garlic, ground beef in oil. Add remaining ingredients, mix well, turn into greased casserole. Refrigerate.

WEDNESDAY NIGHT'S DINNER: Bake casserole in 350 degree preheated oven for 45 minutes. Accompany this with an avocado and grapefruit salad, dinner rolls, sugar cookies and sherbet.

## HAM-NOODLE CASSEROLE

12 oz. "just-cooked" egg noodles
3 cups finely cubed Sunday's leftover ham
1 can cream of chicken soup
1 can consomme
1 small red onion
2 stalks celery, chopped
1 cup grated American cheese
Salt and pepper to taste
1 small jar pimientos
1 small can minced ripe olives

SUNDAY EVENING: Grease a large casserole. Place alternate layers cooked noodles and ham in casserole. Sprinkle minced onion and celery over this. Heat chicken soup and consomme with one soup can of water (try tomato juice sometime in place of water). Pour over contents of casserole. Refrigerate.

MONDAY NIGHT'S DINNER: Sprinkle the grated cheese evenly over top. Garnish with pimiento and olives. Bake in 350 degree oven for 30 minutes covered. Then let simmer uncovered in 325 degree oven 15 minutes. Add more water or tomato juice if dish seems to dry during last 15 minutes. Serve a lime gelatin-pineapple salad, buttered green beans,

# Poached Salmon with Cream Sauce

SERVES 4

*One would think you were dining at the Ritz Hotel when this is served.*

⅔ cup dry white wine or dry vermouth

2 leeks, white part only, finely chopped

4 (6-ounce) 1-inch thick skinless salmon fillets

½ cup whipping cream

1 tablespoon Dijon mustard

Chopped green onion tops

Bring wine and leeks to simmer in a large skillet. Add salmon, cover and simmer until fish is just cooked through, about 8 minutes. Do not overcook. Transfer to plates and tent with foil to keep warm.

Add cream to skillet and bring to boil. Boil until reduced to sauce consistency, stirring occasionally— about 6 minutes. Stir in mustard and whisk to blend. Spoon sauce over salmon. Sprinkle with green onion tops before serving.

# Steamed Salmon

*There is no question but that salmon is a favorite fish. It is delicious fried, broiled, grilled or poached. This is a new fool-proof method that is surprisingly simple and results in a most delicate salmon fillet.*

## SALMON

4 fresh skin-on fillets (about 6 ounces each)

Salt and pepper

Preheat oven to 400 degrees.

Combine all ingredients and spread on a large baking dish taking care not to crowd.

Preheat oven to 350 degrees. Fill a roasting pan half full with boiling water. Coat a small rack with nonstick spray. Arrange salmon, skin side down, on the rack. Season with salt and pepper. Set rack over water, making sure water does not touch the fish.

Carefully place the pan in the oven and steam salmon until firm, about 10 to 15 minutes depending on thickness and personal preference for doneness. Remove and serve each fillet with Lemon Sauce.

## LEMON SAUCE

1 stick butter, melted

¼ cup fresh lemon juice

Whisk butter and lemon juice together and serve with salmon.

*Look for Scottish Duarte salmon—it's the best!*

# Coconut Shrimp

SERVES 6-8                    *Another five –star recipe. Period. The End!!*

## SHRIMP

2 cups shredded coconut

2 cups panko

1 tablespoon curry powder

24 large prawns (15-20 count) peeled, tails intact

1 cup Wondra

2 eggs, lightly beaten

Canola oil for frying

Add coconut to a food processor and pulse until crumbly. Combine with panko and curry powder.

Dip prawns in Wondra, then egg and finally in coconut mixture. Place on parchment-lined cookie sheet and refrigerate 2 hours. This is an important step.

When ready to serve, fry prawns in canola oil. Serve with Cashew Marmalade Sauce.

## CASHEW MARMALADE SAUCE

½ cup cashews, toasted

2 teaspoons black sesame seeds

2 teaspoons sesame oil

2 teaspoons soy sauce

2 tablespoons oyster sauce

½ cup rice vinegar

½ teaspoon minced garlic

1 tablespoon honey

¼ cup olive oil

½ cup orange marmalade

Add cashews to a food processor and chop coarsely. Add remaining ingredients and pulse several seconds taking care to not overly process mixture.

*Wondra is a quick-mixing very fine flour product and there is really no substitute for it in this recipe…NO all-purpose flour! Wondra may be found in blue canister containers on the baking aisle of your grocery store. It is also good for making gravies and as a thickening agent for a lot of dishes.*

# Fried Prawns & Oysters with Cashew Sesame Sauce

SERVES 6

*Ask me to name my top five favorite dishes. This is one of them, bar none! Serve to discerning "foodies"!*

3 yams, peeled and cut into matchstick pieces

Olive oil

Sea salt

1 cup cornmeal

1 cup all-purpose flour

2 teaspoons baking powder

½ teaspoon salt

¼ teaspoon white pepper

18 extra-large prawns (10-15 count), peeled and deveined

Peanut oil for frying

3 jars fresh oysters, drained

2 cups fresh spinach, cut into chiffonade

**CASHEW SESAME SAUCE**

½ cup cashews, toasted

2 teaspoons black sesame seeds

2 teaspoons sesame oil

2 teaspoons soy sauce

2 tablespoons oyster sauce

½ cup rice vinegar

1 clove garlic, minced

1 tablespoon honey

¼ cup olive oil

Preheat oven to 350 degrees.

Place prepared yams on a cookie sheet. Toss with olive oil and sea salt to taste. Bake until crisp—about 30 minutes. Set aside and keep warm.

Combine cornmeal, flour, baking powder, salt and pepper in a bowl. Coat prawns and oysters in cornmeal mixture. In a large pan, heat peanut oil and fry prawns until pink and cooked through. Do not overcook. Remove and set aside. Wipe down pan and heat additional peanut oil. Fry oysters until crisp and brown on both sides—about 2 minutes.

Decoratively arrange spinach chiffonade and yam sticks on individual plates. Top with prawns and oysters and drizzle with Cashew Sesame Sauce.

For Sauce, coarsely pulse cashews in food processor. Add remaining ingredients and pulse several times. Refrigerate until ready to use.

# KOZY KITCHEN

### Kitchen-Tested Recipes From The Kitchen Of
### x JO REID x

The long-awaited season is here! Fresh crabs are on the market and whether yours is a jaunt to the City's Fisherman's Wharf or just a trip down to the local fish store, there's a treat in store for you! Serving the first crab of the season should be pure and unadorned--a platter of cracked crab, fresh green salad with oil and vinegar dressing, french bread, and white wine.

But after the first week or so, go on to one of these recipes for the most delectable of seafoods.

## DEVILED CRABS

3 tablesp. butter
1 medium onion, chopped
1/4 cup flour
1 can condensed tomato soup
1 cup heavy cream
1/2 cup sherry
1 tblsp. lemon juice
1 tsp. salt
1/8 tsp. pepper
Dash paprika
4 cups fresh crab meat
6 or 8 scrubbed crab shells
1/2 cup butter cracker crumbs
Pepper
Parsley for garnishing

In melted butter in saucepan, saute' onion for 5 min.; sprinkle with flour and mix until smooth. Now stir in tomato soup cream, sherry and lemon juice. Add salt, pepper and paprika. Carefully fold in crab meat. Mix well. Spoon mixture into crab shells and sprinkle with cracker crumbs and a little pepper. Bake in 350 degree oven for 15 min. Garnish with parsley and serve hot.

## CRAB MEAT WITH SPECIAL LOUIS SAUCE

1 small onion
3 sprigs parsley
1 cup mayonnaise
1/4 cup chili sauce
Dash cayenne
1/3 cup heavy cream
1 head iceberg lettuce
1 pd. fresh crab meat
4 hard-cooked eggs, grated
4 tblsps. finely cut chives

Wash, peel, and grate onion. Cut parsley as fine as possible. Mix with mayonnaise, chili sauce, and cayenne. Whip cream stiff. Blend into mayonnaise mixture and refrigerate.

Wash lettuce and discard outer leaves. Cut lettuce crosswise in four thick slices. Place on chilled plates. Spoon generous mounds of crab meat on lettuce. Add spoonful of grated egg around crab meat. Sprinkle with chives. Spoon sauce lavishly over crab meat. Serves 4.

## SPANISH CRAB

2 lbs crab meat
1 med. onion
2 tblsp. butter
1 tblsp. flour
1 large can shole tomatoes
1/2 lb. sauteed mushrooms
1 can sliced black olives
Salt and pepper to taste
1 tsp. sugar
1 tsp. Worcestershire sauce

Saute' the onion in butter 'til tender, add the flour and tomatoes. Simmer for 30 minutes and puree the sauce. Add the mushrooml, olives, seasonings, and crab meat to the sauce. Heat thoroughly and serve in a rice ring. Serves 6 generously.

Good Day!

# Glazed Scallops with Butternut Squash

SERVES 4

*Impress!*

## BUTTERNUT PUREE

3 cups large-chunks butternut squash
Olive oil
Salt and pepper
3 tablespoons butter
3 tablespoons heavy cream

Preheat oven to 375 degrees.

Rub squash pieces with olive oil, salt and pepper and bake for 35 minutes or until tender. Cool 10 minutes and mash with butter and cream. Keep warm.

## SCALLOPS

12 large scallops, dried completely
Olive oil

Massage each scallop generously with olive oil. Heat skillet, add scallops and sear on one side—do not disturb. It may be necessary to do this in 2 batches. Turn scallops over and continue cooking until they are golden brown, taking care to not overcook. Remove and keep warm. Do not rinse pan.

## GLAZE

1 cup ruby port
½ cup balsamic vinegar

Pour port and balsamic in reserved pan and reduce to syrup consistency.

To serve, spoon Butternut Puree in the center of 4 plates. Place 3 seared scallops over puree and drizzle with Glaze. Garnish with parsley sprigs, if desired.

# Mussels a la Dennis

SERVES 4

*Dennis loves "batching" when Libbie is away for the occasional evening. One creative evening he produced this zesty dish and now the family stays close to the hearth when they learn he is grooving in the kitchen!*

1 onion, finely chopped

3 tablespoons olive oil

4 fresh tomatoes, chopped

3 cloves garlic, minced

¼ teaspoon crushed red pepper flakes

1 can anchovies, chopped

Crushed black pepper

1 cup clam juice

1 cup wine

1 cup marinara sauce

4 pounds mussels

1 (16-ounce) package linguini, cooked al dente

Chopped parsley

Sauté onion in olive oil until soft. Add the chopped tomatoes, garlic and red pepper flakes and cook 3 minutes, stirring constantly. Stir in anchovies and crushed pepper. Cook gently for 10 minutes stirring often.

Stir in clam juice, wine and marinara sauce and cook for 5 minutes. Add mussels, cover and cook until all mussels are open, discarding any that remain shut.

Serve over cooked linguini and sprinkle with parsley.

*A fly on the wall when Dennis emoting would hear loud music, see an open bottle of Chardonnay and, close by, his beloved bulldog, Louie!*

# Petrale Sole Amandine

*Classic!*

4 large petrale sole fillets (about 3-4 ounces each)

Salt and pepper

All-purpose flour for dredging

4 tablespoons vegetable oil

1 stick unsalted butter, divided

4 tablespoons sliced almonds

2 tablespoons fresh lemon juice

Lemon wedges

Pat fish dry and season with salt and pepper. Dredge in flour, knocking off excess.

Heat oil and 4 tablespoons butter in a heavy skillet. Cook fish, turning once, until browned and just cooked through, about 2½ to 3 minutes total. Do not crowd fillets in pan; cook in 2 batches if necessary. Remove and set aside.

Reduce heat and add remaining 4 tablespoons butter and almonds to the skillet, stirring until almonds are golden brown. Remove from heat and stir in lemon juice. Season with salt and pepper.

Pour sauce over fish and serve with a lemon wedge.

# Buttermilk Fried Chicken

SERVES 6-8

*Fried Chicken with an Attitude!*

| | |
|---|---|
| **1 tablespoon salt** | Combine buttermilk with salt. Add chicken and refrigerate overnight. |
| **3-4 cups buttermilk** | |
| **10-12 chicken pieces of choice** | Mix flour, paprika, garlic powder and pepper. Remove chicken from buttermilk and shake off excess. Roll in flour mixture. |
| **2 cups self-rising flour** | |
| **1 teaspoon paprika** | |
| **½ teaspoon garlic powder** | |
| **Pepper** | Preheat oven to 350 degrees. |
| **Oil for browning** | Brown chicken in hot oil. Place on baking sheet and bake for 45 minutes or until brown and crispy. |

*To make your own self-rising flour, stir together 3 cups all-purpose flour, 1 ½ tablespoons baking powder and 1 teaspoon salt.*

# Grandma Annie's Chicken

*So many of us have loved Janice's specialty. She writes, "This is a great dish to take to a sick friend or neighbor. It's my version of 'chicken soup' handed down from my mother, Annie." This is delicious alongside Green Bean Salad Provençale.*

**8 boneless and skinless chicken breasts**

**¾ cup seasoned bread crumbs**

**½ cup Parmesan cheese, grated**

**3 tablespoons, chopped fresh parsley**

**1 stick butter, melted**

**1 clove garlic, finely minced**

Preheat oven to 350 degrees.

Between two sheets of waxed paper, pound chicken breasts to flatten.

Combine bread crumbs, Parmesan cheese and parsley and set aside.

Melt butter and add garlic. Dip chicken breasts in butter, then in crumb mixture, coating both sides. Roll up chicken breasts end to end and place seam side down in a glass baking dish. Drizzle with remaining butter. Bake uncovered for 45 to 50 minutes.

These may be served hot, as a dinner entrée, or sliced when cooled and served as a luncheon dish. Serve with a dollop of sauce made from ½ cup mayonnaise, 1 teaspoon Dijon mustard and lemon juice to taste. Whisk lightly with a fork to blend.

*Believe it or not, that Parmesan in "the green can" works perfectly for this recipe… you don't have to be a "cheese snob"!*

# Chicken 'N Onions

SERVES 4

*This is a homey recipe you can "pull-out-of-the-hat" at just a moment's notice. It was one of my Mother's staples. I have never put it in print since it was always just "there". You need to make it only once for it to always be "there" for you, too!*

**8 pieces chicken with skin and bones**

**Salt and pepper**

**2 red onions, sliced**

**8 small red potatoes cut in thirds**

**1 tablespoon chopped fresh rosemary**

Salt and pepper chicken pieces. Heat a very large skillet and sauté chicken, skin side down, until brown. It is not necessary to use any oil since the chicken skin renders down a goodly amount of fat. Add onions and stir. Sauté for 5 minutes.

Add potatoes and rosemary. Cover and cook 20 to 25 minutes or until the chicken and potatoes are cooked and golden brown. Add ½ cup water, cover immediately and cook on high heat for 5 minutes. Remove cover and continue cooking and stirring until all ingredients result in a beautifully glazed dish of Chicken 'N Onions.

# Homey Chicken

SERVES 6

*Libbie updates this family favorite—quintessential soul food!*

6 whole chicken legs

Salt and pepper

½ cup dry vermouth

2 red onions, sliced and separated into rings

4 tablespoons butter

1 teaspoon thyme

2 cups half-and-half

2 ½ tablespoons all-purpose flour

Sprigs of parsley

Preheat oven to 375 degrees.

Season chicken generously with salt and pepper. Place onions in a large roasting pan. Top with chicken. Pour vermouth over all and dot with butter. Sprinkle with thyme.

Bake 1 hour. Remove chicken to a warm platter; keep warm.

Skim fat from drippings in pan and then move the pan to the stovetop. In a small bowl, stir half-and-half and flour until smooth and add to pan drippings and onions. Stir well to loosen brown bits from bottom of the pan. Cook over medium heat until sauce thickens, stirring constantly.

Serve chicken with a generous amount of gravy. The perfect accompaniment is rice and shredded zucchini, steamed and buttered.

*The fat-free version of half-and-half works fine for this dish.*

# KITCHEN KAPERS

Kitchen-Tested Recipes from the Kitchen of
JO REID

Once upon a time there lived a little chick who was very, very beautiful.

Even before she was hatched, everyone in the barn commented on the delicate translucence of her shell, and when she finally arrived they came from far and wide and just clucked and crowed over her natural beauty.

As is always the case with a newborn, there were many predictions—she would marry well, she would have many, many beautiful eggs, she certainly wouldn't ever be in a stew! She would end up on an exquisite China plate as Chicken Kiev and everyone who ate her would live happily ever after.

## CHICKEN KIEV
### Serves 4 to 6

| | |
|---|---|
| 4 medium chicken breasts | 8 butter sticks |
| 1 tbsp. finely chopped green onion | Salt |
| 1 tbsp. finely chopped parsley | 1 cup flour |
| 1 cube butter formed into | 2 beaten eggs |
| | 1 cup dry bread crumbs (fine) |

Cut chicken breasts lengthwise in half. Remove skin and bone. Don't tear meat (each half should be one piece). Place chicken on board between 2 pieces of wax paper and working from center out, pound each chicken breast with wood mallet to form cutlet, about ¼ inch thick. Sprinkle meat with salt and divide the onion and parsley equally and sprinkle on each cutlet. Place a butter stick near end of cutlet. Roll as jellyroll, tucking in sides of meat. Press to seal well. Dust with flour; dip in beaten egg; roll in fine bread crumbs. Chill rolls in the refrigerator overnight. Fry in deep hot fat (340 degrees) about 5 minutes until golden brown. (This is equally good, prepared as above and eliminating the onion and parsley).

Serve with Elegant Rice, Broccoli Hollandaise, and Relish Peaches.

## ELEGANT RICE
### Serves 4 to 6

| | |
|---|---|
| 4 tbsp. butter | 1¾ cups water |
| ½ cup white rice | 1 tsp. salt |
| ½ cup wild rice, well washed and drained | Pepper |
| 1 can chicken and rice soup | ¼ cup chopped parsley |
| | ¼ cup pine nuts |

Melt butter and add both kinds of rice and saute' gently at least 5 minutes. Heat chicken soup with water and add salt. Add rice and sprinkle with pepper. Pour into casserole with tight cover. Bake in moderate oven 40 minutes. (350 degrees.) Do not stir until ready to use. Just before serving, mix in parsley and pine nuts.

# Prego Chicken

SERVES 4

*This wonderful restaurant in San Francisco closed down years ago. This is the best interpretation of their famous chicken.*

## CHICKEN

2 chickens, cut in half

Salt and pepper

2 tablespoons olive oil

Generously season chicken halves with salt and pepper. Place a small amount of olive oil in a large roasting pan and bake chicken 1 hour or until golden brown and crispy. Serve topped with Rosemary Cream Sauce and decorate with fresh rosemary sprigs. Small cut roasted potatoes are the perfect accompaniment.

## ROSEMARY CREAM SAUCE

2 tablespoons olive oil

6 cloves garlic, crushed

1 tablespoon chopped fresh rosemary

1 ½ cups whipping cream

1 tablespoon Dijon mustard

Heat olive oil in skillet. Add garlic, rosemary and black pepper and cook 1 minute. Add whipping cream and reduce to sauce consistency. Add the Dijon just before serving, as Dijon gets bitter if cooked too long. Heat sauce gently.

# Quick Chick

*Easy, crisp, moist—the best.*

**1 whole fryer**
**Salt and pepper**
**Olive oil**

Season fryer inside and out with salt and pepper. Set on a rack and refrigerate overnight. Do not cover.

Bring bird to room temperature an hour before baking. Preheat oven to 475 degrees.

Rub olive oil over entire surface of chicken and bake 45 minutes.

*I have allowed this to refrigerate as long as two days before baking with the same great results.*

# A Chicken Thigh Reminder

*That's right! This is simply a reminder that perfectly-cooked chicken thighs are as good as it gets! They always seem like such a treat for so little money.*

**8 chicken thighs with skin and bones**
**Salt and pepper**

Season thighs generously with salt and pepper. Heat a large cast-iron or heavy oven-proof non-stick skillet over high heat. Add chicken, skin side down, and cook until skin is golden brown. Turn pieces over and continue to cook 10 minutes.

Preheat oven to 350 degrees. Transfer skillet to oven and cook 30 minutes longer, turning after 15 minutes.

*On the day before cooking chicken, season it with salt and pepper and refrigerate overnight to amplify moisture and flavor.*

# Claudia's Chicken with Lemon & Rosemary

*Enjoying this chicken once a week is not often enough—it is delicious.*

1 (3½ to 4 pound) chicken, butterflied

Salt

3 long sprigs rosemary

6 cloves garlic, crushed

Juice of 2 lemons

2 red onions, quartered

8 tablespoons olive oil

Maldon or sea salt

6 peeled Yukon gold potatoes cut in half

Sprinkle butterflied chicken with salt and place in a large zip top bag. Add rosemary, garlic, lemon juice, lemon halves, red onions and olive oil. Turn bag several times to distribute marinade over the chicken. Refrigerate overnight or up to 2 days.

Preheat oven to 425 degrees. Once chicken is at room temperature, place chicken, skin side up, along with lemon rinds, potatoes and onions in a foil-lined roasting pan. Tuck additional rosemary sprigs under the legs and breast of chicken.

Cook 45 minutes or until done. Chicken should be crisp-skinned and tender. Cut chicken into 4 pieces. Arrange on a plate along with onions and potatoes. Pour pan juices over all and sprinkle generously with sea salt before serving.

# KITCHEN KAPERS

### Kitchen-Tested Recipes from the Kitchen of JO REID

Now's the time! For autumn leaves and zesty downpours, for crackling fires and bowls of popcorn, for bright rain togs and steamy hot chocolate, for crisp red apples and an exciting new book. Ah, to come home to a warm, cozy bath with the wonderful smell of chicken and dumplings, a boiled dinner, banana fritters. They'll never forget it!

## CHICKEN 'N DUMPLINGS
(Serves 6)

2 2-lb. or larger chickens
½ cup flour
3 tablespoons chicken fat
2 teaspoons salt
2 stalks celery, chopped
Boiling water to half cover

Clean chicken and cut into serving portions; dredge with flour and brown in fat. Add remaining ingredients with enough water to half cover chicken. Simmer, tightly covered 1½ to 2 hours or when chicken is tender. Add more water if necessary during cooking. **Dumplings:** Mix 1½ cups sifted flour, 3 teaspoons baking powder, ¾ teaspoon salt, 1 tablespoon dehydrated onion, ½ teaspoon minced parsley. Add ¾ cup milk to make a thick batter and drop from spoon onto boiling chicken. Cover tightly and cook 20 minutes with raising lid. Place chicken on platter and surround with dumplings. Serve with steamed carrots.

## MINESTRONE

2 lbs. beef shank
¼ pound bacon
2 onions, chopped
2 tomatoes, chopped
½ cup rice
½ cup dried beans
(soaked in water 3 hours)
¼ cup diced celery
1 cup diced carrots
¼ head cabbage, shredded
½ cup fresh peas
½ cup Lima beans
½ cup string beans
8 cups water
2 teaspoons salt
⅛ teaspoon pepper
1 teaspoon dried basil
1 clove garlic, mashed

Put it all in a large kettle and simmer until the soup is thick and vegetables are soft. About three hours. Better the next day and serve with grated parmesan cheese and lots of French bread!

## BANANA FRITTERS

1¼ cups flour
¼ teaspoon salt
½ cup sugar
2 teaspoons baking powder
1 egg
⅓ cup milk
2 teaspoons melted shortening
Bananas (4 or 6)

Sift 1 cup flour with sugar, salt and baking powder. Mix egg and milk; add to flour mixture gradually, stirring until smooth. Add shortening. Peel bananas; cutting crosswise into half or quarters. Roll in remaining flour; cover with batter. Fry in hot, deep fat (375) 4 to 6 minutes. Sprinkle with powdered sugar or serve with maple syrup. Serves 6.

Have a happy day!

# Chicken Thighs with Glazed Lemons on Linguini

SERVES 4

*Elvera's method ensures chicken is succulent and the skin crispy.*

2 lemons, thinly sliced

8 skin-on boneless chicken thighs

Salt and pepper

3 sprigs oregano or 1 teaspoon dried

1 large shallot, minced

2 cloves garlic, minced

¼ teaspoon crushed red pepper flakes

½ cup dry vermouth

½ cup chicken broth

1 (8-ounce) package linguini, cooked al dente

Preheat oven to 435 degrees. Season chicken with salt and pepper. Heat a large oven-proof skillet over medium heat. Add chicken, skin side down, and cook until skin is brown. Pour out any excess fat and continue cooking chicken for 10 minutes.

Slide half of lemon slices under chicken and put half over the chicken. Transfer skillet to oven, leaving chicken skin side down (lemons on bottom of skillet will caramelize).

Transfer chicken, skin side up, and caramelized lemon slices from bottom of skillet to a warm platter. Leave remaining lemon slices in skillet. Allow skillet to cool.

Return skillet to medium heat. Add oregano, shallot, garlic and red pepper flakes. Cook until fragrant—about 1 minute. Add dry vermouth and broth and cook over medium heat until slightly thickened. Return chicken to skillet to rewarm.

Serve over linguini and top with reserved caramelized lemon slices.

*These may be made early in the day, refrigerated and then reheated just before serving. After reheating, place skillet under the broiler for a few minutes to crisp chicken skin.*

*Also, it may be necessary to debone the thighs yourself. If so, combine the bones with 2 or 3 cups of cold water and a little salt. Cook for 15 minutes to have a quick and easy chicken broth.*

# Jean's Chicken

SERVES 2-4

*The recipe everyone wants—prepared in minutes with a beautiful result.*

4 large chicken thighs

2 cups mixed color peppers, cut in 2-inch pieces

1 cup sliced mushrooms

2 cups sliced onion

3 tablespoons olive oil

½ cup white wine or dry vermouth

Preheat oven to 350 degrees.

Place vegetables in 9x13-inch glass baking dish. Pour olive oil over all and toss. Place chicken, skin side down, on top of vegetables and pour wine over all. Cover tightly with foil and bake for 1 hour, basting once or twice. Remove foil, turn chicken and cook for 15 minutes or until chicken is brown and tender.

*Jean suggests serving with polenta and broccoli.*

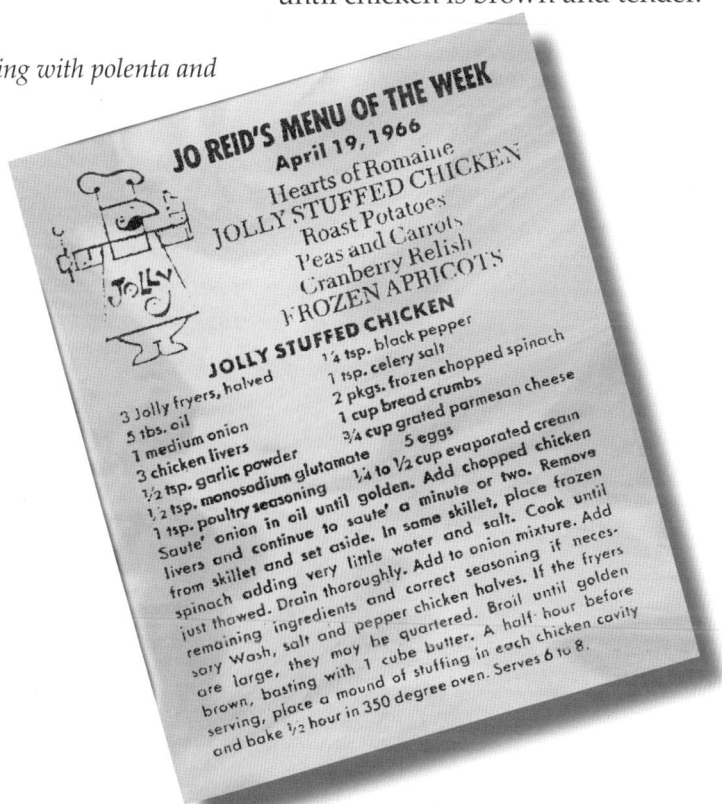

JO REID'S MENU OF THE WEEK
April 19, 1966
Hearts of Romaine
JOLLY STUFFED CHICKEN
Roast Potatoes
Peas and Carrots
Cranberry Relish
FROZEN APRICOTS

JOLLY STUFFED CHICKEN

3 Jolly fryers, halved
5 tbs. oil
1 medium onion
3 chicken livers
½ tsp. garlic powder
½ tsp. monosodium glutamate
1 tsp. poultry seasoning
¼ tsp. black pepper
1 tsp. celery salt
2 pkgs. frozen chopped spinach
2 cups bread crumbs
1 cup grated parmesan cheese
¾ cup grated parmesan cheese
5 eggs
¼ to ½ cup evaporated cream

Saute' onion in oil until golden. Add chopped chicken livers and continue to saute' a minute or two. Remove from skillet and set aside. In same skillet, place frozen spinach adding very little water and salt. Cook until just thawed. Drain thoroughly. Add to onion mixture. Add remaining ingredients and correct seasoning if necessary. Wash, salt and pepper chicken halves. If the fryers are large, they may be quartered. Broil until golden brown, basting with 1 cube butter. A half hour before serving, place a mound of stuffing in each chicken cavity and bake ½ hour in 350 degree oven. Serves 6 to 8.

# Chicken Marbella & Roasted Onions

SERVES 6

*This is such an old stand-by and added to this collection by popular demand! Libbie's touch makes this one of our favorite chicken-onion dishes—a marriage made in Heaven!*

12 chicken thighs with skin and bones

Salt and pepper

20 cloves garlic

¼ cup dried oregano

½ cup balsamic vinegar

½ cup olive oil

1 cup pitted prunes

1 cup pitted Spanish green olives

½ cup capers

3 bay leaves

2 cups brown sugar

1 cup white wine or dry vermouth

½ cup finely chopped Italian parsley

Sprinkle salt and pepper generously over chicken. In a jumbo zip top bag, combine chicken, garlic, oregano, vinegar, olive oil, prunes, olives, capers and bay leaves. Refrigerate 8 hours or overnight.

Preheat oven to 350 degrees. Place chicken and entire contents of bag into a 12x18-inch baking pan in a single layer. Do not use a high-sided pan.

Sprinkle evenly with brown sugar. Pour wine or vermouth over all. Bake 1 hour and 15 minutes. Using a slotted spoon, place all ingredients on a large platter. Surround with Roasted Onions and pour pan juices over the dish. Sprinkle with chopped parsley.

# *Chicken Marbella (continued)*

## ROASTED ONIONS

6 tablespoons butter

3 tablespoons balsamic vinegar

½ cup honey

½ bunch fresh thyme

Salt and pepper

4 red onions, quartered

Preheat oven to 350 degrees.

Combine butter, vinegar, honey, thyme, salt and pepper in a small saucepan. Bring to a simmer and cook 1 minute. Place onions, cut side up, in a single layer on a baking pan. Drizzle with butter-vinegar mixture and roast until soft and slightly caramelized, about 45 minutes.

Serve with Saffron Parsley Rice.

## JO REID'S MENU OF THE WEEK
### 4th of July, 1964

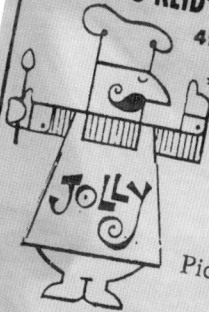

★ ★ ★ ★ ★ ★ ★ ★ ★ ★ ★ ★ ★ ★ ★ ★ ★ ★ ★ ★

**BARBECUED CHICKEN, JOLLY STYLE**

Potato Salad
Sliced Tomatoes
Pineapple Slaw
Pickles, Olives, Celery Hearts
Chocolate Ice Cream

### BARBECUED CHICKEN, JOLLY STYLE.

½ cup Jolly Salad Oil
⅓ cup lemon juice
¼ cup soy sauce
1 clove garlic, peeled and minced

1 tsp. oregano
1 tsp. salt
¼ tsp. salt
2 Jolly fryers, split in half

Combine all ingredients. Pour over chicken halves in a large dish. Cover and marinate 4 to 5 hours. Drain chicken and barbecue to golden goodness, brushing with marinade every 10 minutes and turning the chicken frequently—about 40 minutes in all. Serves 4.

### PINEAPPLE SLAW

In a large bowl, combine 1 cup commercial sour cream, ½ tsp. sugar, 1 tbsp. vinegar, 1 tbsp. finely cut chives, 2 tbsp. pickle relish, 3 cups shredded cabbage and 1 cup drained crushed pineapple. Stir to mix evenly. Wonderful combination of flavors!

# Chicken and Artichoke Paella

SERVES 6

*There is more than one use for that wonderful paella pan which one is apt to use only once a year. This is a real winner—a weekday meal yet very guest-friendly!*

8 boneless and skinless chicken thighs

2 tablespoons olive oil

1 medium onion, finely chopped

1 ½ cups Arborio rice

2 cans chicken broth (not low-sodium)

1 package frozen artichoke hearts

Parmesan

Chopped parsley

Preheat oven to 325 degrees.

Brown thighs in skillet—there is enough fat on the thighs to brown nicely without any additional fat. Place browned thighs on a baking sheet and put in oven for 20 minutes. Remove and slice. Set aside.

Sauté onion in olive oil until soft. Add rice and cook until golden. Add broth and do not stir any longer. Cook on medium heat until broth is almost absorbed.

Place artichokes and sliced chicken around rice. Continue to cook until all broth is absorbed and a nicely-browned crust has formed on the bottom of the pan.

Sprinkle with a generous amount of Parmesan and parsley.

# KITCHEN KAPERS

Kitchen-Tested Recipes from the Kitchen of
JO REID

Today is the day for a new chicken recipe!

This is an exciting blend of ingredients that will do for chicken what a new hat does for a woman! It's Sunday-best, fresh and crisp, subtle in flavor and very definitely will become your "specialty of the house."

It is best when assembled the night before, allowing the wine flavor to seep into the chicken, making it succulently tender and moist. This is chicken at its most glamorous!

Serve with browned rice, stringbeans and slivered almonds, a simple fruit salad first course and Brandied Cherries as a last course, of course!

## HERBED CHICKEN

3 large chicken breasts
(Cut in half)
Salt and pepper
¼ cup butter
1 can cream chicken soup
¾ cup sautern

1 5-oz. can water chestnuts,
drained and sliced
1 3-oz. can broiled sliced
mushrooms, drained
¼ tsp. crushed thyme

Lightly season chicken with salt and pepper; brown slowly in butter in skillet. Arrange browned chicken, skin side up in 11½x7½x1½ in. baking dish. For the sauce, add soup to drippings in skillet, slowly add sauterne, stirring until smooth. Add remaining ingredients, heat to boiling. Pour sauce over chicken. Cover with foil and at this point dish can be refrigerated overnight or baked immediately with the foil on 25 minutes (350°) and then uncover dish, baking 25 to 35 minutes or until chicken is tender. So-o-o Good!

## BROWN RICE

3 cups brown rice
6 cups bouillon (or chicken or
lamb broth)

1 cube butter
Salt and pepper to taste

Melt butter, add dry rice and braise well until butter begins to bubble. Add broth and seasonings if needed. Mix well. Bake in oven for 30 minutes at 400 degrees. Take out of oven, mix well, and bake for 15 minutes more.

## BRANDIED CHERRIES AND CREAM

Drain 2 cans of pitted cherries, the larger the better. Add 1 teaspoon lemon juice, 2 tablespoons sugar, and a few grains cinnamon. Put in a glass pie plate and cover with a small jar of currant jelly. Sprinkle with finely chopped walnuts and bake 10 minutes in 350 degree oven. Pour ½ cup brandy over the cherries and serve lighted. Pass the cream!

## FROZEN CREAM

Pour ½ pint whipping cream into a freezing tray in the refrigerator. Sprinkle 2 tablespoons confectioners sugar over cream. Let freeze until crystals form—no harder. Place in a bowl and serve with the Brandied Cherries. This cream is delicious served with any fruit. Try APRICOTS IN KIRSCH in place of the Brandied Cherries. Drain large can of chilled apricots. Mix ¼ cup of kirsch with some of the apricot juice and pour over the apricots. Serve with Frozen Cream.
Good Day!

# Drunken Chicken

SERVES 6-8

*Voted a favorite when Renee served this at our Book Club. It seems we spend as much time discussing the food as we do the book. It is definitely "soul food" and perfect for a large group since it is easily doubled.*

1 ½ cups uncooked rice

2 cans cream of mushroom soup

2 cans cream of celery soup

½ package dry French onion soup mix

1 cup sherry

1 cup water

1 can mushrooms

8-10 chicken thighs with bone and skin

Paprika

Preheat oven to 325 degrees.

Mix all ingredients except chicken and paprika and pour into a large baking dish with high sides.

Place chicken on top and press gently into rice.

Sprinkle with paprika and cover the pan tightly with foil. Bake for 2 hours.

# Glazed Cornish Game Hens

*Best described as "outstanding"!*

### HERB BUTTER

1 stick butter, softened

1 teaspoon each dried thyme, rosemary, basil and curry powder

### HENS

6 (2 ½-pound) Cornish game hens

1 tablespoon salt

1 lemon, cut lengthwise into 6 wedges

6 sprigs fresh rosemary

4 tablespoons melted butter

### CHUTNEY GLAZE

1 cup mango chutney

1 teaspoon lemon juice

Two days before preparing, defrost hens in a sink filled with cold water. Pat dry. Generously sprinkle each with salt. Place hens in a jumbo zip top bag and refrigerate at least 1 day.

Before preparing hens, make the Herb Butter. Stir seasonings into softened butter and blend well.

After the day of refrigeration, starting at cavity end of each bird, slide index finger between skin and flesh to loosen skin, taking care not to tear it. Slide 1 teaspoon Herb Butter under the skin. Place a lemon wedge and sprig of rosemary in each cavity.

Tie legs with kitchen twine and tuck wings under the body, securing with additional twine if necessary. Brush each hen with melted butter.

Preheat oven to 400 degrees. Using two baking pans, place 3 hens in each allowing as much space around them as possible. Roast for 45 minutes. Reduce temperature to 350 degrees. Brush hens with Chutney Glaze and roast an additional 15 to 20 minutes.

Place chutney and lemon juice in a food processor and process until smooth.

Serve with Rice Medley with Spinach. Decorate plate with rosemary sprigs.

# Barbecued Thai Chicken with Coconut Milk Sauce

*This is Bill's Lake Tahoe creation. One fine summer day he rescued miscellaneous ingredients from the fridge and this delicious dish was created. A must every year.*

**6 whole chicken legs and 6 chicken breasts with skin and bones**

**5 tablespoons peanut butter**

**1 tablespoon Thai curry paste**

**1 ½ cups low-sodium soy sauce**

**2 tablespoons honey**

**12 cloves garlic, finely minced**

## COCONUT MILK SAUCE

**1 can coconut milk**

**1 tablespoon Thai curry paste**

Combine all ingredients and marinate up to 5 hours. Given the seasoning properties of the salt in the soy, the longer the better of course. Remove chicken from marinade reserving the mixture. Grill chicken using the method below. While chicken is cooking, bring reserved marinade to a full boil. Baste chicken with reserved marinade only after the skin has crisped; about 20 minutes into the process. Pour remaining marinade over chicken to serve.

Serve over steamed rice with a broccolini/red pepper sauté and a large dollop of Coconut Milk Sauce spooned over all.

Combine coconut milk and curry paste and gently heat and serve, adding more curry paste if desired.

## BILL'S NEVER-FAIL BBQ METHOD

- *Turn on all grill burners. Heat on high for 20 minutes (covered)*

- *Open lid*

- *Turn off one or two adjacent burners, and place chicken over those burners*

- *Close the lid*

- *Cook chicken about 10 minutes or so, making sure there are no flare-ups*

- *After 10 minutes, transfer chicken to the hot "On" side, turning them "off" and turning on the other burners. Continue this back-and-forth, indirect cooking method until the chicken is done. Implemented methodically, conscientiously, judiciously and—perhaps most critically—soberly, this is the ONLY way to grill chicken.*

# Asian Chicken Drumsticks

*Better than candy! Serve with steamed rice and a spinach salad.*

16 drumsticks

Salt and pepper

2 tablespoons oil

1 teaspoon 5-spice powder

¾ cup hoisin sauce

½ cup pepper jelly or Asian chili
sauce

¼ cup rice vinegar

¼ cup chicken broth

2 tablespoons minced fresh ginger

2 cloves garlic, minced

1 tablespoon sesame oil

1 cup toasted sesame seeds

Greens for garnish

Preheat oven to 425 degrees.

Season chicken with salt and pepper. Combine oil and 5-spice powder in a large mixing bowl and add chicken. Toss well.

Place drumsticks on foil-lined baking sheet and roast 35 minutes.

In a blender, combine hoisin sauce, pepper jelly or Asian chili sauce, rice vinegar, chicken broth, ginger, garlic and sesame oil. Transfer to saucepan and cook 5 minutes.

Transfer cooked chicken to a large bowl and toss with sauce.

Preheat broiler. Return chicken to same baking sheet and broil 10 minutes, brushing with sauce. Drumsticks will be glazy and sticky.

Place sesame seeds in a small bowl and dip the end of the chicken legs in the seeds. Place on a serving dish and garnish with sprigs of greenery.

# Baked Mexican Chicken

SERVES 6

*Some chips, a little guac, a "rita" and a mini fiesta is born!*

6 boneless, skinless chicken breasts

2 cups thick salsa

4 cups fresh bread crumbs or panko

2 cloves garlic, minced

1 teaspoon oregano

½ teaspoon salt

1 teaspoon ground chili powder

Olive oil

4 tablespoons melted butter

Place chicken in a single layer in glass baking dish. Pour salsa over and coat well. Refrigerate and marinate at least 2 hours.

Preheat oven to 375 degrees.

Combine crumbs, garlic, oregano, salt and chili powder in a food processor.

Remove chicken from marinade, leaving as many salsa chunks as possible. Discard remaining salsa. Cover with crumb mixture, pressing down with fingertips.

Place pieces on an oil-rubbed baking sheet and drizzle with melted butter.

Bake 35 minutes; chicken should be golden around the edges. Serve over steamed rice.

# Chicken Enchiladas

*This is a great dish alongside a chilled Margarita!*

3 cups cooked chopped chicken

1 (4-ounce) can chopped green chiles

1 (7-ounce) jar green chile salsa

Salt to taste

2 cups whipping cream

12 corn tortillas

1 ½ cups grated Monterey Jack cheese

Combine chicken, green chiles and salsa. Mix salt and heavy cream in a shallow baking dish. Heat about ½-inch oil in a small skillet. Dip each tortilla into hot oil for about 5 seconds to soften. Drain on paper towels and dip each fried tortilla into cream, coating each side.

Preheat oven to 350 degrees.

Fill each tortilla with chicken mixture. Roll and place in ungreased baking dish. Pour remaining cream over enchiladas and sprinkle with cheese. Bake, uncovered, for 25 minutes.

# Spinach Stuffing for Turkey

*A really old handed-down recipe from my Mother. Stuffed turkey was her specialty. Nowadays we seem to be cooking the dressing separately, but this all-time favorite is best stuffed into the bird.*

1 large loaf white bread

2 pounds fresh (not frozen) spinach

1 ½ pounds pork sausage

1 yellow onion, chopped

2 cloves garlic, minced

1 bunch parsley, chopped

3 stalks celery, diced

1 teaspoon Bell's Seasoning

Salt and pepper to taste

1 cup evaporated milk

1 stick butter

2 eggs, beaten

½ cup Parmesan cheese

½ teaspoon baking soda (maintains color of spinach)

Cube bread including crusts. Chop raw spinach very fine. Combine bread and spinach and set aside.

Place sausage, onion, garlic and parsley in a skillet and cook about 10 minutes. Add to the bread/sausage mixture. Stir in the uncooked celery.

Heat evaporated milk and butter. Add to bread mixture. Add seasoning and eggs. Stir in baking soda and cheese. Mix thoroughly. This is enough stuffing for a 20-pound turkey.

A 20-pound turkey should be baked in a 325 degree oven for 5 ½ to 6 hours. Internal temperatures should be 165 for stuffing, 170 for the breast and 180 degrees for the thighs. Allow to rest 20 minutes before carving.

*About an hour before the turkey was done, Mother added potatoes and yams to the pan. The flavor of those crispy potatoes was delectable.*

*Also, if Bell's Seasoning is not available in your area, simply combine ½ teaspoon sage and ½ teaspoon thyme as a substitute.*

# Bread Dressing for Turkey

*Libbie "throws" this together in minutes.*

1 stick butter

1 large onion, chopped

5 stalks celery, chopped

2 cups turkey broth

4 ounces dried cranberries

1 large package herbed stuffing mix

Preheat oven to 350 degrees.

Sauté onion and celery in butter until soft. Add remaining ingredients and mix well.

Place in a buttered dish and bake for 30 minutes.

## Jo Reid's Kitchen-tested Recipes
### HEAVENLY FLUFF STUFFING
#### for a
### JOLLY FRESH TURKEY

½ cube butter
6 green onions including tops
1 heart of celery including leaves
3 tblsp. chopped parsley
1 lb. sliced fresh mushrooms

1 lb. bulk sausage
2 lge. loaves unsliced white bread for stuffing
2 teaspoons poultry seasoning
1½ cubes butter, melted
15-lb. Jolly turkey

In ½ cube butter, gently saute' finely chopped onions and celery. Add chopped parsley and mushrooms and saute' 5 minutes If desired, chopped cooked turkey giblets may be added. Set aside. Now crumble sausage and brown until all redness disappears. Drain browned sausage on paper toweling. Add to first mixture. Add melted butter. Mix thoroughly. Trim all crusts from bread. Tear apart in small pieces. Add to sausage mixture along with poultry seasoning. Gently mix together, do not pack down.
This stuffing is delicately seasoned, still light when you spoon it out. It may be made the night before and stored in the vegetable crisper.
Happy Holiday!

JOLLY MARKETS

Kentfield

Fairfax

# Shellie's Chicken Pot Pies

*The chicken pie we always dream about—full flavored, simple to prepare, beautiful to behold!*

4 cups chicken broth

1 chicken bouillon cube

1 stick butter

2 leeks, sliced

2 large carrots, sliced into ½-inch rounds

2 ribs celery, sliced

3 tablespoons chopped chives

2 cloves garlic, minced

3 Yukon gold potatoes, peeled and diced

Salt and pepper to taste

½ cup all-purpose flour

¼ cup heavy cream

3 tablespoons cream sherry

1 (2 to 3-pound) deli rotisserie chicken, shredded

1 (9-ounce) box frozen peas

2 (9-ounce) packages refrigerated pie crust

1 egg, beaten with 1 tablespoon water

Kosher salt

Preheat oven to 375 degrees.

In a large saucepan, heat chicken broth and bouillon cube over medium heat until hot.

In a Dutch oven, melt butter over medium heat. Add leeks, carrot, celery, chives, garlic and potatoes. Sauté until tender. Season with salt and pepper. Add flour and stir together until it becomes pasty and lump free, about 2 minutes. Stir in the hot broth, heavy cream, sherry, chicken and frozen peas. Bring to a boil, reduce to simmer and cook for 15 minutes.

With a ladle fill 6 ovenproof ramekins with the filling. Place on a baking sheet.

Sprinkle flour on countertop. Roll out dough an extra inch. Using a biscuit cutter or mold, cut out crust to cover tops of the ramekins with about ½-inch overlap. Crimp dough over the edge of the ramekin. Brush with egg wash and make 4 small slits on the top of each. Sprinkle with kosher salt and place on a baking sheet. Bake for 35 minutes. Remove from oven and serve.

*Puff pastry or phyllo dough may be used in place of the pie crust.*

# Libbie's Joe's Special

SERVES 4-6

*Joe's Special is on every Italian restaurant menu in San Francisco. It is Italian soul food. Libbie's recipe makes it Italian heart-healthy comfort food!*

½ pound sliced mushrooms

3 tablespoons olive oil

1 red onion, chopped

2 pounds ground turkey

4 cloves garlic, finely minced

Salt and pepper to taste

2-3 pounds freshly washed spinach

4 eggs, lightly beaten

Sauté mushrooms in olive oil until golden. Set aside. In same pan, sauté onion until soft. Add ground turkey and cook until crumbly and cooked through.

Stir in garlic, salt and pepper and mix well. Add spinach and cook until thoroughly combined with meat mixture. Stir in eggs and cook for several minutes.

*This is a meal in itself but is most delicious with a side of country-fried potatoes!*

# Turkey Meatloaf

*If you are looking for a great little meatloaf, this is it!*

1 pound ground turkey (preferably dark meat)

½ cup Italian-seasoned bread crumbs

⅓ cup chopped sun-dried tomatoes

2 cloves garlic, minced

2 eggs, lightly beaten

2 tablespoons milk

½ cup crumbled feta cheese

¼ teaspoon pepper

Preheat oven to 350 degrees.

Combine all ingredients and place in a 9x5-inch loaf pan. Bake 45 minutes or to an internal temperature of 165 degrees. Allow to rest 5 minutes before slicing to serve.

# Noni's Chicken Curry

SERVES 6-8

*Create a feast with very little effort. One of my all-time favorites—tweaked recently in the spice department with a fabulous result!*

6 chicken breasts with skin and bones

6 chicken thighs with skin and bones

1 large yellow onion, diced

4 tablespoons butter

2 green apples, peeled and diced

3 tablespoons curry powder

1 teaspoon cumin

1 teaspoon turmeric

1 tablespoon garam masala

2 cans cream of chicken soup

1 pint whipping cream

Preheat oven to 350 degrees. Place chicken pieces in a large baking pan.

In a large skillet sauté onion in butter until soft. Add apple and cook until soft. Stir in spices and sauté 3 minutes, mixing well. Add soup and cream. Simmer 2-3 minutes, stirring to blend well.

Pour over chicken and bake 1 hour.

Serve with steamed rice and pass bowls of several Sambals.

### SAMBALS

- *Mango chutney (a must)*

- *Scallions, chopped*

- *Raisins*

- *Chopped peanuts or cashews*

- *Diced hard-cooked eggs: yolks and whites*

- *Chopped sweet gherkins*

- *Diced bananas*

- *Toasted coconut*

# Breaded Pork Chops

8 thick-sliced bone-in pork chops

Salt and pepper

2 eggs

1 ½ cups dry bread crumbs

1 teaspoon garlic powder

1 teaspoon salt

½ teaspoon pepper

3 tablespoons olive oil

1 cup sweet vermouth

Sprinkle chops with salt and pepper. In a shallow bowl, beat eggs with 2 tablespoons water. In another bowl combine bread crumbs with garlic powder, salt and pepper. Dredge chops in egg and then in bread crumb mixture.

Preheat oven to 350 degrees. Meanwhile, sauté chops in oil until golden brown on each side. Place chops in a baking dish. Deglaze sauté pan with vermouth and pour over chops. Cover dish with foil and bake for 1 hour. Remove foil and bake an additional 15 minutes.

*Another time you may want to substitute whole chicken thighs. Equally as delicious!*

# Zesty Pork Chops

SERVES 6

*A company-worthy dish.*

**MARINADE**

Juice and zest of 2 oranges

6 cloves garlic, crushed

3 tablespoons fresh ginger, mashed

½ cup molasses

1 cup tamari

6 tablespoons light soy sauce

1 cup rice vinegar

6 tablespoons olive oil

½ teaspoon pepper

**CHOPS**

6 extra-thick bone-in pork chops

Olive oil

2 eggs, lightly beaten

1 cup panko

1 cup sweet vermouth

Combine marinade ingredients and mix well. Pour into an extra-large zip top bag. Add pork chops and refrigerate at least 4 to 6 hours, turning occasionally.

To prepare, remove chops and reserve marinade. Pat chops dry.

Dip chops in beaten egg, then in panko. Sauté in olive oil until browned on both sides. Place browned chops on a shallow rimmed baking pan. Deglaze sauté pan with vermouth and reserve.

When ready to serve, preheat oven to 400 degrees and bake chops 15 minutes. Pour reserved vermouth over chops and bake an additional 5 to 7 minutes.

Meanwhile, boil reserved marinade then reduce it to sauce consistency and serve over baked chops.

# Peking Pork

*A perfect pairing with Spicy Peanut Noodles. You may also double the recipe for a buffet entrée.*

2 pork tenderloins

2 cloves garlic, mashed

2 tablespoons peeled and chopped fresh ginger

2 tablespoons soy sauce

2 tablespoons sugar

¼ cup honey

1 cup sesame seeds

Place tenderloins in a shallow glass baking dish. Combine garlic, ginger, soy sauce and sugar. Pour over meat and cover the dish. Refrigerate 4 to 6 hours, turning occasionally.

Drain and reserve marinade. Bring meat to room temperature and pat dry.

Preheat oven to 375 degrees. Pour honey on a plate. Roll tenderloins in honey and evenly coat them with sesame seeds. Transfer tenderloins to an oiled roasting pan. Bake for 40 to 45 minutes.

In the meantime, bring reserved marinade to a boil then quickly reduce heat and simmer 10 minutes to use as a dipping sauce.

Remove cooked tenderloins to a carving board and let rest for 10 minutes. Cut into diagonal slices and serve with cooked marinade.

# Pork Roast with Sausage & Apple Stuffing

*Company will love this! Ours does!*

1 (3-pound) boneless pork loin

½ pound mild Italian sausage

1 onion, chopped

2 stalks celery, chopped

1 apple, peeled and diced

Salt and pepper

2 cloves garlic, minced

3 slices French bread

2 teaspoons chopped fresh sage

2 teaspoons chopped fresh rosemary

1 teaspoon chopped fresh thyme

2 tablespoons butter

1 tablespoon oil

1 cup Marsala wine

In a large sauté pan, cook sausage until crumble and no longer pink. Remove and set aside. Leaving drippings in the pan, add onion, celery and apple. Sprinkle with salt and pepper. Cook until apple is no longer crisp, about 5 minutes. Add garlic and cook an additional 2 to 3 minutes. Remove from heat and add sausage.

In a food processor, pulse bread with sage, rosemary and thyme into large, coarse crumbs. Heat butter in a medium sauté pan and cook crumbs until lightly toasted. Add to sausage mixture.

Prepare roast as if making a jellyroll. Place the roast with the short side toward you and the fat side facing down toward the counter or cutting board. Using a sharp knife, slice the roast open at about ½-inch from the bottom of the roast (parallel to the cutting board), being careful to not cut all the way through. Continue cutting, unrolling the roast as you work until you have a large thin piece of meat. Place the rolled-out meat between 2 sheets of waxed paper and lightly pound with meat mallet to increase the surface area of the meat by 10 to 20 per cent but taking care not to pound completely through the meat.

Salt and pepper meat and top with prepared sausage filling, spreading evenly across the pork, leaving a 1-inch margin around the edges. Starting with the short side, roll up tightly, jellyroll style, and secure with kitchen twine.

## Pork Roast (continued)

Preheat oven to 350 degrees.

Heat a large sauté pan over medium heat and add oil. Place tied roast in pan and brown on all sides. Place in a roasting pan fitted with a rack and add Marsala to the bottom of the pan. (This prevents drippings from burning.)

Bake 45 minutes to 1 hour or until internal temperature reaches 145 degrees. Remove and allow to rest for 10 minutes before slicing. Serve with sauce made by heating pan drippings, adding more Marsala if needed.

*Pork tenderloins work well prepared this way with simple adjustments made to cooking time.*

## Pork Rib Roast

*Nothing unusual here but I like this fast method in cooking a bone-in pork roast. It is done to perfection and, best of all, it is moist.*

**1 (5 ½-pound) bone-in pork roast**

**1 tablespoon salt**

**½ teaspoon pepper**

**½ teaspoon garlic powder**

Preheat oven to 435 degrees.

Combine salt, pepper and garlic powder. Rub entire surface of roast with mixture.

Roast 20 minutes, and then reduce oven temperature to 375 degrees and bake an additional 45 to 50 minutes. Remove when internal temperature registers 150 degrees.

Tent with foil and allow to rest 10 minutes. Roast should then register 160 degrees and be perfectly done.

# Braised Pork

*I watched a super chef on TV make this wonderful pork dish. I tweaked it a bit with an outstanding result. Just terrific!*

1 (5 to 6-pound) pork shoulder, trimmed and cut into large pieces

Salt and pepper

4 tablespoons olive oil

2 onions, chopped

4 celery stalks, chopped

3 carrots, chopped

4 cloves garlic, chopped

4 tablespoons tomato paste

2 cups red wine

3 cups beef broth

SLURRY

3 tablespoons Wondra

4 tablespoons water

Preheat oven to 325 degrees. Pat pork dry and season with salt and pepper.

Place olive oil in a skillet and brown pork on all sides. It will take 2 or 3 batches. Transfer to a large bowl and set aside.

In the same skillet add onion, celery and carrot and cook until softened. Add the garlic and mix well. Stir in tomato paste and cook 3 minutes; whisk in wine and reduce by half. Stir in beef stock and mix well.

Transfer the pork to a large braising pan or skillet. Add vegetable mixture. Liquid should come up to the top of the pork. If there is not enough liquid, add water but do not cover the pork with liquid.

Cover the pan and place it in the oven to braise—about 2 ½ to 3 hours. Turn off oven.

Combine Wondra and water to make a slurry. Stir into pork. Cover pan and return to the oven (with NO heat) and allow it to sit all day. When ready to serve, gently reheat over a burner.

*This is great served over mashed potatoes or polenta.*

# Leg of Lamb with Garlic & Anchovies

*We all know that slivers of garlic imbedded in a leg of lamb before roasting produces a delicious roast. Adding the anchovies only deepens the "umami" depth of flavor.*

1 (5-pound) leg of lamb

½ lemon

1 teaspoon Dijon mustard

1 teaspoon freshly ground black pepper

8 cloves garlic, cut into thick slivers

8 anchovy fillets cut into pieces

3 tablespoons all-purpose flour

2 cups chicken broth or milk

Salt and pepper

Mint jelly

Rub lemon, then mustard over entire surface of the roast. Sprinkle with pepper. With a very sharp knife, put 1-inch deep slits about 2 inches apart evenly over surface of roast. Insert garlic sliver in first slit and alternate garlic and anchovies until all slits are filled.

Preheat oven to 450 degrees. Immediately after putting meat in oven reduce temperature to 350 degrees. Roast 1 ½ hours. Check temperature. Internal temperature should be 160 degrees for slightly rare. Do not cover or baste. Allow to rest 10 minutes before slicing.

To the pan drippings, add flour a little at a time, stirring with a whisk until flour is lump free. Slowly add warmed chicken stock or milk to make 2 cups, stirring constantly until gravy is thickened. Season with salt and pepper.

Serve slices of lamb with gravy and a dollop of mint jelly.

# Leg of Lamb with Spicy Peanut Sauce

*This is Carole's signature dish. Now that she has generously shared the recipe, you can make it yours!*

1 leg of lamb, butterflied

**MARINADE**

4 cloves garlic, minced

1 medium shallot, chopped

1 teaspoon dry mustard

¼ cup dry red wine

1 ½ tablespoons curry powder

1 teaspoon chopped fresh thyme or
   ½ teaspoon dried thyme

Zest of 1 lemon

Juice of 1 lemon

1 tablespoons honey

Freshly cracked pepper

1 bay leaf

Prepare Marinade by combining all ingredients. Pour over meat, refrigerate and marinate 4 to 6 hours, turning a few times. Remove lamb and discard Marinade. Grill lamb as you like and serve with Peanut Sauce and Lemon Rice with Capers.

**PEANUT SAUCE**

1 cup crunchy peanut butter

¼ cup soy sauce

4 cloves garlic, minced

½ cup chicken broth

3 tablespoons honey

2 tablespoons hot pepper oil

3 tablespoons finely chopped cilantro

¼ cup lemon juice

2 tablespoons green curry paste
   (should have chili in ingredient
   list)

Combine all ingredients. Whisk together until blended—this may take a while. The oils should be well incorporated, not separate. May be made a day ahead of using but bring it to room temperature before serving.

*Leg of Lamb (continued)*

## LEMON RICE WITH CAPERS

1 cup long-grain white rice

3 tablespoons butter, softened

½ teaspoon salt

⅓ teaspoon finely ground black pepper

1 tablespoon lemon juice

1 tablespoon capers, drained

Chopped parsley

Cook rice as directed on package. Stir in remaining ingredients. Adjust seasonings as needed.

### JO REID'S MENU OF THE WEEK
#### August 24, 1965

Cucumber Slices in Sour Cream
JOLLY ROAST LEG O' LAMB
French Peas
Roast New Potatoes

Mint Sauce
Lemon Meringue Pie

### JOLLY ROAST LEG O' LAMB

Crush a clove of garlic with 1 tsp salt and freshly ground pepper. Mix with 2 tbsp olive oil and spread on Jolly leg o' lamb. Sprinkle lamb with 1 tsp each marjoram, thyme, rosemary and 2 tbsp flour. Now pour 1 cup dry white wine in roasting pan along with 1 cup of water and the lamb . . . Roast in slow oven (325°) 2½ to 3 hours, basting frequently. Serves 6.

### FRENCH PEAS

6 to 8 fresh lettuce leaves
¼ tsp pepper
1 small white onion, sliced
½ tsp chicken stock base

1 tsp sugar
3 tbsp butter
2 pkgs. frozen peas

Wash lettuce leaves. Put half the still-damp lettuce leaves in bottom of pan and sprinkle with salt, sugar, and stock base. Cover over peas and spread slices of onion over peas and sprinkle with salt, sugar, and stock base. Cover with more lettuce leaves. Do not add water. Cover and cook over low heat 10 minutes. Remove top lettuce; add butter and pepper. Serve with onion and lettuce. This is a winner!

### CUCUMBER SLICES IN SOUR CREAM

Thinly slice 2 large cucumbers and sprinkle with 1 tsp. salt. Let stand 30 minutes, shaking occasionally. Drain thoroughly. Now combine ½ cup dairy sour cream, 1 tbsp vinegar, 2 tbsp chopped chives, 1 tsp dill seed and a dash of freshly ground pepper. Pour over cucumbers. Chill well about 30 minutes . . . Cucumbers at their best.

# Reid's Leg of Lamb

*This is a basic recipe for leg of lamb. It can be grilled or broiled or baked in is equally delicious using any method.*

**1 boned and butterflied leg of lamb**

### MARINADE

¾ **cup olive oil**

¼ **cup red wine vinegar**

½ **yellow onion, sliced**

2 **teaspoons Dijon mustard**

2 **teaspoons salt**

½ **teaspoon dried oregano**

½ **teaspoon dried basil**

**Pepper to taste**

1 **bay leaf**

Combine all Marinade ingredients in a blender or food processor and pulse until well blended. Place leg of lamb in an extra-large zip top bag along with the Marinade and refrigerate for 8 hours or as long as 2 days, turning periodically. Remove and discard Marinade. Cook lamb using method of choice.

- Grill with coals close to meat
  5 minutes each side

- Grill with coals lowered
  20-25 minutes each side

- Oven (under broiler)
  10 minutes each side

- Bake (400 degrees)
  25 minutes

LAMB

# Breaded Lamb Chops

*Not fancy but just plain delicious! Great flavor.*

½ cup olive oil

2 tablespoons lemon juice

3 cloves garlic, chopped

1 tablespoon Dijon mustard

1 tablespoon chopped fresh rosemary

8 lamb chops or 2 racks of lamb cut
   into double chops

Salt and pepper

CRUMB TOPPING

2 cups fresh sourdough breadcrumbs

2 tablespoons melted butter

Make a marinade by combining oil, lemon juice, garlic, mustard and rosemary. Sprinkle chops with salt and pepper. Place chops in large zip top bag and pour in marinade. Marinate chops in refrigerator at least 4 hours or up to 1 day. Meanwhile, prepare crumbs for topping the chops.

Preheat broiler. Remove chops from marinade and pat dry with paper towels. Broil chops 2 minutes per side. Remove pan from broiler and press crumbs over each chop; return to broil until crumbs are golden (watching carefully).

Toss crumbs with melted butter.

*My mother's method: Brush chops with olive oil, roll in dry breadcrumbs, place on baking sheet and bake in 400 degree oven to desired doneness.*

# Melinda's Spicy Lamb Stew with Couscous

*There are many gifts at the end of the rainbow—one such is this recipe!*

2 tablespoons olive oil, divided

1 (3-pound) boneless leg of lamb, cubed

Salt and pepper to taste

1 onion, chopped

1 red pepper, seeded and chopped

1 whole leek, cleaned and chopped

2 cloves garlic, minced

1 ½ teaspoons ground cinnamon

1 ½ teaspoons ground cumin

1 teaspoon ground ginger

¾ cup pitted kalamata olives

½ cup chopped dried dates

1 (14.5-ounce) can stewed tomatoes

2 cups beef broth

⅓ cup chopped flat-leaf parsley

1 (16-ounce) box couscous

½ cup sliced almonds, toasted

Heat 1 tablespoon oil in Dutch oven over medium high heat. Season lamb with salt and pepper. Working in batches, brown lamb on all sides. Transfer to a bowl using a slotted spoon.

Add remaining oil to Dutch oven and sauté onion, pepper, leek and garlic 4 to 5 minutes. Stir in cinnamon, cumin and ginger and continue cooking until vegetables are tender, about 3 to 4 minutes. Return lamb to Dutch oven.

Stir in olives, dates, tomatoes and beef broth. Break up tomatoes with wooden spoon. Bring mixture to a boil. Reduce heat. Simmer, covered, for 1 hour or until lamb is tender. Stir in parsley.

Prepare couscous following package directions; stir in toasted almonds. Serve stew with couscous.

*Melinda's note: I tend to use vegetables I have in the fridge. I may add carrots and leave out red pepper. However, you must NEVER leave out the dates. They are the secret ingredient for this delicious stew! Also quinoa or rice may be substituted for the couscous.*

# Lamb with Black Olives

SERVES 6-8

*Picture a farm in Tuscany surrounded by grapevines and olive trees where you have the good fortune of being invited to dinner. You will love the main course.*

1 (3-pound) leg of lamb, cut into small pieces

Salt and pepper to taste

3 tablespoons olive oil, divided

1 red onion, chopped

2 shallots, chopped

4 cloves garlic, chopped

2 sprigs rosemary, chopped

1 cup dry white wine or dry vermouth

1 cup black ripe or kalamata olives

½ cup currants or raisins

2 tablespoons tomato paste, thinned with ¼ cup water

1 cup chicken or beef broth

Season lamb with salt and pepper. In a large skillet, add 2 tablespoons olive oil and brown lamb thoroughly on all sides. Remove lamb from skillet and set aside.

In the same skillet add 1 tablespoon olive oil and gently sauté onion and shallots until soft. Add garlic and rosemary and simmer about 10 minutes. Add wine or vermouth, return to simmer and cook until reduced by half.

Add lamb, olives, currants or raisins and tomato paste. Cook on very low heat for about 1 hour or until sauce is quite thick and lamb is cooked through. Check periodically. Add broth as needed if the sauce seems too thick.

*Polenta is the natural accompaniment.*

## JO REID'S MENU OF THE WEEK
### July 14, 1964
★ ★ ★ ★ ★

### LAMB CURRY CASSEROLE
Buttered Green Beans
Fresh Pineapple

Frosted Angel Food Cake
Iced Tea

★ ★ ★ ★ ★

## LAMB CURRY CASSEROLE

8 lamb shanks
  Instant meat tenderizer
2 tsp. salt
4 tsp. curry powder
½ tsp. ginger

2 onions, chopped
2 apples, chopped
3 cups water
2 cups uncooked rice
2 tbsp. lemon juice

1. Sprinkle meat with tenderizer and pierce with a fork. Brown in a very hot oven (450) about 30 minutes. Pour off fat.
2. Combine salt, curry and ginger; sprinkle over meat. Add onion, apple and water. Cover and bake 1 hour or until tender.
3. Add rice and lemon juice to liquid in bottom of pan. Bake, covered 45 minutes longer or until rice is tender; adding more water if necessary.
4. Serve with green beans and cubes of fresh pineapple! Serves 8.

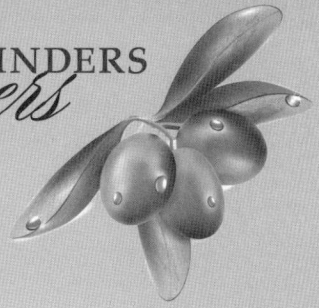

# Prime Rib

SERVES 10+

*Finally, a method that has proven successful every time.*

**2 (5 ½-pound) boneless prime ribs at room temperature**

**Salt, pepper and garlic powder**

Preheat oven to 250 degrees.

Brown roasts on all sides in a very hot pan. Sprinkle with a mixture of salt, pepper and garlic powder. Place both roasts in a large metal pan (such as a paella pan).

Place in oven and bake for 2 hours. Internal temperature should be 125 to 130 degrees for medium rare. Depending on the oven, additional time may be required. Remove and allow meat to rest at least 40 minutes.

Remove as much fat as possible from pan drippings. Add 2 cans beef consommé to drippings for au jus.

*In testing this recipe, I found that it was more successful when I used the two smaller roasts as opposed to one larger one. It is definitely the "cook's choice".*

# Steak Au Poivre

SERVES 4

*Ta Da! Here it is! The steak makes anyone who serves this—famous! It is the best company dish ever! Marilyn first served this to us many, many years ago. The ultimate thanks to her!*

**4 filet mignon steaks, 1 ¾-inches thick, well-trimmed**

**Jane's Krazy Mixed-up Pepper**

**1 cup red wine**

**1 cup cognac or brandy**

**1 can beef consommé**

**1 cup whipping cream**

Press pepper on both sides of steak, flattening steak with the heel of your hand. Set aside.

Place wine, cognac or brandy and consommé in large fry pan and cook over medium heat, stirring often. Cook down to 1½ cups. This will take quite a while. Watch carefully and often.

Add cream and continue cooking until reduced to the consistency of thick melted chocolate. Set aside. The sauce takes time but the slow cooking is necessary for the proper result.

Sauce may be made early in the day and reheated. Recipe can also be doubled for more servings or more steaks.

Heat a non-stick skillet and sauté steaks (do not use fat or oil). Brown nicely on both sides but do not overcook. They must be rare.

Remove from pan and tent steaks with foil to retain heat.

To serve, reheat sauce and place steaks in sauce, turning quickly to lightly cover both sides with sauce. Do not cook together; this is not a steak and gravy presentation. It may also be served by spooning a puddle of sauce on a plate and placing the steak over it.

Decorate with sprigs of parsley or fresh rosemary. Best served with Accordion Potatoes.

*Want to talk like a culinary pro? The technical term for turning the steak in the sauce is to "nap" it. The definition of that is "to coat food lightly with a sauce so that it completely covers the food with a thin, even layer."*

## KITCHEN KAPERS

**Kitchen-Tested Recipes from the Kitchen of
JO REID**

Anticipation better than realization? Maybe. But some of our best times are when we have invited guests to stay on to dinner on the spur-of-the-moment.

How nice to serve a dinner that is inexpensive, quick to prepare, and simply delicious. Try this. Realization is better than anticipation here!

### IN-A-MINUTE CANAPES

Mayonnaise
Grated parmesan cheese
Onion, peeled and finely
   chopped

Tiny rounds of bread cut with
   1-inch cooky cutter, toasted on one side

Mix mayonnaise and cheese (equal amounts) to consistency of softened butter. Place little chopped onion in center of each round of bread. Cover with mayonnaise-cheese mixture. Put under broiler until puffed and brown. Serve immediately. (Can be made the day before, covered with waxed paper, and stored in refrigerator.) Broil before serving.

### STEAK-ROLLS

(Serves 4)

1 onion, peeled and cut fine
1 green pepper, cut fine
1 clove garlic, peeled and cut
   fine
¼ pound butter
1 7-ounce can tomato paste

30 crackers, crumbled
1 teaspoon salt
½ teaspoon pepper
4 cube steaks
¾ cup hot water

Saute onion, green pepper, and garlic in half the butter in large skillet until golden brown. Combine half tomato paste with cracker crumbs, salt and pepper. Add to onion mixture. Spoon mixture onto steaks. Roll each and fasten with small skewer or toothpicks. Brown rolls on all sides in remaining butter. Blend remaining tomato paste with ¾ cup hot water. Pour over steaks and cover skillet. Simmer covered over low heat 40 to 50 minutes. Remove skewers before serving. Makes 4 servings. Washed, drained, cut string beans may be cooked with steaks. Add to skillet last 20 minutes of cooking. Add little hot water if necessary.

### CHOCOLATE PIE SUPERB

Graham cracker crust for
   9-inch pie
1 9-ounce Hershey almond bar

⅔ cup milk
12 marshmallows
1 cup heavy cream, whipped

Prepare crust. Melt chocolate bar in top of double boiler over boiling water. Stir in milk and marshmallows. When smooth, remove from heat. Let cool. Fold in whipped cream. Pour into crumb shell. Chill. Serve topped with additional whipped cream if desired. Makes 6 servings.

Have fun—see you next week!

# Filet of Beef Bourguignon

SERVES 8-10

*Finally! A glorious make-ahead entrée. This is a lighter version of a French classic. There are quite a few steps but the result is outstanding. Ina reworked Julia's recipe and I reworked Ina's!*

12 (1-inch thick) slices filet of beef

4 ounces pancetta, diced

4 cloves garlic, minced

2 tablespoons butter

2 tablespoons olive oil

1 pound mushrooms, sliced ¼-inch thick

1 bottle good dry red wine

3 cans beef consommé

3 tablespoons tomato paste

2 tablespoons fresh thyme leaves

3 tablespoons butter at room temperature

3 tablespoons all-purpose flour

1 pound pearl onions, cooked al dente

12 carrots, sliced diagonally into 1-inch thick slices, cooked al dente

Sauté filet slices in batches until browned on outside and very rare inside. Remove and set aside.

In the same pan, sauté pancetta on medium low heat until browned and crisp. Remove and add to beef. Cook garlic for 30 seconds and add to beef.

Again, in the same pan, heat 2 tablespoons butter and olive oil. Add mushrooms and cook until golden. Add to meat mixture.

To make the sauce, deglaze pan with wine and cook on high heat for 5 minutes. Add consommé, tomato paste and thyme. Bring to a boil and cook uncovered on medium heat for 20 minutes.

Mash 3 tablespoons softened butter with 3 tablespoons flour into a paste and whisk it gently into sauce. Simmer for 2 minutes to thicken.

Add pre-cooked onions and carrots and simmer uncovered for 20 minutes or until sauce has thickened and vegetables are cooked to desired tenderness.

Remove filets from mushroom mixture to a separate container and refrigerate. Add the mushroom mixture to the sauce and mix well. Pour sauce into another container and refrigerate overnight.

## Filet of Beef Bourguignon *(continued)*

On the following day, remove containers from the refrigerator and bring all ingredients to room temperature. When ready to serve, simmer sauce for 12 to 15 minutes—just until heated through. Add filets and simmer 5 minutes longer. Do not overheat so that beef will remain rare.

*If we are going to "cook like Julia" then we will learn to talk like her, too! The French terminology for mashing the softened butter and flour together is making a* beurre manie, *or kneaded butter. You can even make up a batch of this and keep it on hand in the refrigerator for use as a thickening agent in any heated sauce.*

## Filet Steak with Anchovy Garlic Butter

SERVES 4

*Amazing flavor. Superb.*

**4 (1-inch thick) fillet steaks**

**Salt and pepper**

**3 tablespoons olive oil**

Pat steaks dry. Season with salt and pepper and sauté in oil for a total of 8 minutes for medium rare. Transfer to a cutting board and let rest 5 minutes.

**ANCHOVY GARLIC BUTTER**

**1 stick butter, softened**

**4 cloves garlic, minced**

**1 can anchovies, drained and patted dry**

**3 tablespoons lemon juice**

**½ teaspoon pepper**

**4 tablespoons finely chopped Italian parsley**

To serve, top each steak with a dollop of Anchovy Garlic Butter.

Mix all ingredients until well blended.

173

# BEEF

# KITCHEN KAPERS

**Kitchen-Tested Recipes from the Kitchen of**
**JO REID**

"You can discuss Veal Scallopini with 50 people and you'll hear 50 different opinions on how it should look, what it should contain, how it should taste. And what's more, if the 50 people are Italians, you'll get 100 opinions! Go to 50 restaurants — the same thing.

Here's what we have to say on the subject. The first is simple to prepare, excellent. The second, delicious and more typical of the restaurant type of Veal Scallopini. Which do you prefer?

## VEAL SCALLOPINI CLASS I

2 pounds veal (steak off of the leg ⅛" thick)
4 tablespoons butter
4 tablespoons olive oil
3 cups fresh mushrooms
1 lemon
¾ cup Marsala Wine
Flour, salt and pepper

Cut the veal in serving size, cover each portion with wax paper, and pound slices with the flat side of a cleaver until very thin. Season the meat with salt and pepper, and flour light on each side. Brown veal in butter and oil. Add the mushrooms, which have been thinly sliced, and cook all for 10 minutes. Add the juice of lemon and the Marsala wine and simmer 5 minutes more. Serves 6.

## VEAL SCALLOPINI CLASS II

1½ lbs. veal steak, thinly sliced
Flour, salt and pepper
2 tbs. butter
2 tbs. shortening
1 4-oz. can mushrooms (1 cup fresh, sliced)
1 clove garlic, mashed
1 small onion, sliced
1 cup chicken stock or bouillon
½ cup dry white wine
¼ cup tomato juice
⅛ tsp. nutmeg
¼ cup grated Parmesan cheese
2 tbs. chopped parsley

Trim skin and gristle from veal. Dredge in seasoned flour and pound thin. Season. Cut into 1x3" strips. Melt butter, add oil and saute garlic and onion. Brown veal on both sides. Remove garlic; add mushrooms, chicken stock, wine, tomato juice, and nutmeg. Reduce heat to low and cover. Cook ½ hour or until tender, stirring occasionally. Add more liquid if necessary. Sprinkle with cheese. Cover and let stand 10 minutes before serving. Garnish with parsley.

A perfect accompaniment to Scallopini:

## NOODLES DE LUXE

Cook ½ pound noodles as described on package. Drain thoroughly. Add 4 tablespoons butter and 2/3 cup slivered toasted almonds. Toss lightly to coat noodles with butter and serve on heated platter around veal.
Good Day!

174

# Filets in Puff Pastry

*Martha's kids love this for the Holidays. So will you and your kids!*

8 filets

4 tablespoons butter

6 tablespoons Madeira, divided

1 package frozen puff pastry Duxelles

Egg wash (1 egg beaten with small
   amount of water)

Sear filets briefly in butter. Pour 2 tablespoons Madeira over meat, cover and chill. This is an important step. In the same frying pan, add 4 tablespoons Madeira and Duxelles. Cook until liquid evaporates. Cover and chill. When ready to assemble, defrost pastry according to package directions. From this, cut 8 (8-inch) circles. Divide the Duxelles evenly over the 8 pastry circles and top each with a filet. Enclose filet with pastry and place, seam side down, on a baking sheet. Cover and chill for 1 hour. (The chilling is necessary to prevent the filets from becoming overcooked.)

Preheat oven to 425 degrees. When ready to serve, brush packets with egg wash. Place them on a baking sheet on the lower rack of the oven and bake 10 minutes. Move to highest rack and bake 8 to 10 minutes longer. Serve with Béarnaise Sauce.

## DUXELLES

2 tablespoons butter

1 pound mushrooms, chopped

2 shallots, finely diced

Salt and pepper to taste

In a large sauté pan, heat butter. Add mushrooms and sauté for 6 minutes. Add the shallots and continue to sauté for 4 minutes. Season with salt and pepper. Remove Duxelles from the pan and cool completely. Place in a clean kitchen towel and squeeze out all liquid.

# Short Ribs with Red Wine & Hoisin Sauce

SERVES 6

*Deep, rich flavor here—best made a day ahead.*

4 tablespoons olive oil, divided

3 large yellow onions, chopped

5-6 pounds short ribs with bone

Salt and pepper

1 ½ cups red wine

2 cans beef consommé

½ cup hoisin sauce

1 (14.5-ounce) can petite diced tomatoes, undrained

2 bay leaves

8 cloves garlic, minced

6 carrots cut diagonally into 1-inch lengths

1 tablespoon cornstarch mixed into 2 tablespoons cold water

Chopped parsley

Preheat oven to 400 degrees.

Heat 2 tablespoons oil in a large pan over high heat. Sauté onion slowly until cooked through. Remove to a large bowl.

Sprinkle salt and pepper over short ribs. Brown the meat in two batches adding remaining oil as needed. Add to reserved onion. Discard any fat.

Add wine, consommé, tomatoes and hoisin sauce to the pan. Bring to a boil, scraping up browned bits in the pan. Add meat, onions, bay leaves and garlic to the wine mixture.

Pour into a large LeCrueset-type casserole or a large braising pan. Cover and bake 1 hour. Reduce temperature to 350 degrees and bake 30 minutes. Add carrots, cover and cook an additional 30 minutes.

Remove to stovetop and discard bay leaves. On medium heat, add cornstarch mixture and cook until sauce is slightly thickened, stirring constantly.

Making this dish a day ahead of serving really helps the flavors blend nicely. Cool slightly and chill uncovered until completely cooled. Cover and refrigerate. Bring to room temperature and simmer before serving, stirring occasionally.

Sprinkle with parsley and serve, preferably, over polenta.

## KOZY KITCHEN
### KITCHEN TESTED RECIPES
### FROM THE KITCHEN OF
### JO REID

An economy move is considered by most of us somewhere on our list of resolutions for the new year.

Women attack the food budget first! Certainly a challenge with today's food prices but one well worth the little extra effort spent in planning and time devoted in the kitchen.

It is absolutely soul-satisfying to serve a really good meal to the family and to know it was done so inexpensively.

So often we American housewives decide to cut down by having "just hamburgers" but perhaps serving hamburger as our Swedish or Russian counterparts do would warrant a little more acclaim from the family.

### SWEDISH MEATBALLS
Soak:

1 cup bread crumbs in 1-1/3 cup milk

Add:

1 egg
1 pound ground beef
1 tsp. salt
1/8 tsp. pepper
1/4 tsp. nutmeg

Form small balls and brown in 2 tbs. butter. Remove meatballs and add 2 tbs. flour to drippings, stirring until well-blended. Gradually add 1½ cups bouillon and 1/3 cup cream (half & half, canned milk). Stir well. Return meatballs and simmer for 15 minutes.

### RUSSIAN MEATBALLS
1 large loaf fresh bread
1½ cups milk
1 pound beef, ground
1 pound pork, ground
1 pound veal, ground
4 eggs
1 tablesp. finely cut fresh dill (use dried dill if fresh is unavailable)
1½ tsp. salt
½ teasp. pepper
1 teasp. Kitchen Bouquet or Worcestershire sauce
¼ cup water
¾ cup bread crumbs
3 tablsp. butter or margarine
1½ cups commercial sour cream

Remove crust from bread. Break bread coarsely. Moisten with milk and let stand until very soft. Combine meats, mixing thoroughly with the hands. Beat 2 eggs lightly and work into meats.

Add dill, salt, pepper, and Kitchen Bouquet or Worcestershire to the softened bread and combine with meat mixture. Form loose balls the size of a small orange. Beat remaining 2 eggs lightly. Mix with about ¼ cup water. Dip meatballs into egg, then into crumbs. Saute' in butter or in a metal-base casserole on moderate heat 10 minutes. Turn meat balls and brown 10 minutes longer.

Start oven at moderate (375 degrees). When meat balls are lightly browned, pour sour cream over them. Cover casserole. Bake 45 min. Makes 6 to 8 servings. Thank you for your nice comments. See you next week. For breakfast?

# Spaghetti Sauce

1 tablespoon olive oil

1 small onion, finely chopped

2 cloves garlic, minced

1 carrot, grated

1 zucchini, grated

½ cup red wine

1 (28-ounce) can crushed tomatoes

1 tablespoon fresh basil or parsley

Salt and pepper

1 tablespoon butter

1 tablespoon sugar

Pinch of baking soda

Heat olive oil in a large skillet. Add onion and sauté until translucent. Add garlic, carrot and zucchini and cook for 3 minutes, stirring constantly. Add wine and cook 3 minutes or until liquid evaporates. Stir in tomatoes, basil, salt and pepper. Cook over low heat for 30 minutes.

Add butter, sugar and baking soda. Stir well and simmer a few minutes. Add meatballs and heat 5 minutes. Spoon over spaghetti that has been cooked al dente.

*A little food "chemistry" is involved in this dish. The use of both sugar and baking soda serves to lower the acidity level of the tomatoes. Sugar alone may cause more of a sweet taste than desired but adding the baking soda balances the flavor of the sauce perfectly. Look for the mixture to bubble up a bit when the baking soda is added.*

# Sicilian Meatballs and Spaghetti

## MAKES 12 MEATBALLS

*These meatballs win the Oscar. Do not question the ingredients. Just go for it and enjoy the tastiest meatballs this side of Hollywood (or anywhere in the Universe)!*

2 tablespoons pine nuts

2 tablespoons dried currants or raisins

⅔ cup fresh bread crumbs

3 tablespoons milk

⅓ cup grated Parmesan

½ small red onion, coarsely chopped

1 egg

2 cloves garlic

3 tablespoons fresh basil

⅛ teaspoon red pepper flakes

1 pound mild Italian sausage (or half sausage and half ground chuck)

Place all ingredients except sausage in food processor and process until well combined.

Add mixture to the sausage. Wet hands and form into 12 meatballs.

Preheat oven to 350 degrees. Place meatballs on lightly oiled baking sheet. Bake until light brown— about 25 to 30 minutes. Add to Spaghetti Sauce and simmer gently.

*There is no need to add salt and pepper to these meatballs. The combination of other ingredients provides perfect seasoning. The recipe also doubles very well.*

# Baked Corned Beef with Braised Red Cabbage

*You will never go back to preparing Corned Beef the old-fashioned way. No need to wait a whole year for St. Patrick's Day as this is delicious any day of the year.*

**3 to 5-pound corned beef**

**1 cup marmalade**

**½ cup Dijon mustard**

**½ cup brown sugar**

**¼ teaspoon red pepper flakes**

Simmer corned beef according to directions on package. Drain and place in baking dish.

Preheat oven to 350 degrees.

Combine marmalade, mustard, brown sugar and red pepper flakes and spread over entire surface or corned beef. Bake 30 minutes.

Slice and serve with Braised Red Cabbage and Perfect Mashed Potatoes.

## BRAISED RED CABBAGE

**1 large head red cabbage, shredded**

**2 cups boiling chicken broth**

**4 tablespoons butter**

**2 tablespoons vinegar**

**2 apples, peeled and grated**

**2 whole cloves**

Place cabbage in large saucepan or skillet. Add chicken broth and butter. Cook for 30 minutes. Add remaining ingredients except cornstarch and water. Cook 30 minutes longer, stirring often.

Mix cornstarch with water and stir into cabbage. Cook several minutes until well combined and heated through.

*At times, I feel the "round" cut is almost too lean—a matter, again, of cook's preference.*

# Grilled Flank Steak

SERVES 8

*A simply grilled flank steak is always good, but Carol's steak is out-of-this world! So flavorful—so rich. This will surely become your "go-to" steak recipe.*

⅓ cup olive oil

⅓ cup red wine vinegar

4 tablespoons Dijon mustard

6 cloves garlic, minced

2 large shallots, chopped

1 tablespoon coarsely ground pepper

1 tablespoon minced fresh thyme

1 tablespoon minced fresh rosemary

1 teaspoon salt

1 teaspoon pepper

3 flank steaks (about 1 ¼-pounds each)

Combine all ingredients except steak and whisk together well. Pour into a plastic zip-top bag and add steaks. Refrigerate overnight.

Prepare grill to medium high heat. Remove steaks from bag and discard marinade. Season steaks well with salt and pepper. Grill to desired doneness, about 5 to 7 minutes per side for medium-rare (best for flank steak).

Transfer cooked steaks to a cutting board and allow to stand 10 minutes.

Cut steak at 45-degree angle across the grain into thin slices. Garnish platter with fresh thyme and rosemary sprigs.

Serve with Potato Gratin with Boursin.

# KITCHEN KAPERS

**Kitchen-Tested Recipes from the Kitchen of**
**JO REID**

Please! Won't some of you go along with the fact that tripe is out-of-this world?

At this point, half of our readers have turned the page, but the remaining troupers might like to fix it this way. It is best made one day and heated and eaten the next. Double the quantity and freeze part of it. This is a delicious, full-bodied dish and the writer would love to start a Tripe Crusade. Any joiners?

## SPANISH TRIPE

3 lbs. honeycomb tripe
1 large onion, chopped
3 tbsp. chopped fresh parsley
1 teaspoon dried rosemary
2 cloves garlic, finely chopped
1 8-oz. can tomato sauce

No. 2½ can whole tomatoes, sieved or blended
1 cup chopped celery
6 carrots, cut in large pieces
4 potatoes, cut in large pieces

Wash tripe thoroughly under cold running water. Cut in 2-inch pieces. Cook in boiling salted water 1 hour or longer or until tender. Drain. Meanwhile, saute onion in salad oil. Add parsley, rosemary, garlic, tomatoes and tomato sauce. Simmer ½ hour. Add tripe and cook ½ hour more. Now add vegetables and simmer until tender. According to the French, tripe can't be overcooked! Serves 6.

Since we are crusading, why not discuss the merits of liver! Liver is another food-great which is only too often overlooked in meal planning.

## SAUTEED LIVER

1 lb. calves liver, cut in
2 in. strips
3 tablespoons oil
Salt and pepper

1 large onion
½ teasp. dried rosemary
½ cup water

Brown onion. Salt and pepper the liver. Add to onion mixture and saute turning as it browns, about 5 minutes in all. Add rosemary, water. Mix thoroughly. Cover pan and simmer 2 or 3 minutes. Turn off burner and serve 5 minutes later over mounds of hot, buttered mashed potatoes. Serves 2 if you just love liver, 3 if you can take it or leave it, and 4 if you can't stand the stuff!

# Grandma Arata's Braciola

*Every Italian family has a personalized braciola recipe. Some are stuffed with Italian sausage, others with pancetta, another with hard-cooked eggs. Chris's Grandma's is a favorite in which she uses a light touch stuffing the steak with carrots and celery.*

1 flank steak, butterflied

Salt and pepper

4 tablespoons olive oil, divided

¼ cup chopped Italian parsley

1 teaspoon dried oregano

1 teaspoon dried thyme

1 teaspoon dried sage

2 stalks celery, sliced into narrow strips

2-3 carrots, sliced into narrow strips

3 cloves garlic, minced

8 fresh Roma tomatoes, chopped

1 (28-ounce) can tomato sauce

1 cup dried porcini, reconstituted and chopped

1 teaspoon dried rosemary

½ teaspoon dried oregano

Salt and pepper to taste

3-4 packages frozen cheese ravioli, cooked according to package

To prepare the braciola, open flank steak and sprinkle with salt and pepper. Rub with 1 tablespoon olive oil, parsley, oregano, thyme and sage. Arrange celery and carrots over herbs. Roll meat and tie at 2-inch intervals

Heat remaining 3 tablespoons olive oil and sauté steak until brown on all sides. Add tomatoes, tomato sauce, porcini, rosemary and oregano and bring to a boil. Add salt and pepper to taste, cover and reduce heat. Cook gently for 1 hour. Remove braciola and reduce sauce to 4 cups.

Slice braciola into 1-inch slices and arrange over cooked cheese ravioli. Top with sauce. Mangia!

## KITCHEN KAPERS

Kitchen-Tested Recipes from the Kitchen of
**JO REID**

"Gee, Mom, there's never anything good to eat in this house." Ever heard this lament?

There may be cold chicken in the refrig, fruit of every variety, ice cream in the freezer, and caviar on the pantry shelf, but something "good" to teenagers means a hamburger, a chilled Coke, and freshly-baked anything chocolate. You'd be really "tough"* if you prepared some of these specialties.

(*Teen-Age Jargon meaning, the best.)

### HAMBURGER BBQ

3 lbs. ground chuck
1 cup chopped onion

¾ cup chopped green pepper
2 cups hot barbecue sauce

Combine ground chuck with onion and green pepper and ½ cup barbecue sauce. Shape into 12 hamburgers. Broil, turning once and basting frequently with hot barbecue sauce. Serve with remaining sauce.

### CHEESE AND CHILI-BURGERS

3 lbs. ground beef
½ cup wine vinegar
1 teaspoon salt
Freshly ground black pepper
12 hamburger buns

Butter
Onion rings
Cheese sauce
Chili sauce

Combine beef, wine vinegar, seasonings. Mix well. Divide into 12 burgers and broil. Butter buns. Serve burgers on buns with onion rings and a choice of cheese sauce or chili sauce.

### ROCKY ROAD FUDGE COOKIES

1 cup sifted all purpose flour
1 cup sugar
½ teaspoon salt
⅔ cup shortening
2 eggs
2 squares unsweetened chocolate, melted

1 tsp. vanilla
½ cup chopped nuts
24 marshmallows, cut in quarters
1 6-oz pkg. semi-sweet chocolate bits

Sift flour, sugar, salt. Add shortening and eggs and beat with mixer until fluffy. Add vanilla and the 2 melted squares of chocolate. Beat thoroughly. Then stir in nuts. Spread in lightly greased 11x7x1½" pan. Bake at 350 degree oven 20 to 25 minutes. Remove from oven and immediately cover top with marshmallows which have been quartered. Cool in pan. Then melt over warm water the chocolate bits. Pour over marshmallows. Cool and cut in bars or squares. If there are any left over, store in air-tight container.

### CAKE BARBIA

1 pkg. chocolate cake mix
1 pkg. raspberry gelatin
4 eggs

¾ cups oil
¾ cups water

Mix all ingredients and beat with electric mixer 5 minutes. Pour into ungreased angel food pan and bake 50 minutes, 350° oven. Remove from oven, poke holes with a fork over the entire surface of cake while still hot. Do not remove from pan. Pour frosting over top, making sure some of the frosting drips down along the side of pan. Frosting: Dissolve 1½ cups powdered sugar with 7 or 8 tablespoons fruit juice (Hawaiian punch, grape, lemon, or any juice you may have open). Try this cake with a white cake mix and any flavor gelatin for a change.

Good Day!

# Cheese 'N Crackers Meatloaf

SERVES 6

*Bear with me! I go on and on about meatloaf. If it is on a menu, I order it. This is one of my all-time favorites (circa 1965). Old-fashioned, quick and easy to prepare and truly a winner!*

24 round buttery crackers

2 pounds ground chuck

2 eggs, lightly beaten

1 package dry onion soup mix

1 can Cheddar cheese soup, undiluted

¼ teaspoon pepper

Preheat oven to 350 degrees.

Roll crackers into coarse crumbs. Add to ground chuck along with remaining ingredients, blending well.

Pack into a 12x5-inch loaf pan and bake 50 minutes. While meatloaf is baking, prepare a topping by mixing 1 cup catsup with ½ cup brown sugar. After the 50 minutes of baking time, spread sauce over meatloaf and return it to the oven to bake an additional 10 minutes. Allow to rest 10 minutes before removing from pan.

# Meatloaf & Gravy

SERVES 10-12

*I will choose this over fillet mignon any day. You will, too.*

3 pounds ground chuck

1 pound ground pork

1 tablespoon canola oil

1 large onion, finely chopped

2 large carrots, finely chopped

1 celery rib, finely chopped

3 cloves garlic, minced

1 ½ cups panko

4 large eggs

2 tablespoons Dijon mustard

2 tablespoons catsup

2 tablespoons Worcestershire sauce

1 teaspoon Tabasco

1 teaspoon salt

1 teaspoon pepper

8 ounces Monterey Jack cheese, cut into ½-inch cubes

Preheat oven to 400 degrees. In a skillet, sauté onion, carrots and celery until softened. Add garlic and cook 1 minute longer. Place in a large bowl and cool. In a separate bowl combine panko, eggs, mustard, catsup, Worcestershire, Tabasco, salt and pepper. Stir to form a paste. Using hands, work in the meats and vegetables until well combined. Line a roasting pan with parchment. Form mixture into 2 loaves (10 inches long). Push cheese cubes down into the middle of the loaves, taking care to cover cheese completely. Bake 1 hour and allow to rest. Cut into thick slices and serve with Creamy Onion Gravy.

# Meatloaf & Gravy (continued)

## CREAMY ONION GRAVY

2 tablespoons butter

2 tablespoons olive oil

2 large white onions, thinly sliced

¼ cup all-purpose flour

1 quart chicken broth

1 cup cream

Salt and pepper to taste

In a large saucepan, melt butter with olive oil. Add onion, cover and cook 10 to 12 minutes. Stir in flour and cook 2 minutes. Add chicken broth, whisking frequently. Cook about 5 minutes. Season with salt and pepper.

Transfer gravy to a blender and pulse very carefully until smooth. Return gravy to saucepan, stir in cream and simmer until reduced to 5 cups.

*Gravy may be made days ahead and refrigerated until ready to use.*

# KITCHEN KAPERS

Every once in awhile don't you just "feel" like Mexican food! It usually hits our house on slack Saturday nights, and the results depend on pantry supplies. We've had repeat performances on these dishes, and all are wonderfully suitable for unexpected guests.

## ENCHILADA CHA-CHA
### with mushrooms

1 pkg. frozen tortillas
1½ lbs. chuck ground
1 onion, coarsely chopped
1 clove garlic, finely chopped
1 8-oz. can tomato sauce

1 large can enchilada sauce
1 can sliced olives
½ cup grated Parmesan cheese
½ cup shredded cheddar cheese

Brown chuck with onion and garlic. Add the tomato and enchilada sauce. Mix well and heat. Set aside. Cut the tortillas in half and line an 8x12 baking dish in a single layer. Now spread half of the meat mixture and half the remaining ingredients over the tortillas. Place a layer of tortillas over this and repeat with meat mixture and so on! Cut remaining tortillas in quarters and arrange in design over the top of the casserole. Brush the tortillas with oil. Bake in 350 degree oven ½ hour. Serves 4 to 6.

## TOMATO-CHILI TORTILLAS

Yellow corn meal
Sesame seeds
1 can refrigerated biscuits

2 16-ounce cans chili with beans
1 16-oz. can stewed tomatoes

On square of wax paper pour about ¼ cup corn meal; add sesame seed if desired. Press each side of a biscuit into the corn-meal, then on the meal-covered paper, roll biscuit out to thin 6-inch circle. On ungreased hot griddle or skillet, cook about 1 minute on each side. Then remove from heat and roll up at once. Repeat, using more corn meal if necessary. Cover and store at room temperature until needed. About 10 minutes before serving: In saucepan combine chili and tomatoes. Cook stirring once or twice 'til hot. Serve in bowls with tortillas on side. Serves 4.

## EMPANADAS (Beef Turnovers)

Sifted all-purpose flour
Salt
½ tsp. baking powder
Shortening
Cold water
3 medium onions, minced
1 clove garlic, minced
2 medium green peppers, minced

1 lb. chuck ground
½ tsp. Tabasco
½ tsp. chili powder
⅛ tsp. pepper
1 tsp. sugar
6 stuffed olives, sliced
1 hard-cooked egg cut into 8 slices, then halved
1 beaten egg

In a medium bowl, combine 2 cups sifted flour and ½ tsp. salt with baking powder. With pastry blender cut in 2/3 cup shortening until like corn meal. Now add 3 tbsp. cold water, toss together quickly, then form into smooth ball. Wrap in wax paper and refrigerate.

Now in 1 tbsp. shortening in large skillet, saute onions, garlic and green peppers until tender. Then add beef and saute until it loses its pink color. Stir in Tabasco, 1 tsp. salt, chili powder (more or less) pepper, sugar and 1 tbsp. flour. Remove from heat, stir in olives and set aside. Start heating oven to 400 degrees. On floured, cloth-covered pastry board, roll out half of chilled dough about ⅛-inch thick. With a 4½-inch round cookie cutter, or cardboard pattern and sharp knife, cut out rounds.

Now cover one-half of each round with about 1 heaping tbsp. meat, making half-moons; with floured fork, firmly press pastry edges together. Place on large ungreased cookie sheet. Repeat with other half of dough. Brush Empanadas with beaten

2

# Beef Enchiladas

MAKES 20

*Everyone needs a few "no brainer" recipes. Can't get much better than this goodie.*

2 ½ pounds ground chuck

1 large onion, chopped

1 (15-ounce) cans enchilada sauce

1 can cream of mushroom soup

1 can tomato soup

20 (8-inch) flour or corn tortillas

2 ½ cups shredded Mexican-blend cheese

Additional cheese for topping

Preheat oven to 350 degrees.

Brown ground chuck and onion. Drain any remaining fat.

Combine sauce and soups. Pour 1 cup sauce in each of two 9x13-inch baking dishes. Stir 1 ½ cups sauce into beef mixture. Reserve remaining sauce.

Spoon ¼ cup beef mixture down the center of each tortilla. Top with 2 tablespoons shredded cheese. Roll tortillas tightly and place 10 enchiladas, seam side down, in each prepared dish. Top with remaining sauce.

Cover with foil and bake 25 to 30 minutes. Uncover and sprinkle with additional cheese and bake 5 to 10 more minutes until cheese is melted and begins to brown.

# Mexican Delight

*An oldie but a cutie!*

1 ½ pounds ground chuck

1 large onion, chopped

1 (28-ounce) can tomatoes

2 (4-ounce) cans green chiles

1 pound Monterey Jack cheese, grated

1 (10-ounce) bag tortilla chips

1 cup whipping cream

1 tablespoon vinegar

Whole tortilla chips

Sliced tomatoes

Preheat oven to 350 degrees.

Sauté onion and ground chuck together, stirring often. Add tomatoes and green chiles. Mix thoroughly. In a 9 x13-inch glass baking dish, arrange tortilla chips in a single layer. Top with meat mixture and sprinkle cheese over all. In a small bowl, combine whipping cream and vinegar. Pour over meat/cheese mixture. Bake 30 minutes.

Garnish with whole tortilla chips and sliced tomatoes.

# Italian Delight

*It is doubtful the Italians have this recipe. It is an American 1960s staple and never out of flavor.*

1 ½ pounds ground beef

1 small onion, chopped

½ teaspoon garlic salt

1 (28-ounce) can tomato puree

1 can cream-style corn

1 can pitted black olives

Grated Cheddar cheese

½ pound large elbow macaroni, cooked al dente

Preheat oven to 350 degrees.

Sauté onion and ground beef together. Add garlic salt. Drain any excess fat. In a large casserole dish, make 2 or 3 layers in this order: macaroni, beef, corn, tomato puree, olives and cheese.

Bake uncovered for 30 to 45 minutes or until top layer of cheese is lightly browned.

# Hamburger Pie

*It is memory lane time with this recipe. It was a "regular" then and we devotees continue to relish it!*

1 medium onion, chopped

1 tablespoon oil

1 pound ground beef

Salt and pepper to taste

½ pound cooked green beans

1 can condensed cream of tomato soup

5 medium-size potatoes, cooked

½ cup warm milk

1 egg, lightly beaten

Preheat oven to 350 degrees. Grease a casserole dish and set aside.

Brown onion in oil. Add ground beef, salt and pepper and brown until meat crumbles. Add cooked green beans and soup. Mix well and pour into prepared dish.

Mash potatoes, adding milk, egg and more salt and pepper as needed. Spoon potatoes in mounds over beef mixture. Bake for 30 minutes.

*In the olden days when we made this dish the green beans were canned! Now along with most other vegetables, the "fresher the better."*

The Santa Rosa News, Santa Rosa, Calif., May 30, 1963

# KOZY KITCHEN

### Kitchen-Tested Recipes From the Kitchen of JO REID

Aren't there some days when you feel you've just been running around in circles! It's either a dash to the orthodontist or your week for carpool, or the car has to be serviced and it's Bluebird day. Nothing, but nothing, has been done around the house and the thought of fixing dinner is unbearable! Wouldn't it be great if the budget could stretch to take the family out to dinner but payday is three days away. Isn't there a dinner that can be "thrown" together that the family would thoroughly enjoy and wouldn't clue poor ole' Dad in on the daytime pandemonium? Maybe these suggestions will do the trick and you might find yourself using them even on the "good" days!

## PORCUPINE STEW
(Serves 4)

1 lb. lean ground beef
¼ cup dehydrated onions (always keep them on hand)
½ cup raw rice
1 tsp. salt
¼ tsp. pepper
1 tsp. dried basil
1 tsp. dried parsley
1 No. 1 can tomato puree
2 cups water
6 carrots, scraped and sliced
2 bay leaves

In medium size saucepan mix together tomato puree, water and bay leaves. Simmer gently. Now mix the ground beef, onions, rice, salt, pepper, basil and parsley thoroughly. Form into medium-size meatballs and drop into simmering sauce. Add carrots. Cover and cook over slow heat 15 to 20 minutes. (Even better when made in the morning and partially cooked, then heated 10 minutes before serving.)

## ROMAINE SALAD

In a salad bowl rubbed with a cut clove of garlic, toss broken romaine leaves with dressing made of about 3 parts olive oil to 1 part wine vinegar. Season with salt and freshly ground black pepper.

If you accompany the Porcupine Stew and Salad with hot rolls and an elegant dessert like our Nut Mold Pudding, even you will agree with the family that you are a whiz!

## NUT MOLD PUDDING

2 cups cold water
2 tbsp. cornstarch
1½ tbsp. floor
1½ cups brown sugar
2 egg whites
1 tsp. vanilla
½ cup chopped walnuts

Mix cornstarch and flour. Add ½ cup water and mix well. Place in saucepan with remaining water and add brown sugar. Mix thoroughly and cook mixture until it comes to a boil, stirring constantly. It should boil 10 minutes. Remove from stove. Beat egg whites until stiff. Add brown sugar mixture gradually over egg whites. Add

# KOZY KITCHEN
### Kitchen-Tested Recipes From The Kitchen Of
### JO REID

A Very Important Person is coming to dinner — good ole' G. W. (that's George Washington). We wouldn't want to give him the impression that we can "afford" steak and champagne.

As Father of our Country he might get a notion that he could tax us in some way, say a tax on our income or the like.

So when George arrives he'll have a good dinner, but it will not be lavish!

We've checked with some of his Army pals and learned that he has a passion for cherries and any kind of game meat. But who has any game? Perhaps we can satisfy him with this Hunter's Beef recipe. The combination of sauce, wine, and mushroom gives it a gamey flavor.

We'll toss in a salad with Green Goddess Dressing, hot French bread, Vin Rose', and after we've planned the future of the Colonies, we'll wow him with G.W.'s Cherry Cheese Cake!

## HUNTER'S BEEF
2 pounds round steak (¾ in. thick)
1 tesp. salt
½ cup flour
3 tablesp. shortening or bacon drippings
1 bunch green onions (cut in 2-inch lengths)
3 stalks celery (cut diagonally in 2-inch lengths)
2 carrots (quartered and cut in 2-inch lengths)
1 pound fresh mushrooms (or two 6-ounce cans mushroom caps)
3 tablesp. soy sauce
1/3 cup red table wine
Dash of cayenne pepper and ½ teasp. powdered ginger

Cut the meat into serving size pieces. Sprinkle with salt, dust with flour, and then brown on both sides in shortening. Arrange green onions, celery, carrots, and mushrooms over meat. Mix together soy sauce, wine, cayenne pepper and ginger and pour over all. Cover and simmer for one hour, or until meat is tender. Serves four to six, depending on

## GREEN GODDESS DRESSING
2 tablesp. chives
2 tablesp. parsley (chopped)
1 can flat anchovy
1 cup mayonnaise
¼ teasp. coarsely ground pepper
Dash garlic powder
1/3 cup tarragon vinegar
1 tablesp. Worcestershire

## CHERRY CHEESE CAKE
18 graham crackers
½ cube butter
1 large can extra large, pitted, dark cherries.
1 small package cream cheese
½ pint whipping cream
1 box black cherry gelatin
½ cup sifted powdered sugar

Make crust (according to directions on box of graham crackers. Bake and cool.

Drain cherries thoroughly. Make gelatin according to directions, remove the gelatin (about ½ cup) and jell only half-way (a quivering consistency). Whip cream; Whip cream cheese and add powdered sugar. Blend with whipped cream, being careful not to over beat. Put into crust. Place cherries over this mixture. Gently pour the ½ cup of gelatin over the cherries, as evenly as possible. Refrigerate.

Next week with Lent in view — an incomparable Souffle'. See you then!

193

# KITCHEN KAPERS

## Kitchen-Tested Recipes from the Kitchen of
### JO REID

We've had more requests for menu planning! Today's woman is a good cook, always trying something new, and certainly earns the "oh's" and "ah's" she receives after serving an unusual meal. She isn't afraid to serve an Italian, Chinese, or Indian dinner and we really can't very honestly say that many of our mothers would do this!

This is a delicious dinner but not so off-beat that the "meat and potato" man won't enjoy it!

### MAY MENU
Grapefruit and Avocado Salad
Polynesian Pot Roast
Fluffy Rice
Baked Tomato Halves
Marmalade Bread
Coffee    Tea    Milk

### POLYNESIAN POT ROAST

The day before: Take a 4 to 5 pound semi-boneless chuck roast; moisten meat and sprinkle with tenderizer as label directs. Place 1 large onion, sliced in rings in bottom of 3-quart casserole or bowl. Set meat on top. Combine 1 cup canned pineapple juice, 3 tbsp. soy sauce, 1½ tsp. ginger and ½ tsp. salt and pour over meat. Cover and refrigerate. About 2½ hours before serving: place onions and meat in Dutch oven, pour on sauce and cover. Place in 350 degree oven and cook until meat is tender. About 15 minutes before meat is done add 4 stalks celery, sliced in small diagonal pieces, 4 carrots, sliced in thin diagonal pieces, ½ pound fresh washed spinach, stems removed, and cook until all vegetables are tender-crisp and spinach wilts. Remove meat and vegetables to heated platter. Blend 1 tbsp. cornstarch (or more if you prefer a thicker gravy) with 2 tbsp. cold water and stir into gravy and cook until gravy thickens. Pour some over meat and pass rest. Serve with rice. Serves 8.

### BAKED TOMATOES

Cut a lid from the required number of tomatoes and scoop out the pulp. Sprinkle the inside of the tomato with salt. Mix the tomato pulp with fresh or canned whole kernel corn and ½ green pepper, chopped fine. Season with grated onion, celery salt, and freshly-ground black pepper. Fill the tomato shells, sprinkle with buttered bread crumbs and bake in a moderate oven (350 d.) until tomato is cooked through but is not too soft—about 20 minutes.

### MARMALADE BREAD**

Sift together 3 cups flour, 3 tsp. baking powder, 1 tsp. salt and ¼ tsp. soda. Combine 1¼ cups orange marmalade, 1 beaten egg, ¾ cup orange juice, and ¼ cup salad oil. Add to flour mixture, stirring 'til moistened. Add 1 cup chopped walnuts . Turn into loaf pan and bake 1 hour at 350 d. When done, spread top with ¼ cup marmalade and return to oven for 1 minute or until glazed. Cool on rack.

**This bread can also be baked in three small-sized loaf pans reducing baking time to 35 minutes. Wonderful for breakfast too. Our favorite way of using leftovers of any nut bread, is to slice the bread, and toast it on a buttered waffle iron, until crisp. Serve it this way with fruit salad.

Have a very nice day!

## KITCHEN KAPERS

SEBASTOPOL TIMES 3
THURSDAY MARCH 19, 1964

Kitchen-Tested Recipes from the Kitchen of
**JO REID**

California sunshine! We've had more than our share this winter, but the weather experts do promise many rainy days ahead, just to keep California green!

Rainy days are fun days—the children arrive home from school bustling with unused energy and clammering for mugs of hot cocoa and marshmallows and Dad arrives from work hoping for renewed energy and thinking that a rainy day calls for a big kettle of beans and cornbread. And he's right!

### CHILI CON CARNE

1½ cups dry red or kidney beans
1 large onion, sliced
1 green pepper, chopped
1 pound ground beef
1 1-lb can (2 cups) tomatoes
1 8-oz. can tomato sauce
2 cups tomato juice
1½ tbsp. chili powder
1½ tsp. salt
1 bay leaf
Dash each paprika and cayenne

Rinse beans; then add to 1½ quarts cold water and let stand overnight. Add 1 tsp. salt to beans and the soaking water; cover and simmer 'til tender, about 1 hour. Drain reserving the bean liquid. Now brown onion, green pepper and meat in a small amount fat. Add beans and remaining ingredients. Cover and simmer 1½ hours, adding reserved bean liquid or water if needed. Test bean for doneness. Make cornmeal dumplings, drop batter by rounded tablespoon into the hot, bubbling chili. Cover tightly and steam (do not peek) for 10 minutes. Serves 6. Corn Meal Dumplings: Add 2 tbsp. minced parsley to a package of corn-bread mix and prepare batter according to box directions. Proceed as above.

How long has it been since you've made Lamb Stew? This is our favorite.

### FRENCH LAMB STEW

4 lbs. lean lamb stew
15 small carrots, quartered
5 large potatoes, quartered
½ cup chopped celery
1 large, yellow onion, chopped
1 clove garlic, minced
1 bay leaf
1 clove
Salt and pepper to taste
1 tbsp. butter
1 tbsp. flour
1 lb. fresh mushrooms, sliced
1 tbsp. chopped parsley
1 tsp. lemon juice
⅛ tsp. powdered thyme

Place meat, carrots, potatoes, celery, and onion in heavy pan and add water to cover. (No browning with this stew!) Add seasonings. Bring to a boil and reduce heat and allow to simmer for 45 minutes. Remove meat, carrots, and potatoes from the mixture and reserve in a warm container. Strain broth through cheesecloth into a second pan and bring it again to a boil. Now cream together the butter and flour. Add to mixture and boil 5 minutes over high heat to thicken. Reduce the heat and replace the meat and vegetables. Add the sliced mushrooms, parsley and lemon juice and simmer for another 15 minutes or until meat is tender. Yields 6 to 8 hearty portions.

### STUFFED FLANK STEAK

1 2-lb. flank steak
Salt and pepper
2 medium apples, peeled and sliced
¼ cup finely-chopped onion
8 prunes, pitted
2 tbsp. oil
2 cups water
1 envelope hearty beef soup mix
¼ cup light cream

Trim membrane from steak. Score both sides of steak and sprinkle with salt and pepper. Pound thin. Sprinkle top with onion and arrange apple and prunes down center. Roll up and tie securely. Heat oil in Dutch oven and add steak and cook over low heat until lightly browned on all sides. Add 1 cup water. Bring to boil; reduce heat and simmer until meat is tender, about 1 hour. Blend soup mix with remaining water. Stir into liquid in pan. Simmer 5 minutes, stirring constantly. Add cream; heat. Makes 4 to 6 servings.

Have a happy day!

SEBASTOPOL TIMES
THURSDAY APRIL 2, 1964

## KAPERS

**Kitchen-Tested Recipes from the Kitchen of**
**JO REID**

Really, a hamburger steak can be just as scrumptious as a "name" steak! All it needs is a little dressing up both in preparation and in title and you serve hamburger with fanfare and without apology. And for burger know-how, remember:

- Look for bright red color with some fat for flavor.
- Medium or coarsely-ground meat gives light textured burgers.
- Handle the meat lightly, the more gently you treat the patties, the more tender your burgers.

### THE "STEAK" CAPER

2 lbs. ground chuck
½ cup evaporated milk
1 slightly beaten egg
1 tsp. salt
¼ tsp. pepper
¼ tsp. monosodium glutamate
3 tbsp. butter
Small jar capers

Mix meat, evaporated milk, egg, and seasonings. Shape into 5 oval patties. Broil 5 inches from heat 12 minutes, turn, and broil about 8 minutes more or 'til done to your liking. Remove to warm dish. Now melt the butter, drain the capers and add to the butter. Heat and pour over meat.

### COUNTRY CLUB BURGERS

2 lbs. ground beef
1 3-oz. pkg. cream cheese
1 tbsp. crumbled blue cheese
1 tbsp. finely chopped onion
1 tsp. prepared horseradish
1 tsp. prepared mustard
12 slices bacon, precooked slightly
Salt and pepper
6 large mushrooms, scored and stems removed

Divide ground beef in 12 mounds. Flatten each to ½ inch thick. Cream cheeses together; stir in onion, horseradish, and mustard. Top half the patties with filling, leaving ½-inch margin for sealing. Cover filling with remaining patties, sealing edges well. Wrap edges of each burger with bacon, using 2 slices and securing ends with toothpicks. Broil 5 inches from heat about 6 minutes, sprinkle with salt and pepper, turn and broil 5 minutes more. Season the second side. While burgers cook, lightly brown mushroom caps in small amount of butter. Top each burger with a mushroom. Makes 6 servings.

### GALA MEAT LOAF

1½ lbs. ground beef
⅔ cup diced, process sharp cheese
1 cup cracker crumbs
2 beaten eggs
1 8-oz. can tomato sauce
½ cup finely chopped onion
2 tbsp. chopped green pepper
1½ tsp. salt
1 medium bay leaf, crushed
Dash thyme and marjoram
Chili sauce

Combine all ingredients except chili sauce; mix well. Shape mixture in a loaf in shallow baking dish. Score the loaf by pressing top with handle of wooden spoon. Fill the score marks with chili sauce. Bake in moderate oven (350 degrees) 1 hour. Serves 6 generously.

Good Day!

# JO REID'S MENU OF THE WEEK
## September 28, 1965

SO-SIMPLE SUKIYAKI
Fried Rice and Shrimp
Soy Sauce
Mustard
Mandarin Oranges
Sake

## SO-SIMPLE SUKIYAKI

1½ pounds sirloin tip
1 bunch fresh spinach
½ pound fresh mushrooms
1 large onion
1 bunch green onions
1 stalk celery

2 carrots
1 can bamboo shoots
Soy Sauce
Salt and pepper
Undiluted canned consomme
Cooking Oil

Slice meat paper thin into bite-sized strips. (Try freezing meat and then slice with a very sharp knife). Remove center stems from large spinach leaves. Slice some mushrooms and leave some whole. Slice onion thinly. Slice green onions lengthwise and then cut into 2 or 3-inch lengths. Slice celery diagonally. Pare carrots and cut into thin lengthwise strips. Drain bamboo shoots. Arrange artistically in large shallow bowl or on tray, keep each food separate. COOKING: Do not try to cook all meat and vegetables at one time. Cook about one-third or a quarter at a time giving everyone some of the first cooking. Put a couple tablespoons oil in an electric skillet pre-heated to 260 degrees. Add some of the meat and cook until brown. Then add some of the vegetables, adding soy sauce, salt and pepper and a little consomme. Cover and cook about 5 to 8 minutes until vegetables are crisp tender. Repeat. Makes enough for four. So simple!

## JO REID'S MENU OF THE WEEK
### September 21, 1965

Tomato Wedges

### CHEESE 'N CRACKERS MEAT LOAF

Fluffy Mashed Potatoes
Herb-Buttered Zucchini

Baked Apples

### CHEESE 'N CRACKERS MEAT LOAF

2 pounds Jolly ground chuck
24 Ritz-type crackers
2 eggs
1 pkg. dehydrated onions

1 can cheddar cheese soup, undiluted
¼ tsp. pepper

Roll crackers into coarse crumbs. Add to chuck ground along with remaining ingredients blending together with wooden spoon. Pack in foil-lined loaf pan and bake in 350° 45 to 60 minutes. Allow meat loaf to rest 10 minutes before removing from pan. Garnish with stripes of chili sauce and springs of parsley. Serves 6 generously.

### JOLLY BACK-TO-SCHOOL DAYS REMINDERS

For the
**Lunch-Packing Set**
... Sliced Cheese 'N Crackers
Meat Loaf Sandwiches
... Carrot Sticks
... Delicious Apples
... Oatmeal Cookies
... Milk

For the
**Snack-Packing Set**
... Small Boxes Raisins
... Small Packages
Potato Chips
... Pears, Apples, Bananas
... Small Baggies
... Colored Bags!

# Grandma Reid's Icebox Cookies

*Brought over on the boat from bonnie Scotland! We could always count on the cookie jar being filled with these crisp treats.*

**1 stick butter**

**1 cup sugar**

**2 cups all-purpose flour**

**½ teaspoon baking soda**

**1 teaspoon vanilla**

**1 egg**

**1 cup walnuts, chopped**

Cream butter and sugar until fluffy. Add remaining ingredients. Form into two rolls, wrap in plastic wrap and refrigerate overnight.

When ready to bake, preheat oven to 375 degrees. Slice and bake 10 to 15 minutes until light golden.

# Biscotti

*Every cookbook should contain a recipe for biscotti and every pantry should have a cookie jar filled with these Italian staples. Yummy eaten straight from the jar, dipped in coffee and over-the-top dipped in red wine!*

3 ¼ cups all-purpose flour

1 tablespoon baking powder

½ teaspoon salt

1 ½ cups sugar

1 ¼ sticks unsalted butter, melted

3 eggs

1 tablespoon vanilla or anise extract

2 tablespoons aniseed, ground

2 cups almonds, toasted and chopped

1 large egg white

Preheat oven to 350 degrees.

Sift flour, baking powder and salt. In a large bowl, mix sugar with melted butter, eggs, vanilla or anise extract and ground aniseed. Add flour mixture and stir well. Add almonds.

Divide dough in half. Shape each half into a 13 ½ x 2 ½-inch log. Transfer to parchment lined baking sheet. Whisk egg white and brush over each log.

Bake until golden brown—25 to 30 minutes depending on oven. Remove and cool logs completely on the sheet placed on a rack—a full 25 minutes. Maintain oven temperature during cooling. Transfer logs to work surface and discard parchment.

Using a serrated knife, cut logs diagonally into ½-inch slices. Arrange biscotti, cut side down, on baking sheet. Bake 8 to 10 minutes. Turn slices over and bake an additional 6 to 8 minutes. The timing here is a little tricky since each oven if different. The biscotti should be light golden on both sides.

Transfer to rack to cool.

*For a colorful change of pace, use a blend of pistachios and dried cherries in place of the almonds*

## New this week

# Kitchen Column Aids Busy Cooks

**KOZY KITCHEN**
Kitchen Tested Recipes
From the Kitchen of
Mrs. Jo Reid

Christmas! A most wonderful holiday and so often because of the pressures of shopping for Christmas gifts, we find ourselves tired by Christmas week, and just not up to doing any baking. Now is the time. Plan on devoting an hour, twice a week, in your own Kozy Kitchen, and storing your baked delicacies to be brought out for your family and friends for Christmas week. This week's recipes are ones which have been requested of me year after year by any and all who have tasted them. They are not fancy, but just plain good.

I have collected many recipes for scotch shortbread, but none has ever compared with this one which was given me many years ago by a member of the family. It is quick to prepare, makes a good-sized quantity, and is excellent for gift giving.

SCOTCH SHORTBREAD
Bake at 300 degrees for one hour. Makes at least 4 dozen cookies.
1 pound butter (no substitutes)
1 cup sugar
5½ cups all-purpose flour, sifted.
Mix butter with sugar until well-blended. Add the flour, a little at a time, kneading thoroughly, until the flour is used forming a large ball of dough. Place the dough on a large, ungreased cooky sheet, and roll out with a rolling pin to within an inch of the pan's edge. It will be about ½ inch thick. With the back of a fork, press a design along the entire outer rim of the dough. Prick across the entire surface with the fork. Bake at 300 degrees for one hour or until delicately brown. Remove from oven and cut into 1½-inch squares while still warm. Cool thoroughly before storing in tightly covered containers.

The following recipe for a simple and light fruitcake is wonderful all year long. The glaced' fruit may be omitted and the raisins increased accordingly. Nuts or currents may be substituted.

ENGLISH FRUITCAKE
Bake 325 degrees for 1 hour and 20 minutes.
Makes 2 regular sized loaf cakes or 3 small-sized loaf cakes.
2½ cups all-purpose flour, sifted.
1 tsp. baking powder
1¼ cups granulated sugar
2 cubes butter or margarine.
2 eggs
2/3 cups milk
2/3 cup white raisins
2/3 cups glaced' fruit

Sift flour with baking powder. Combine the raisin and glaced' fruit with the flour mixture. Set aside. Beat butter and sugar until light and fluffy. Add eggs, one at a time, beating thoroughly after each addition. Add flour mixture a little at a time to the butter mixture, beating thoroughly. Then beat in milk. Pour into greased and floured pans and bake at 325 degrees for one hour and 20 minutes. Cool on rack when done.
Now hide everything until Christmas week.
See you next week! We'll talk about a Persimmon Pudding.

# Chocolate Sea Salt Cookies

MAKES 41/2 DOZEN

*The chocolate cookies that Ritz-Carlton Chef Rob Wilson made delivered two surprises: tiny nuggets of chopped dark chocolate and little bursts of fleur de sel, a coarse French salt extracted by hand from sea water. The salt, although unexpected, seemed to heighten the chocolate flavor. Using cake flour makes the cookies especially tender. Serve with Crème Fraiche Sorbet or, in a pinch, vanilla ice cream would complement them as well.*

1 ¾ cups sifted cake flour

2 tablespoons sifted unsweetened cocoa powder (not Dutch process)

1 ¼ teaspoons fleur de sel

½ teaspoon baking soda

10 tablespoons unsalted butter, softened

½ cup raw sugar

3 tablespoons granulated sugar

1 ½ teaspoons vanilla extract

1 ½ cups finely chopped dark chocolate (about 2.5 ounces)

In a bowl, combine cake flour, cocoa, fleur de sel and baking soda. Whisk to blend.

In an electric stand mixer or with a hand-held mixer, cream butter, raw sugar and granulated sugar on medium speed just until smooth.

Do not overbeat—the mixture need not be fluffy. Beat in vanilla, then reduce mixer to low speed and add dry ingredients. Mix on low until dough comes together. It will be crumbly at first—then mix in the chopped chocolate. Divide dough in half, shape into a log and roll up in a sheet of parchment or wax paper into a 1 ½-inch cylinder. Chill for 30 minutes until firm but not too hard.

Preheat oven to 375 degrees.

Cut dough into ½-inch slices and transfer to baking sheets lined with parchment or a silicone baking mat.

Bake cookies until they look dry on top and are dry to the touch—about 15 minutes. Let cookies cool completely on the baking sheet and then transfer them to an airtight container.

# COOKIES

SEBASTOPOL TIMES SEPT. 17, 1964 THURSDAY

## KITCHEN KAPERS

**Kitchen-Tested Recipes from the Kitchen of**
**JO REID**

They're back to school! We breathe a sigh of relief in one way; but those relaxed mornings and jaunts to the swimming hole were kind of fun, weren't they! Until they are in the 5th or 6th grade, the most important decision to be made before going back to school is which lunchbox to choose and even if you try to convince them that last year's is still as good as new, it doesn't work! A nutritious lunch consists of a raw carrot or celery stick, fresh fruit, a high-protein sandwich on whole grain bread, a few nuts or vitamin-packed cookies. They won't brush their teeth after lunch at school, therefore, the fewer sweets the better. These are our best vitamin-packed cookies.

### SPICY OATMEAL COOKIES

½ cup shortening
1 tsp. salt
1 tsp. cinnamon
1 tsp. vanilla
1 tbsp. molasses
1 cup sugar
2 tbs. wheat germ

1 egg, unbeaten
1½ cups flour
¾ tsp. baking soda
1 cup rolled oats
⅓ cup chopped dates
⅓ cup chopped walnuts
⅓ cup raisins

Cream shortening with sugar and blend in remaining ingredients. Mix well. Drop level tablespoon of dough on greased cookie sheet. Bake in 350 degree oven 10 to 15 minutes. Makes 3 dozen of the best cookies you have ever tasted! Really!

### CORN FLAKE MACAROONS

2 egg whites
1 cup brown sugar
2 tbsp. melted butter
1 tbsp. vanilla

1 cup cocoanut
½ cup chopped nut meats
⅓ tsp. salt
4 cups corn flakes

Beat egg whites until stiff and dry, add sugar. Add remaining ingredients and mix thoroughly. Drop by teaspoonfuls onto a greased cookie sheet and bake in 350 degree oven 8 to 10 minutes. Watch closely.

### HONEY CAKES

½ cup butter
⅓ cup sugar
1 egg
1 cup honey
2 tbsp. lemon juice

3½ cups flour
2 tsp. baking powder
¼ tsp. salt
⅔ cup chopped almonds

Cream butter with sugar. Add 1 egg and beat until fluffy. Warm the honey and add to butter mixture along with lemon juice and flour, salt. Stir in almonds and mix well. Chill the dough for 2 hours. Now roll out ¼ inch thick and cut into strips or squares. Bake the cookies on a butter cooky sheet in 350 degree oven 10 to 12 minutes. May be glazed with confectioners sugar-water icing.

### OATMEAL SHORTBREAD

1½ cups flour
2/3 cup rolled oats
1 cup butter

2/3 cups brown sugar (have you tried the new Brownulated?)

Combine all the ingredients and knead with your fingers until well-blended. Press evenly in a lightly buttered cooky sheet (about 10x15). Poke surface with fork for design. Bake in 300 degree oven about 45 minutes. Cut into squares while warm, then cool in pan.

Have a nice day!

# Oatmeal Cookies

MAKES 72

*How could anything this good be good for you?*

3 eggs, beaten

1 cup raisins

1 teaspoon vanilla

2 sticks butter

1 cup brown sugar

1 cup granulated sugar

2 ½ cups all-purpose flour

1 teaspoon salt

1 teaspoon cinnamon

2 teaspoons baking soda

2 cups oatmeal

¾ cup chopped walnuts

Combine eggs, raisins and vanilla in a small bowl. Cover and let sit one hour.

Preheat oven to 350 degrees.

Cream butter and sugars. Combine flour, salt, cinnamon and soda. Add to sugar mixture then mix in egg/raisin mixture, oatmeal and chopped walnuts.

Roll into small balls and flatten slightly on cookie sheet. Bake for 10 to 12 minutes or until lightly browned.

*No need to bake all the cookies at one time. Refrigerate some of the dough to be baked when needed—or wanted!*

# Oatmeal Carmelites

MAKES 48 BARS

*Judi's sinfully healthy bars!*

2 ¼ cups all-purpose flour, divided

2 cups oatmeal

1 ½ cups brown sugar

1 teaspoon baking soda

1 teaspoon salt

2 sticks butter, melted

1 (12-ounce) package chocolate chips

1 cup chopped pecans

1 (10-ounce) jar caramel ice cream topping

Preheat oven to 350 degrees.

Combine 2 cups flour, oatmeal, brown sugar, soda, salt and butter together. Pat half of mixture into the bottom of a 9x13-inch baking pan. Bake 10 minutes and remove from oven.

Sprinkle with nuts and chocolate chips. Stir remaining ¼ cup flour into ice cream topping and spread over the hot crust. Add remaining half of mixture for top crust.

Bake 15 minutes until golden brown. Chill 1 hour before cutting into bars.

# Patti's Sweet Pretzels

*The only description: Sinful—Addictive—Wonderful*

**1 (12-ounce) package Guittard white chocolate chips**

**2 cups broken pretzel pieces**

Carefully melt chocolate chips. Combine with pretzel pieces until they are coated with chocolate. Spread on a cookie sheet and cool. Break into pieces to serve.

*Chocolate may be melted in the top of a double boiler. Just be careful to not let any water hit the chocolate as that could cause it to seize and be unusable. You can also put the chips in a glass measuring cup and microwave them. Microwave for 30 seconds and stir. Repeat as necessary to get chocolate to the right consistency.*

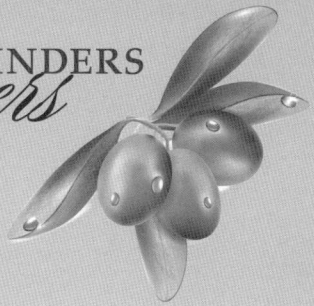

# Raspberry and Almond Tart

*One of the priciest, most delicious offerings in fancy bakeries. Now we throw it together in minutes!*

**2 cups sliced almonds, divided**

**⅔ cup sugar**

**1 ¼ sticks unsalted cold butter**

**1 ¼ cups all-purpose flour**

**¼ teaspoon salt**

**2 eggs**

**1 cup seedless raspberry jam**

Preheat oven to 400 degrees. Line a 9-inch tart pan with parchment paper and set aside.

In a food processor, grind 1 ¾ cups almonds with sugar. Cut butter into small pieces and add to processor along with flour and salt. Process until mixture is crumbly.

Remove 1 cup of mixture and add to reserved ¼ cup almonds. Set aside.

To the remaining flour mixture, add egg and pulse until mixture binds. Press mixture into prepared tart pan with the palm of your hands making it level and smooth. Bake 15 minutes.

Spread jam over baked crust and sprinkle with reserved almond mixture. Bake 15 minutes; cool in pan.

*Small slices and a dollop of whipped cream make this the perfect dessert.*

# Marilyn's Walnut Tart

SERVES 10-12

*Just a sliver and you will be transported to Dessert Heaven!*

## TART SHELL

⅓ cup butter

¼ cup sugar

1 large egg yolk

1 cup all-purpose flour

## FILLING

2 cups coarsely chopped walnuts

⅔ cup light brown sugar, packed

¼ cup butter

¼ cup dark corn syrup

2 tablespoons heavy cream

Preheat oven to 350 degrees.

For the shell, in a medium bowl, beat butter with sugar until light and fluffy. Add egg yolk and beat well. Gradually beat in flour just until blended (mixture will be crumbly). Press dough evenly over bottom and up the side of a 9-inch fluted tart pan with removable bottom. Bake in center of oven 12 minutes or until lightly browned.

Cool on rack.

Spread walnuts on a cookie sheet in a single layer. Toast in oven at 375 degrees for 5 minutes. Cool. Spread walnuts into bottom of baked tart shell.

To finish filling, in a heavy 2-quart saucepan, stir sugar with butter, corn syrup and heavy cream. Stirring constantly, bring mixture to boiling over medium heat. Boil one minute.

Pour mixture over walnuts and bake in center of oven for 10 minutes or just until mixture is bubbly. Remove tart to a wire rack to cool. Serve with a dollop of slightly sweetened whipped cream.

# Peaches and Almond Tart

*The kind of dessert you sigh over when peering into the bakery window in Paris.*

1 purchased pie crust

2 tablespoons all-purpose flour, divided

¾ cup slivered almonds

⅓ cup sugar

1 teaspoon almond extract

2 tablespoons butter

1 egg

5 peaches

½ cup peach preserves

Preheat oven to 400 degrees. Rub 1 tablespoon flour over crust and then place crust, floured side down, in a 9-inch tart pan. Trim edges and pierce all over with a fork. Bake 10 minutes. Cool.

In a food processor, grind almonds; add remaining 1 tablespoon flour, sugar, extract, butter and egg. Process until well blended. Pour into baked crust and bake 15 minutes longer. Cool on rack.

Blanch peaches 30 seconds and immediately transfer to a bowl of cold water. Peel and cut into slices; drain well.

Warm preserves until slightly thickened. Brush half of preserves over tart filling. Arrange peaches on top, overlapping slices. Brush with remaining preserves. Do not refrigerate—this is best served at room temperature.

*Almond liqueur may be substituted for the almond extract.*

# Heavenly Lemon Pie

*It is universally agreed that this is one of the best of the best! This was featured at the long-gone Bullock's Department Store Café.*

## MERINGUE CRUST

4 egg whites

1 cup sugar

1 teaspoon lemon juice

Nonstick cooking spray

Preheat oven to 200 degrees. Coat a 9-inch pie pan with cooking spray and set aside.

Beat egg whites until soft peaks form—3 to 4 minutes. Gradually add sugar, beating until stiff but not dry. Blend in juice. Spoon meringue into prepared pan and using a tablespoon, push mixture up around edges to form pie shell. Bake for 2 hours. Cool.

## FILLING

4 egg yolks

½ cup sugar

Grated zest and juice of 1 large lemon

2 cups whipping cream, whipped, divided

1 tablespoon confectioner's sugar

Beat egg yolks with sugar, lemon zest and juice until light in color and slightly thickened. Cook, stirring, in top of double boiler set over, but not touching, simmering water until thickened, about 10 minutes.

Remove from heat and cool thoroughly. Fold in half of whipped cream. Turn into Meringue Crust and refrigerate at least 2 hours to set. Fold confectioner's sugar into remaining whipped cream and spread over chilled pie.

# Apple Pie with Crumb Topping

*Apple pie aficionados profess this to be the best of apple pies. Join the crowd!*

## APPLE PIE

1 purchased pie crust

3 pounds assorted types apples, peeled, cored, sliced ¼-inch thick

⅔ cup sugar

2 tablespoons all-purpose flour

1 teaspoon cinnamon

¼ teaspoon nutmeg

¼ teaspoon allspice

2 tablespoons butter, melted

## TOPPING

1 cup all-purpose flour

½ cup sugar

¼ cup light brown sugar

1 teaspoon cinnamon

½ teaspoon salt

⅔ stick chilled unsalted butter cut into small cubes

Preheat oven to 400 degrees. Place pie crust into a deep-dish pie pan and crimp edge decoratively.

Combine all Apple Pie ingredients and place in crust, mounding in center. Sprinkle Topping over all. Place pie on foil-covered baking sheet to catch drippings. Bake 40 minutes. (Cover top with foil if pie browns too quickly.) Reduce temperature to 350 degrees and continue baking until apples are tender—about 45 minutes longer. Cooking time varies according to oven.

Blend flour, sugar, brown sugar, cinnamon and salt in food processor. Add butter cubes, pulsing until mixture is crumbly.

*All apple pies are tastier when using a variety of apples—Gala, Fuji, Braeburn and Granny Smith. This also makes for a "taller" pie as some of the apples cook down more than others.*

# Italian Pumpkin Pie

*Leave it to the Italians to gild the lily!*

1 refrigerated pie crust

1 cup solid pack pumpkin (not pie mix)

1 cup brown sugar

2 eggs

1 teaspoon lemon juice

1 teaspoon cinnamon

1 teaspoon ginger

½ teaspoon nutmeg

1 teaspoon vanilla

¼ teaspoon salt

8 ounces mascarpone cheese

### MASCARPONE TOPPING

¼ cup mascarpone cheese

1 cup whipping cream

2 tablespoons sugar

1 teaspoon vanilla

Preheat oven to 350 degrees.

Beat pumpkin and sugar until well blended. Add eggs, lemon juice, spices, vanilla and salt and blend well. Add mascarpone cheese and mix until filling is smooth. Pour into pie crust and bake until filling is set—about 50 minutes. Cool. Serve with dollops of Mascarpone Topping.

Combine all ingredients and beat until soft peaks form.

# Peanut Butter Pie *(Highland Ranch, 1973)*

*The horseback riding was great but, oh, that Peanut Butter Pie!*

1 (8-ounce) package cream cheese, softened

¾ cup peanut butter (creamy or crunchy according to taste)

1 ½ cups confectioner's sugar

1 large container non-dairy whipped topping

1 graham cracker crust

In a large mixing bowl, beat cream cheese, peanut butter and confectioner's sugar. Fold in topping and pour into prepared crust.

# Fran's Lemon Bundt Cake

*Very easy. Very moist. Very delicious.*

## CAKE

1 package lemon cake mix

1 (3.4-ounce) package instant vanilla pudding mix

¾ cup canola oil

4 eggs

1 cup lemon-lime soda

Preheat oven to 325 degrees. Grease and flour Bundt pan and set aside.

In a large bowl, combine cake mix and pudding mix. Stir in oil. Beat in eggs, one at a time. Stir in soda and pour mixture into prepared pan. Bake 35 to 40 minutes. Immediately drizzle Glaze over hot cake. Cool on a wire rack.

## GLAZE

1 teaspoon lemon zest

2 tablespoons lemon juice

1 cup confectioner's sugar

Combine all ingredients until smooth.

Pour over hot cake.

## KITCHEN KAPERS

**Kitchen-Tested Recipes from the Kitchen of**
**JO REID**

It's a sweet and simple statement of fact, desserts are here to stay! Amen.

Who can resist a sweetie, even if it's "just a sliver?" Dessert calories count, but who cares? The true devotee will forego anything in the food line including potatoes, butter, bread, but never dessert.

You can have leftovers for dinner but if the dessert is special, you are more than redeemed. Dessert is soul-satisfying and energy giving -- this is a sweet and simple statement of fact.

There are favorite cake recipes that are easy to prepare because they are not "made from scratch" but no one, not even your best friend, would guess! Clip these for your permanent file.

### CHOCOLATE CRUNCH CAKE

2/3 cup chopped walnuts
½ cup melted butter
½ cup granulated sugar
2/3 cup bread crunch
1 package devil food mix
1 cup cream, whipped and sweetened

Chop nuts, and combine with melted butter, sugar, crumbs. Mix well with fork. Divide between 2 ungreased cake pans. Press firmly.

Prepare cake as directed on label. Bake. Cool in pans 10 to 15 minutes. Then cool on racks. Place the first layer crunch side down. Spread with one-half of the whipped cream. Place the second layer over this, crunch side up. Top with dollops of whipped cream placed in a spaced circle around the edge of cake with one dollop in the middle.

### PEACHY UPSIDE DOWN CAKE

¼ cup butter or margarine, melted
1 No. 2½ can sliced cling peaches, well-drained
½ cup brown sugar, firmly packed
1 package yellow cake mix
1 cup whipping cream
2 tablespoons confectioners sugar
½ teaspoon almond extract

Spread butter or margarine evenly over bottom of 2 nine-inch cake pans. Arrange peaches in a single, patterned layer on top of butter. Sprinkle with brown sugar. Mix cake according to directions. Pour batter over peaches, dividing evenly.

Bake in moderate oven 25 minutes, or until center of cake springs back lightly. Cool on wire cake rack 10 minutes loosen around edges with knife, invert onto cake racks; cool, slightly. Whip cream adding sugar and almond extract. Put warm layers together, fruit side up. Pass the whipped cream.

Have a perfect day. We'll encounter a Chic Chick next week!

# Almond Cake Treasure

*Claudia shares her copy of the famous Narsai's Almond Cake with us. It is truly a treasure.*

## CAKE

7 ounces almond paste

¾ cup sugar

1 stick butter

3 eggs

1 tablespoon orange liqueur

¼ cup all-purpose flour

½ teaspoon baking powder

Confectioner's sugar for dusting

Preheat oven to 350 degrees.

In a food processor, combine almond paste, sugar and butter. Process until smooth. Add eggs and liqueur and process again until very smooth. Add flour and baking powder and mix until just blended.

Pour into a parchment-lined 8-inch square cake pan. Bake 40 to 50 minutes—until knife inserted in center comes out clean. Cool in pan and then turn out. Dust with confectioner's sugar and serve with Raspberry Amaretto Sauce.

## RASPBERRY AMARETTO SAUCE

2 cups fresh or frozen raspberries, thawed if frozen

¼ cup confectioner's sugar

1 tablespoon fresh lemon juice

¼ cup amaretto liqueur

Puree raspberries in a food processor or blender. Strain to remove seeds and return to blender. Add confectioner's sugar, lemon juice and liqueur. Continue to process until smooth.

# Mrs. Brown's Banana Cake

*This Mrs. Brown was the wife of California Governor Edmund G. "Pat" Brown and the mother of Governor Jerry Brown. She kept the men in her life happy with this delicious cake while they managed the state.*

## CAKE

2 eggs, separated

1 stick butter

1 ½ cups sugar

2 cups all-purpose flour

1 teaspoon baking soda

½ teaspoon salt

2 teaspoons baking powder

½ cup buttermilk

1 teaspoon vanilla

3 bananas, mashed

1 cup chopped nuts

Preheat oven to 350 degrees. Grease and lightly flour 3 cake pans and set aside.

Beat egg whites and set aside. In a separate small bowl, lightly beat egg yolks and reserve. Cream butter and sugar. Combine flour, baking soda, salt and baking powder; add to creamed butter mixture. Add buttermilk, beaten egg yolks and vanilla. Stir in mashed bananas and nuts. Fold in egg whites and pour mixture into prepared cake pans. Bake for 25 to 30 minutes. Cool layers on a rack before frosting.

## FROSTING

2 ½ cups confectioner's sugar

2 tablespoons softened butter

1 teaspoon vanilla

Half-and-half (as needed for smooth consistency)

Combine all ingredients and mix, adding half-and-half as needed until Frosting reaches spreading consistency. Spread between cooled cake layers and over the top and sides.

*What a delicious way to incorporate bananas that may be a little "too ripe" for other purposes!*

# Glazed Pear Cake

*This is the all-time crowd pleaser. Be prepared to hand out the recipe.*

## CAKE

2 sticks butter

1 cup granulated sugar

1 cup brown sugar

2 eggs

1 teaspoon vanilla

2 ½ cups all-purpose flour

2 teaspoons baking powder

1 teaspoon baking soda

½ teaspoon salt

2 teaspoons cinnamon

1 (16-ounce) can pears, drain and
   reserve syrup

1 cup raisins

1 cup chopped walnuts

Preheat oven to 350 degrees. Grease a 9x13-inch baking pan and set aside.

Cream butter and sugars. Blend in eggs and vanilla. Sift together dry ingredients and add to butter mixture alternately with ½ cup reserved pear syrup. Coarsely chop pears and add to the mixture along with raisins and walnuts. Pour into prepared pan and bake for 25 minutes or until the center tests clean. While cake is still warm, spread with Glaze.

## GLAZE

¼ cup brown sugar

1 tablespoon butter

2 tablespoons reserved pear syrup

½ cup confectioner's sugar

Bring brown sugar, butter and syrup to a boil. Stir in confectioner's sugar and spread over cake.

# KITCHEN KAPERS

Kitchen-Tested Recipes from the Kitchen of
**JO REID**

A sheer catastrophe! For the woman who loves to cook, it is an absolute tragedy to misplace a favorite recipe and nothing will do until it is found. This is what happened with this recipe and after making it once you, too, will prize it above all else. It's a truly elegant German cheesecake and deserves your finest China, your strongest coffee, your nicest friends!

## KASE KUCHEN

| | |
|---|---|
| 1 cup sifted flour | 1 cube butter |
| 3 tablespoons sugar | 1 egg yolk |
| ¼ teasp. salt | 1 tablespoon cream or milk |

Sift flour, sugar and salt together into a mixing bowl. With pastry blender, cut in butter until particles are fine. Beat egg yolk with cream or milk and add to crumbs. Press dough into bottom of springform pan. Bake 325 degrees for 30 minutes and cool on rack.

## CHEESECAKE LAYER

| | |
|---|---|
| 4 small packages (3 oz.) softened cream cheese | ¼ teaspoon salt |
| | 2 eggs |
| 1½ teasp. vanilla | ½ cup sugar |

Stir together cream cheese, vanilla, salt. Beat in eggs until thick and light. Add sugar, beating until mixture is lemon-colored. Spread evenly over cooled crust and bake 350 degrees for 20 minutes. Allow to cool.

## POPPY SEED LAYER

| | |
|---|---|
| 1 cup poppy seeds (whirled to a powder in blender) | ½ cup milk |
| | grated peel of 1 lemon |
| ¾ cup golden raisins | ½ teaspoon vanilla |
| ¾ cup sugar | |

Measure poppy seed powder and place in saucepan. Plump raisins by allowing them to stand in warm water few minutes; drain well and add to poppy seeds along with ¾ cup sugar, milk, and lemon peel. Cook over low heat, stirring until thickened, about 20 minutes. Stir in vanilla; allow to cool. Very gently spread evenly over top of cooled cheesecake.

## STREUSEL CRUMB TOPPING

| | |
|---|---|
| 6 tablespoons brown sugar | 3 tablespoons butter |
| 6 tablespoons flour | |

Blend into coarse crumbs with pastry blender. Sprinkle evenly over poppy seed layer. Bake 350 degrees for 12 minutes. Toppy should be golden brown (Slip under broiler a minute, watching carefully, if necessary).

Cool pastry thoroughly and chill. Cut into strips or wedges. This is a long recipe but worth every effort.

# Melinda's Almond & Lemon Cake

*An extra-light cake that is gluten free—the lemon glaze makes a tangy texture contrast. At times Melinda simply dusts the top with confectioner's sugar and adds fresh berries.*

**2 cups almond meal (from 1⅓ cups whole almonds)**

**4 tablespoons cornstarch**

**½ teaspoon baking powder**

**4 eggs**

**¾ cup sugar**

**Grated zest of 1 lemon**

## LEMON GLAZE

**1¼ cups confectioner's sugar**

**2-3 tablespoons lemon juice**

Preheat oven to 350 degrees. Butter the side of a 9-inch cake pan and line the bottom with a circle of parchment.

Combine almond meal, cornstarch and baking powder. Set aside. (If using whole almonds, grind in batches in an electric coffee grinder for a floury texture.)

Beat eggs lightly to combine; add sugar in small increments. Beat at medium high speed until mixture reaches the ribbon stage—about 7 minutes. (Important step.) Sprinkle lemon zest on top and fold in almond mixture, one third at a time. Transfer batter to prepared pan and smooth the top.

Bake cake until golden and sides pull slightly away from the pan—about 30 minutes. Cool 5 minutes in pan. Run a knife blade around the edge of the cake to loosen and turn on to a wire rack. Peel off paper and let cake cool upside down.

Place cake on a sheet of aluminum foil. Pour Lemon Glaze over the cake and smooth into a thin layer, letting excess drip over the sides. Let cake stand until the glaze has set—about 1 hour.

For Lemon Glaze, sift sugar into a bowl. Add lemon juice and beat until smooth.

*Need a little help with the "ribbon stage" referred to in this recipe? It is a cooking term describing the texture of egg and sugar that has been beaten until it is pale and thick. When the beaters are lifted, the batter falls slowly back on the surface of the mixture, forming a ribbon like pattern that soon sinks back into the batter.*

# Lemon Bites

MAKES 5 DOZEN

*The perfect bite—big flavor and just enough to satisfy that sweet tooth. This is Paula's recipe with just a little bit of tweaking.*

## BITES

1 package yellow cake mix

1 (3.4-ounce) package instant lemon pudding mix

⅓ cup lemon juice

Zest of 1 lemon

4 eggs

¾ cup vegetable oil

Preheat oven to 350 degrees.

Spray non-stick miniature muffin tins with vegetable cooking spray. Be very generous with spray.

Combine cake mix, pudding mix, lemon juice, lemon zest, eggs and oil. Blend 2 minutes; the batter will be sticky. Fill each muffin cup only half way—a scant teaspoonful. Do not overfill to make sure cakes will not bake over the rim. Bake 12 minutes and remove from oven. Allow to sit a minute or so before carefully removing them from the pan.

## GLAZE

1 box confectioner's sugar

½ cup lemon juice

Zest of 1 lemon

3 tablespoons vegetable oil

3 tablespoons water

To make the Glaze, combine all ingredients and mix with spoon until smooth.

While the cakes are still warm, dip each into the glaze covering as much as possible or simply glaze tops only. Place on racks with waxed paper underneath to catch and drips.

Allow to cool for 1 hour.

*I find flavor improves if these are made a day ahead of serving.*

# Mocha Chocolate Icebox Cake

SERVES 10

*The lap of chocolate luxury!*

## CRUST

15 cream-filled chocolate sandwich cookies

4 tablespoons butter, melted

Coarsely break cookies; add cookies and melted butter in food processor and process until very fine crumb mixture is formed. Press crumbs into the bottom of a 10-inch springform pan.

## TOPPING

1 (10-ounce) container whipped cream cheese

½ cup brown sugar

1 tablespoon instant coffee granules

1 (12-ounce) package chocolate chips

½ cup milk

3 eggs, separated

1 envelope unflavored gelatin, softened in ¼ cup warm water

1 teaspoon vanilla

1 cup heavy cream

Process cream cheese, brown sugar and coffee granules until well combined. In a double boiler, melt chocolate chips with milk. Whip egg yolks and mix with softened gelatin. Add vanilla and combine all mixtures in a large bowl. Set aside.

In a small bowl, whip egg whites until soft peaks form and set aside. In an additional bowl, whip cream.

Gently fold egg whites into chocolate mixture. Fold in whipped cream and spoon mixture into prepared springform pan. Cover tightly and freeze.

Remove cake from freezer 15 minutes before serving. To make cutting easier, dip the knife into a cup of warm water before slicing.

# Olive Oil Cake

*Not only does every lady need a perfect little black dress in her wardrobe, she needs the perfect little cake recipe in her recipe file—thanks to Marilyn, here it is!*

5 large egg yolks

4 large egg whites

¾ cup sugar, plus 1½ tablespoons, divided

½ teaspoon salt

3 cups olive oil

1 ½ tablespoons lemon juice

1 ½ teaspoons lemon zest

1 cup cake flour

Place oven rack in center of oven and preheat to 350 degrees. Grease springform pan with oil, then line bottom with parchment paper and oil that as well.

Beat egg yolks with ½ cup sugar until thick and pale—about 3 minutes. Add olive oil and lemon juice, beating until just combined (mixture may look separated). Add lemon zest to flour and stir flour into egg mixture until just combined. Do NOT beat.

Beat egg whites with salt until foamy, then add ¼ cup sugar, a little at a time, beating until egg whites form soft peaks—about 3 minutes.

Gently fold one third of egg whites into yolk mixture to lighten; fold in remaining egg white gently, but thoroughly.

Pour batter into prepared pan and rap gently against work surface once or twice to release any air bubbles. Sprinkle top evenly with remaining 1½ tablespoons of sugar.

Bake until puffed and golden—about 35 to 45 minutes or when wooden pick inserted in center comes out clean. Cool cake in pan on a rack for 10 minutes. Run a knife around edge of pan and remove side of pan. Cool to room temperature—about 1¼ hours. Remove bottom of pan and parchment. Transfer cake to serving plate.

# Petite Fudge Cake

*Jennie shares the perfect little dessert recipe—a glamorous goodie!*

**5 ounces semi-sweet chocolate**

**2 sticks butter**

**1 cup chopped pecans**

**1¾ cups sugar**

**1 cup all-purpose flour**

**4 eggs, unbeaten**

**1 teaspoon vanilla**

**Confectioner's sugar**

Preheat oven to 325 degrees.

Melt chocolate and butter in microwave until just melted. Watch carefully, stirring every 30 seconds. Add pecans and stir until well coated. In another bowl, combine sugar, flour and eggs. Add chocolate mixture and stir until just mixed. Add vanilla.

Pour batter into greased or paper-lined petit four-sized or regular cupcake tins. Bake 12 to 15 minutes for small cakes, 30 minutes for larger ones. Be careful to not over bake. They should be "gooey". Cool and dust with confectioner's sugar before serving.

*For a dramatic presentation, use gold or silver cupcake liners and add a dot of whipped cream to each cake. Beautiful!*

# Prune Cake with Buttermilk Topping

*Joann's recipe for this old-fashioned dessert is the ultimate!*

## CAKE

2 cups all-purpose flour

1 teaspoon baking soda

1 teaspoon salt

1 teaspoon cinnamon

1 teaspoon nutmeg

¼ teaspoon allspice

2 cups sugar

1 cup vegetable oil

1 cup buttermilk

1 teaspoon vanilla

3 eggs

2 cups prunes, quartered

1 cup chopped walnuts

Preheat oven to 350 degrees. Grease a 9x13-inch baking pan and set aside.

Combine flour, baking soda, salt, cinnamon, nutmeg and allspice. In a separate bowl, combine sugar, vegetable oil, buttermilk and vanilla. Beat in eggs, one at a time; add dry ingredients and mix well. Fold in prunes and walnuts.

Pour cake batter into prepared baking pan and bake 35 to 45 minutes. Cool slightly and pierce all over with a wooden skewer. Pour Topping over warm cake.

## TOPPING

⅓ cup sugar

⅓ cup buttermilk

1 tablespoon butter

¼ teaspoon baking soda

Juice of ½ lemon

Combine all ingredients in a saucepan and bring to a boil. Reduce heat and simmer 3 minutes.

# Prune Cake

*This is sweet Auntie Annie's recipe—a family treasure.*

1 cup sugar

⅓ cup vegetable oil

2 eggs

1 cup cooked and chopped prunes, drained and liquid reserved

2 cups all-purpose flour

1 teaspoon baking soda

¼ teaspoon each: cinnamon, cloves, allspice and nutmeg

¾ cup chopped walnuts

Preheat oven to 350 degrees. Grease and lightly flour a Bundt pan and set aside.

Combine sugar, oil and eggs and beat well. Stir in prunes.

In a separate bowl, combine dry ingredients. Combine both mixtures, adding reserved prune liquid to thin batter somewhat.

Coat walnuts with flour, shaking off excess. Add to batter. Pour mixture into prepared pan and bake 45 minutes to 1 hour, depending on oven. Check toward end of baking time.

*This IS an old recipe… we changed the original from "⅓ cup shortening" to vegetable oil to accommodate the language of today's bakers!*

# Pumpkin Sandwich Cake

*Everyone who tastes this cake wants the recipe. Marilyn P. is our hero!*

## CAKE

¾ cup all-purpose flour

1 ½ teaspoons pumpkin pie spice

1 teaspoon baking powder

¼ teaspoon salt

3 eggs

1 cup sugar

¾ cup canned pumpkin

Cream Cheese Filling

Chocolate Cream Icing

Additional pumpkin pie spice for garnish

Preheat oven to 375 degrees. Grease bottoms and sides of 2 (8-inch) round cake pans. Line bottoms with parchment paper. Lightly flour pans and set aside.

Combine flour, pumpkin pie spice, baking powder and salt. Set aside. In a separate bowl, beat eggs and sugar until thick—about 5 minutes. This is an important step. Beat in pumpkin. Add flour mixture and beat just until combined. Spread batter into prepared pans. Bake 16 to 18 minutes or until wooden pick inserted in center comes out clean. Cool on a wire rack for 10 minutes; remove from pan and cool completely.

Place one cake layer on serving platter. Spread Cream Cheese Filling evenly over bottom cake layer then top with second layer.

Spread Chocolate Cream Icing over top and sides of cake. Sprinkle lightly with additional pumpkin pie spice. Chill cake at least 1 hour before serving.

# Pumpkin Sandwich Cake (continued)

## CREAM CHEESE FILLING

½ cup whipping cream
4 ounces cream cheese, softened
½ cup confectioner's sugar

In chilled mixing bowl, beat whipping cream to soft peaks and set aside. In a second bowl, beat cream cheese until smooth; beat in confectioner's sugar. Fold in whipped cream.

## CHOCOLATE CREAM ICING

½ cup whipping cream
1 cup semisweet chocolate chips

In a small saucepan, bring whipping cream until just boiling over medium high heat, watching carefully. Remove from heat and pour in chocolate chips but do not stir. Let stand for 5 minutes; stir until smooth. Cool 15 minutes and then spread on cake. If icing is too thin, cover and chill 30 minutes before spreading. If it is too thick, add a teaspoon of milk or cream to bring it to the desired consistency.

*Be sure to purchase solid pack pumpkin and not pumpkin pie filling for this recipe.*

# Fruit Torte

*This is the easiest, tastiest little cake. It can be "thrown" together in minutes.*

### TORTE DOUGH

¾ cup sugar

1 stick unsalted butter

2 eggs

1 teaspoon vanilla or almond extract

1 cup all-purpose flour

1 teaspoon baking powder

½ teaspoon salt

### TORTE TOPPINGS (SELECT ONE OR A COMBINATION OF CHOICE)

Large plums, halved and pitted

Apricots, halved and pitted

Peaches, peeled, pitted and sliced

Pears, peeled and halved (fresh or canned)

Canned pineapple chunks, drained

Berries

Cherries

Bananas, sliced

½ cup sugar

1 tablespoon cinnamon

Confectioner's sugar

Preheat oven to 350 degrees. Generously grease a 10-inch springform pan and set aside.

In a food processor, cream sugar and butter. Add eggs and vanilla and pulse several times. In a separate bowl, combine flour, baking powder and salt. Add to processor and pulse until just mixed, scraping down sides of bowl. Place in prepared pan. Dough will be quite stiff.

Blend ½ cup sugar and cinnamon. Roll fruit of choice in sugar mixture and arrange decoratively over the dough. Sprinkle any excess sugar mixture over top of fruit. Bake 35 to 40 minutes depending on oven or until center tests done with a wooden pick. Remove from oven and cool on a wire rack.

Sprinkle with confectioner's sugar and serve with vanilla ice cream or a large dollop of sweetened whipped cream.

# Broiled Plums with Mascarpone Cream

*A light (but not too light) finale!*

**5 medium plums, halved and pitted**
**3 tablespoons brandy**
**6 tablespoons brown sugar, divided**
**¼ cup mascarpone cheese**
**¼ cup cream**

Preheat broiler. Place plums, cut side up in a single layer on baking sheet. Pour brandy evenly over plums and sprinkle with 4 tablespoons of the brown sugar. Broil until plums are soft and sugar is caramelized--about 8 to 10 minutes.

Meanwhile, place mascarpone and cream in a small bowl. Mix in remaining 2 tablespoons brown sugar and beat for 2 minutes.

Top broiled plums with whipped mascarpone cheese to serve.

# Butterscotch Sauce Murray

*A much coveted recipe from Cindy's grandmother. Delicious on French Vanilla ice cream or straight from the spoon!*

¾ **cup brown sugar**

½ **cup light corn syrup**

¼ **teaspoon salt**

4 **tablespoons butter**

1 **cup cream, divided**

½ **teaspoon vanilla**

Combine brown sugar, corn syrup, salt, butter and ½ cup cream in a small saucepan and cook over low heat, stirring to soft ball stage (234-242 degrees). Stir in additional ½ cup cream and cook to a thick consistency (228 degrees).

Remove from heat and stir in vanilla. If too thick, more cream may be added.

Pour into a glass jar with a screw-top lid. Cover and refrigerate when not in use.

# Judi's Treats

*A simple recipe that is simply delicious from a lady who knows everything about a kitchen—her shop is the best!*

1 **box round buttery crackers**

1 **jar peanut butter**

1 **pound dipping chocolate**

Spread peanut butter between two crackers while chocolate is melting in a double boiler. When chocolate is ready, dip filled crackers into chocolate and place on a parchment paper-lined cookie sheet. As quickly as possible after dipping, transfer baking sheet to the refrigerator for chocolate to set.

# Cream Cheese Flan with Caramel Sauce

*Another one of our "oldies".*

1 jar rich caramel sauce

1 (8-ounce) package cream cheese, softened

½ cup sugar

1 teaspoon vanilla

6 eggs

2 cups milk

Preheat oven to 350 degrees. Butter a 9-inch glass cake or pie dish that is at least 1½-inches deep. Pour caramel sauce into bottom of dish and set aside.

Whip cream cheese, sugar and vanilla until smooth. Add eggs, one at a time; add milk and blend well.

Pour mixture into caramel-lined baking dish. Set into a large pan half-filled with boiling water, taking care that no water gets into flan.

Bake 45 to 50 minutes. Cool on a rack for 20 minutes then carefully invert on a serving plate.

# Pineapple for Grown-Ups

*An end-of-the-meal sweet without the guilt!*

1 ripe pineapple, peeled, cored and cut into ½-inch slices

¼ cup Golden Rum

Juice of 1 lime

Zest of 1 lime

¼ cup honey

Crème fraiche

Arrange pineapple on a serving plate. Sprinkle with rum, honey, lime juice and zest. Marinate and chill for 1 hour.

Serve each slice with a dollop of crème fraiche.

# Glazed Baked Apples

*We often forget about the simple desserts of yore. This is a delicious reminder!*

**8 Golden Delicious apples**

**½ cup brown sugar**

**1 teaspoon cinnamon**

**½ teaspoon nutmeg**

**6 tablespoons maple syrup**

**4 tablespoons cold butter, cut into small cubes**

Preheat oven to 350 degrees.

Core apples and peel skin off top quarter of each apple. Place in a baking pan.

Combine sugar and spices. Fill apple cavities with this mixture. Spoon maple syrup into each cavity and scatter pieces of butter over apples.

Pour ½ cup water into the pan with apples. Bake 30 minutes. Baste apples and continue baking until tender—25 to 30 more minutes.

Remove from oven. Carefully pour liquid into a small skillet and boil until syrupy. Pour over apples and serve at room temperature with a generous dollop of whipped cream.

*Another tasty filling option—soak raisins in rum overnight and stuff those into the cavity of the apples before baking. Yummy!*

# Mother's Rice Pudding

*I loved this as a little girl and I love it now as a big girl.*

3 eggs
½ cup sugar
¼ teaspoon salt
½ teaspoon vanilla
3 cups scalded milk
¾ cup cooked rice
⅓ cup raisins
Nutmeg

Preheat oven to 350 degrees. Butter a small casserole dish and set aside.

Beat eggs lightly. Add sugar, salt and vanilla. Pour on scalded milk. Strain mixture and pour into prepared dish. Add rice and raisins and sprinkle with a few grains of nutmeg.

Set in a pan of hot water and bake for 1 hour or until center is set.

# Pavlova with Berries

*The perfect finale!*

## SHELLS

**Confectioner's sugar for dusting**

**1 cup superfine granulated sugar**

**½ cup light brown sugar**

**1 ½ tablespoons cornstarch**

**1 ½ teaspoons vanilla**

**2 teaspoons white vinegar**

**¾ cup egg whites (from 5 or 6 eggs) at room temperature**

Preheat oven to 275 degrees with rack placed in the center. Lightly butter 3 (8-inch) round cake pans. Dust sides of pans with confectioner's sugar, tapping out excess. Line bottom of each pan with a round of parchment.

Pulse superfine sugar, brown sugar and cornstarch in food processor until well combined. Beat egg whites with a pinch of salt using an electric mixer at medium speed until they hold soft peaks. Increase speed to medium high and add sugar mixture, 1 tablespoon at a time. After all sugar has been added, beat 1 additional minute. Add vanilla and vinegar; beat at high speed until meringue is glossy and holds stiff peaks—about 5 minutes. Spoon meringue into prepared pans (about 2 ½ cups per pan). Smooth tops.

Bake until meringues have a crisp crust and feel dry to the touch, about 1 hour. (The inside will still be marshmallow-like.) Turn oven off and prop door open with a wooden spoon. Cool meringues in oven for 1 hour. Meringues may sink slightly and crack while cooling. Run a knife along sides of cake pans and carefully turn meringues out of pans. Carefully peel off parchment (meringues will be fragile and the crust may crack further) and turn right side up. Put one meringue on a serving plate and spread with one third of the whipped cream. Spoon one third of the fruit (with juice) over the top. Repeat with remaining meringues, cream and fruit.

# Pavlova with Berries (continued)

## BERRIES

**3 pounds strawberries, trimmed and sliced**

**2-3 tablespoons granulated sugar**

Macerate fruit with sugar and let stand at room temperature.

## CREAM

**2 cups heavy cream, chilled**

**⅔ cup sour cream, chilled**

Beat the cream using an electric mixer until it just holds soft peaks. Fold in the sour cream.

*For individual servings, line baking sheet with parchment and drop 10 rounds onto parchment, spreading each with the back of a spoon. Proceed with about baking instructions, reducing baking time to 40 minutes. Place one meringue on a plate, spread with cream and top with berries.*

# Strawberry Cream Parfaits

*So pretty—so luscious—so easy.*

3 cups sliced fresh strawberries
4 tablespoons sour cream
2 cups chilled whipping cream
4 cups coarsely broken meringues
Fresh mint for garnish
8 whole strawberries, fanned

Mash 3 cups strawberries to a chunky sauce.

Place sour cream in a 2-cup measuring cup. Add enough chilled whipping cream to fill cup completely. Beat until thick. (Make ahead of time and refrigerate). When ready to serve, fold broken meringues into the whipping cream mixture.

Divide half of the strawberries into 8 serving glasses. Spoon half of the cream mixture over this and then repeat layers. Garnish with a whole fanned strawberry and a sprig of fresh mint.

*For those of us fortunate enough to be able to shop at Trader Joe's, their meringues are excellent!*

# Mango or Peach Chutney

*It is my belief that chutney is as important a staple as mayonnaise, mustard or catsup. A perfect accompaniment for curries, roasted pork or lamb, wonderful in salad dressings or spread over a block of cream cheese for an instant appetizer—probably would be delicious over vanilla ice cream!*

**4 mangoes or firm unpeeled peaches, cut into medium dice**

**2 ½ cups granulated sugar**

**1 cup brown sugar**

**1 cup cider vinegar**

**2 tablespoons garlic, minced**

**5 tablespoons ginger, finely chopped (unpeeled)**

**½ teaspoon red pepper flakes**

**1 cup golden raisins**

Combine mangoes or peaches with sugars and stir well. Cover and let stand for 8 hours.

Drain well, reserving syrup. In a heavy saucepan, thoroughly combine syrup with vinegar, garlic, ginger, salt and red pepper flakes. Simmer 30 minutes.

Add reserved fruit and raisins. Simmer 30 minutes, stirring frequently.

Spoon into sterilized jars and refrigerate.

*I do this often—halve peaches and fill cavity with chutney. Bake 10 to 15 minutes and serve alongside roasted pork or lamb.*

# *Tips: Finder's Keepers*

## GARLIC, GINGER AND GREEN ONION PASTE

2 tablespoons chopped ginger

3 tablespoons chopped garlic

6 scallions

Blend all to a paste and use to liven up sautéed chicken or vegetables.

## FISH SAUCE

Add to any dish where garlic plays a role—on Caesar salads, in dipping sauces or on roasted tomatoes.

## KEEP AN AVOCADO GREEN

Rinse or submerge in cold water. This prevents the exposed fruit from browning for hours. Or, you may dip it in a small amount of salad dressing and set aside for later use.

## TO CONVERT ALL-PURPOSE FLOUR OR CORNMEAL TO SELF-RISING

1 cup flour or cornmeal

1 ½ teaspoons baking powder

½ teaspoon salt

## BISCUITS

**2 cups self-rising flour**

**1 cup sour cream**

Blend well, knead slightly, roll, cut and place in a buttered baking pan. Bake at 450 degrees for 15 minutes. For a savory twist, add ¼ teaspoon sage, rosemary or chives—especially good served with pork or chicken.


## ITALIAN STYLE SALSA VERDE

**8 tablespoons olive oil**

**1 large bunch Italian parsley**

**25 large basil leaves**

**5 anchovy fillets**

**4 fresh tarragon sprigs**

**2 teaspoons capers, drained**

**2 teaspoons Dijon mustard**

**2 teaspoons white wine vinegar**

**1 clove garlic**

Blend in food processor or blender until a coarse sauce forms. Add more oil by the tablespoonful to thin, if desired. Adds a fresh and bright flavor to pork, seafood, sliced tomatoes and steamed potatoes.

# INDEX

# Index

# INDEX

# INDEX

# INDEX

# Index

# Index

## W

### WATERMELON

## Z

### ZUCCHINI

The

# *Jam Journal*

## A unique Cookbook
## and Journal
## for the whole family.

*Preserving the fruits of time*

*ISBN 0-9725158-0-1*

Created and published by:  Hollee Eckman

Printed by:  Printech, Salt Lake City, UT

Graphics and Design:  Lee A. Steadman

Words and poetic license:  Heather Higgins

For more information on Holleeberry's Jam or The Jam Journal
Email - holleeberrys@yahoo.com
or write: ✉
Hollee Eckman
P.O. Box 701963
West Valley City, UT  84170-1963

*Preserving the fruits of time*

# Contents

# Excerpts from my journal....

**June 1996**... What a busy week! Fred and I just back from vacation and visiting his sister Evelyn. I found a beautiful patch of wild raspberries and made some jam.

**January 1997**... Happy New Year! Christmas was a great time for family and friends. Fred and I gave away cute gift baskets of my homemade jam... Fred calls it Holleeberry's. I am so lucky...

**September 1998**... Hey this jam idea is not such a bad idea. I think I might try selling it commercially... I love how colorful the jars of jam look on my counter...

**April 1999**... I am so excited! My first customer!! I can't believe it. I took up some jam and bread for them to try last week. And today they called! An order today for 20 jars!! I am Holleeberry's!! I can't wait to tell Fred so we can celebrate.

**September 2000** ... Guess what? I got Planet Rainbow. I'm sure I am more excited than they are... but what great people to work with... this is really turning out to be a dream come true.

**Christmas 2000**... I am so blessed. Holleeberry's is really taking off. I have five flavors now... Sometimes I am so tired I just fall into bed. I don't know what I'd do without Fred..my daughters are so supportive..

**February 2001** ... So I'm not quite sure about this... in fact I'm not even sure I want to write it down... but my friends at Planet Rainbow put an idea in my head and I can't shake it... What about a book...

**September 2001**... I just finished up putting the orders together from the Wholesale Gift Shows...wow! 8 new customers... and I've added 6 more flavors... now about this book idea...

**March 2002** ... EEK! I am going to do it! I found the most amazing artist to work with...the energy between us and the ideas... I feel incredible... I am so excited and scared at the same time... The Jam Journal... will my dream be everything I want it to be?

**July 2002**... I just got back from Lee's. He has the cover done... This is even more amazing than I ever thought it would be. I love how kind people are. The creative ideas just start flowing when I bring up my book...recipes...pictures...stories...this is exactly how I want people to enjoy my book.

**October 2002**... There it goes off to the printer... A journal to preserve family memories while enjoying my jam... I hope everyone loves the journal as much as I have loved creating it for them.... thank you to everyone who has made my dream possible.

# Rise and Shine

*A*cknowlege and record special family occasions; those moments when your children surprise you !

I woke up this morning to my two darling children with smirky looks on their faces and my husband beaming proudly behind them... Happy Birthday, mom! Rise and shine. Look – we cooked you breakfast...

*E*xperiment with your own tastes, try a different flavor jam in one of the recipes!

*P*aste in your favorite family photos and record your memories visually as well! Your children who can't read will also be able to enjoy the journal.

*Preserving the fruits of time*

# Bite-Size Jam Swirls

3 cups all-purpose flour
dash salt
1 - 8 oz. cream cheese
1 cup butter
1/2 cup jam of choice
1 cup chopped pecans
coarse sugar

In large mixing bowl, combine flour and salt using pastry blender, cut in cream cheese and butter until fine crumbs. Form a ball, knead until smooth, divide in half, and wrap in plastic wrap. Refrigerate (chill) one hour. When dough is chilled, roll each half into rectangles. Spread with jam and nuts, fold into thirds, roll, then slice each roll into 1/2 inch pieces. Sprinkle with coarse sugar and bake at 350° for 12-15 min. Bakes about 2 1/2 dozen.

*Jessie Jean's Recipe*

# Your Journal Entry

*Jessie Jean's Coffee Shop, Roy*

# Easy Jam Biscuit Treats

10 oz. can of flaky biscuits
10 tbs. jam
1/4 cup powdered sugar
1 to 2 teaspoons milk

Preheat oven to 375.° Separate dough into 10 biscuits, separate each biscuit into 2 layers. Spoon 1 tbs. jam or peanut butter in center of 1st layer of biscuit. Place other half of biscuit on top and pinch edges to seal. Place biscuits in engrossed 9-inch round cake pan or 8-inch square cake pan. With thumb, make imprint in center of each roll. Fill each indentation with 1 tbs. jam. Bake for 23-28 mins. or until golden. In small bowl, combine powdered sugar and enough milk for desired glaze consistency. Drizzle over warm rolls.

# Your Journal Entry

Ever Pressing Forward
Lest We Forget

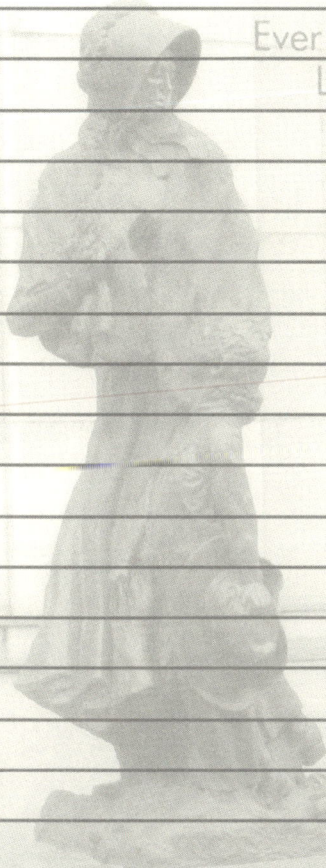

# Jammin with Oatmeal

1 cup old fashion oatmeal
1/4 cup water
3 or 4 egg whites
3 or 4 tbs. of your favorite jam

Mix in medium bowl 1 cup oatmeal, 1/4 cup of water
and let it stand for 5 min.  Stir in 3 or 4 egg whites then pour in
saucepan.  Making a big pancake, cook on medium heat until light
brown.  Cook other side until light brown.  Put on serving plate
and add 3 to 4 tablespoons of your favorite jam.

*Body Success Recipe*

# Your Journal Entry

Body Success, Ogden

# Mormon Muffins

Thoughts...

Life is easier than
you think.
All you have to do is:
accept the impossible,
do without the indispensable,
bear the intolerable,
and
be able to smile at anything.

2 cups boiling water
5 tsp. baking soda
1 cup shortening
2 cups sugar
4 eggs
1 qt. buttermilk

5 cups flour
1 tsp. salt
4 cups 40% bran flakes
1 cup chopped walnuts

Add baking soda to boiling water and set aside. Whip shortening
and sugar until light and fluffy. Add the eggs slowly. Mix well.
Add buttermilk, flour and salt and mix well. Add soda water very slowly.
Gently fold the cereals and the walnuts into the mix. Let muffin mix
sit in refrigerator overnight. Spoon 1/8 cup mixture into greased
muffin tins. Bake at 350°for 30 min. Let cool for five min.
Yields 3 doz. muffins.

*Planet Rainbow Recipe*

8

# Your Journal Entry

*Rainbow Gardens, Ogden*

# Pancakes w/Berry Topping

1 1/4 cups flour
2 tbs. sugar
2 tbs. baking soda
1 1/2 cups buttermilk
1/2 cup egg
3 tbs. corn oil spread

Mix in larg bowl flour, sugar, and baking soda. Stir in buttermilk, egg and 2 tbs. spread until blended. Use remaining spread to brush over the pan to cook pancake on. Use 1/8 cup pancake mix for each pancake. Flip when first side is bubbling, finish cooking until lightly brown.

**Mixed Berry Topping:**
In med. saucepan, heat 1 (12 oz.) Blueberry jam over med.-low heat, 1/4 cup honey and 1/8 tsp. ground ginger. Cook and stir until hot and well blended. Serve hot over warm pancakes.

# Your Journal Entry

*Cassandra & Ed*

# Pumpkin Pancakes w/Peach Jam

2 cup flour
1 tbs baking powder
1/2 tsp. salt
2 tbs. sugar
1 tbs. pumpkin spice
2 eggs
1 3/4 cup milk
3 tbs. oil or melted butter plus 1 tbs.
1/2 cup pumpkin mashed

### Serve w/ Peach Jam

Sift dry ingredients in one bowl. Whisk eggs and milk in another bowl. Add oil or butter and pumpkin. Pour over dry ingredients. Stir, do not beat. Okay if batter is lumpy. Melt tbs. oil or butter on griddle. Waffles: Follow same recipe, but separate the eggs. Combine yolks with milk, 3 tbs. of oil or butter, and pumpkin mashed. Stir into the dry ingredients. Beat egg whites until stiff and gently fold into batter.

# Your Journal Entry

# Silver Dollar Pancakes with Berry Topping

1 1/4 cups flour
1 tbs. sugar
1 tsp. baking soda
1 1/2 cups buttermilk
1/2 cup egg beaters
3 tbs. butter
mixed berry topping

Mix in large bowl flour, sugar, and baking soda. Stir in buttermilk, egg beaters, and 2 tbs. butter until blended. Use remaining spread to brush over the pan to cook pancake on. Use 1/8 cup pancake mix for each pancake. Flip when first side is bubbling, finish cooking until lightly brown.
**Mixed Berry Topping:** In medium saucepan, heat 1 (12 oz.) Blueberry / seedless Raspberry jam over med.-low heat, combine 1/4 cup honey and 1/8 tsp. ground ginger. Cook and stir until hot and well blended. Serve hot over warm Pancakes.

# Your Journal Entry

*Peek-a-boo Sadie*

# Strawberry Crepes

FANCY **KLONDYKE** STRAWBERRIES
THIS CASE CONTAINS 24 PINTS DRY MEASURE. AGRICULTURAL & SU...
FANCY CREAMERY BUTTER

1 - 8 oz. cream cheese
2 tbs. sugar
12 crepes (see recipe pg. 112)
6 tbs. sugar
3/4 cup dairy sour cream
2 tsp. lemon rind, grated
1/4 cup butter
2 cups strawberry jam
1/2 cup fresh strawberries

Mix cream cheese, sour cream and 2 tbs. sugar until smooth.
Stir in lemon rind. Spoon mixture onto crepes and roll up.
Place on plate and keep warm. Combine butter with remaining
sugar and cook in small saucepan until sugar is desolved.
Stir in Strawberry jam. Heat until smooth. Spoon over crepes.
Put fresh strawberries on top of crepes.

# Your Journal Entry

Heidi & Loren in the Little White Chapel

Insert
your own...

...family favorites!

From the kitchen of:_____

# Tea for Two

**M**ake it a special
family weekend -
take everyone on
a "cookie and milk" -
picnic in the backyard.
Have the children
make invitations
for each other and
help make the cookies.

Today, I know why
I became a dad!
My six year old invited
me to a tea party.
We walked into her room.
She had her little table
all set up. Cookies,
Pretzels, Jelly beans
and Kool-aid.
"It's just for you
and me daddy!"

**R**aining outside?
Move the picnic
to the front room.
Push all the
furniture out of
the way and lay
a blanket down.

**I**nvite
someone
over for a
tea party.
Just the two
of you -
for some quality
one on one
time.

## Preserving the fruits of time

# Apricot Swirls

3/4 cup unsalted butter
4 ozs. nonfat cream cheese
1/4 cup non-fat liquid egg substitute
1 3/4 cup flour
3/4 cup apricot jam

Cream butter and cream cheese in bowl on low speed. Add the liquid egg and beat at med. speed until mixture is smooth. Beat in flour at low speed to form dough. Gather the dough into a ball, wrap it in wax paper, and refrigerate for at least 2 hours. Preheat oven to 350.° Lightly coat cookie sheets with light vegatable oil cooking spray, spreading the oil evenly over the surface. Cover a work surface with a sheet of wax paper and lightly flour. Divide dough in half. Roll half into 1/8 inch thick rectangle measuring about 9 x 12 inches. Spread 6 tbs. of jam over dough. Starting at a long end, roll the dough up like a jelly roll. Trim the ragged ends and cut the roll into 1/2 inch slices. Transfer the slices to prepared cookie sheets. Repeat with remaining dough. Bake for 18 - 20 minutes, until lightly browned. Any jam could work with this.

# Your Journal Entry

_Rachel's Tigger_

# Chocolate Raspberry Crumb Bars

1 cup butter, softened
2 cups flour
1/2 cup brown sugar, packed
1/4 tsp. salt
2 cups (12 oz.) semi-sweet choice chocolate
1/4 cup sweetened condensed milk
1/2 cup chopped nuts
1/3 cup raspberry jam

Preheat oven to 350.° Beat butter in large mixing bowl until creamy.
Beat in flour, sugar, and salt until well mixed. With fingers, press
1 3/4 cups crumb mixture onto bottom of greased 13 x 9-inch pan.
Reserve remaining mixture. Bake for 10-12 minutes or until edges are
golden brown. Combine 1 cup Chocolate chips and sweetened condensed
milk in a small saucepan. Melt over low heat until smooth. Spread over
hot crust. Stir nuts into reserved crumb mixture. Sprinkle over Chocolate
filling. Drop teaspoon fulls of jam over crumb mixture. Sprinkle
remaining chocolate chips. Continue baking 25 to 30 minutes or until
center is set. Cool completely on wire rack.

*Landing on a Glacier on Mt. McKinley*

# Cream Cheese and Jam Danish

1 sheet frozen ready-to-bake pastry
6 oz cream cheese
1/4 cup powdered sugar
1 egg
1 tsp. vanilla

## Creamy Glaze

3 oz. cream cheese
8oz jam
1tbs. milk

Cut Pastry to 15x10 inch rectangle.
Place in 15x10x1 inch jelly roll pan. Beat 6 oz.
cream cheese, 1/4 cup sugar, egg, and vanilla in small bowl at med. speed
until well blend. Spread cream cheese mixture over pastry to within 1 inch
of border. Make 2 inch cuts at 1 inch intervals on long side of pastry.
Crisscross strips over filling. Bake at 350° 25-30 minutes or until
golden brown. Cool. Drizzle glaze over it.

# Your Journal Entry

"Jess"

# Jam Roll

3 eggs
1/2 cup sugar
3/4 cup self-raising flour
2 tbs. boiling water
1/3 cup jam
2 tbs. sugar, extra

Grease a roll pan, line base and sides with paper, grease paper well.
Beat eggs in small bowl with electric mixer for about 3 min. or until thick
and creamy. Gradually add sugar, beat until dissolved between
each addition. Transfer mixture to large bowl, fold in sifted flour and water.
Spread mixture into prepared pan, bake in moderate oven for about 10 min.
Warm jam gently in saucepan over low heat. Turn cake immediately on to
paper, sprinkled with extra sugar. Spread hot cake evenly with hot jam,
roll up from the short side using paper as a guide.

# Your Journal Entry

*"Cookin' w/ mom in the kitchen"*

# Lemon - Pistachio Biscotti

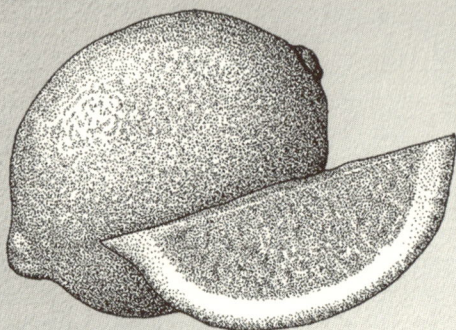

Thoughts...

When life
gives you lemons,
make wassail.

1/3 cup butter
2/3 cup sugar
2 tsp. baking powder
1/2 tsp. salt
2 eggs
1 tsp. vanilla

4 tsp. finely shredded lemon peel
2 cups flour
1 1/2 cups unsalted pistachio nuts
Lemon curd (see recipe pg. 118)

Preheat oven to 375°. Line two cookie sheets with parchment paper and set aside. Beat butter in a large mixing bowl with a beater on med. speed for 30 seconds. Add sugar, baking powder, and salt; beat until combined, scraping sides of bowl. Beat eggs and vanilla until combined. Beat lemon peel and as much of the flour as you can with mixer. Stir in any remaining flour and the pistachios with a wooden spoon. Divide dough into three equal portions on a lightly floured surface. Shape each portion into a 8 inch loaf. Place loaves at least 3 inches apart on prepared cookie sheet(s). Flatten loaves to about 2 1/2 inches. Bake for 20-25 minutes or until golden brown and top is cracked. Reduce oven to 325°. Cool cookie sheet on wire rack for 30 minutes. Cut each loaf into 1/2 inch slices. Bake for 8 minutes. Turn slices over and bake 8-10 minutes more or until dry and crisp. Dip end into or drizzle with lemon curd.

# Your Journal Entry

"I have four reasons to continuously smile..."
L.A. Steadman

# Napoleons

Thoughts...

Circumstance does not make the man, it reveals him to himself.

1 frozen ready-to-bake puff pastry sheet
1 8 oz. cream cheese
1/4 cup powdered sugar
1/4 tsp. almond extract
1 cup whipping cream (whipped)
1/2 cup powdered sugar
1 tbs. milk
8 oz. jam, melted

Thaw puff pastry sheet according to package.  Preheat oven to 400.°
On lightly floured surface roll pastry to 15x12 inch rectangle.
Cut lengthwise into thirds.  Place pastry strips on large ungreased cookie
sheet, each one on a different sheets.  Prick with a fork to let it air and bake
for 8 to 10 minutes or until golden brown.  Stir together cream cheese,
1/4 cup powdered sugar, and almond extract in med. bowl until well
blended.  Fold in whipped cream.  Spread two pastry
strips with cream cheese mixture, stack them one on top of the other.
Top with remaining pastry strip.  Stir together 1/2 cup sugar and milk in
small bowl until smooth.  Spread over top pastry strip.  Drizzle with
melted jam.

*Roger, age 2*

# Peach Blossom Torte

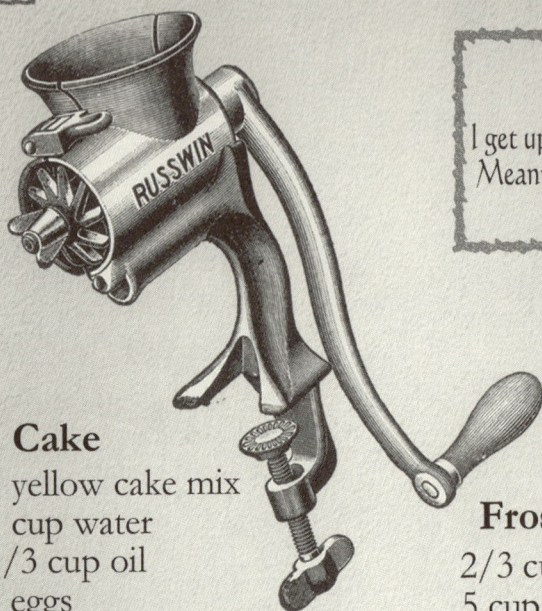

## Cake

1 yellow cake mix
1 cup water
1/3 cup oil
3 eggs
1 tsp. almond extract
2/3 cup peach jam

## Frosting

2/3 cup butter
5 cups powdered sugar
3 to 4 tbs. half-and-half
1/3 cup peach jam

Preheat oven to 350.° Grease 15 x 10 x 1 inch baking pan, line bottom with parchment paper. Grease and flour wax paper. Prepare cake as shown on box using water, oil, and eggs. Fold in almond extract. Pour into pan. Bake for 20-25 minutes. Cool for 30 minutes. While cake cools, toast almonds. Spread almonds on cookie sheet. Bake for 5 to 7 minutes stirring occassionally. Cool. Run knife around edges of cake to loosen. Invert cake onto counter Remove waxed paper. Trim short ends. Cut cake crosswise into 3 equal layers. Place one layer on serving plate spread with 1/3 cup of peach jam. Repeat with second layers.
Place last layer on top. In large bowl mix frosting ingredients together except peach jam add enough half-n-half to desired thickness. Take out 1/3 cup frosting for sides add 1/3 cup peach jam. Frost top and sides of torte with remaining peach jam frosting. Press toasted almonds along sides.

# Your Journal Entry

*"Cora in her fur"*

# Strawberry Tarts

1 8 oz. cream cheese
1 cup powdered sugar
1 tsp. vanilla
1 12 oz. whipping cream
3 pint strawberries
1/2 cup strawberry jam (melted)

## Crust
1 cup butter
2 cups flour
1 cup pecans, finely chopped garnish

Crust: Heat oven to 350°. Grease 10 inch spring form pan. Line with parchment paper. Mix butter, flour, and pecans in med. bowl. Press mixture over bottom of spring form pan. Bake for 20 minutes. With mixer on med. speed, beat together cream cheese and powdered sugar in large bowl for 2 minutes. Beat in vanilla. Fold in whipped topping. Spread over cool crust. Place each strawberry, cut side down on top of filling to cover pie. Brush strawberries with melted jam.

*The Sweet "Tart" Girls*

Insert
your own...

...family favorites!

From the kitchen of: _____

# Let's get saucy

*Go shopping with "the girls" and buy an outrageous hat.*

I gave my mother
a poem about
an old woman
learning to spit
and wearing purple
and red.
It reminds me of
her. She laughed
and clapped her hands.
I am so proud of
the woman she's
become.

*Hat's off to you! Have everyone wear their favorite hat to dinner & tell a story about how they got it or why it's their favorite!*

*Crazy out of your mind? Take time to journal an entry about the most adventurous thing you've ever done!*

## Preserving the fruits of time

# Chinese Apricot Glaze

1/2 cup dried apricots
3/4 cup water
1 1/2 tsp. grated orange peel
1/4 cup apricot jam
3 tbs. dark corn syrup
1 tbs. cider vinegar
1 tbs. soy sauce
1/2 tsp. ground ginger

In a cup measure and combine apricots and water. Cook on high 3-4 min.,
then cook on low for 3-5 min. or until apricots are soft and plump.
Let stand 5-10 min.: drain. Combine plumped apricots and remaining
ingredients in blender. Process on low until smooth.
Use a baste for Cornish hens, pork or chicken.

# Your Journal Entry

*Mom & the girls off on an adventure.*

# Curried Apricot - Pineapple Dip

Thoughts...

If I could sit across
the porch from God,
I'd thank him for
lending me you.

8 oz. cream cheese, softened
1/2 cup mayonaisse
1/3 cup apricot/pineapple jam
1/2 silvered almonds
1/2 cup chopped green onions
1 tbs curry powder
1 tbs lemon juice
1/4 tsp salt

Heat oven to 400.° Blend cream cheese, mayonaisse and jam in food
processor until well blended.  Add 1/4 cup almonds, green onions,
curry powder, lemon juice & salt.  Pulse until blended.
Spread on 9" baking dish.  Sprinkle w/almonds.  Bake 10-15 min.
Serve with sliced fruit or crackers.

# Your Journal Entry

_Scott, Jamie & little Chalice_

# French Salad Dressing

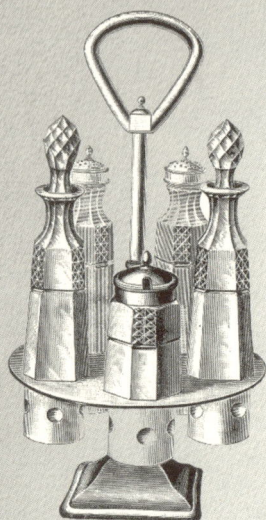

1 can tomato soup
1/2 cup oil
1/2 cup sugar
1/2 cup vinegar
1 tsp. salt, pepper to taste
1/2 cup apricot/pineapple jam

Combine and beat well with beater.

# Your Journal Entry

Liz Ranes & Carly

# Ham Sauce

Thoughts...

As I took this picture of
my beautiful, silly boy,
I thought to myself, he's
got my smile, but those
are his fathers ears.

1 cup apricot / pineapple jam
1 tsp. dry mustard
1 1/2 cup brown sugar
1/4 tsp. ground cloves
1/2 cup pineapple juice

Mix all ingredients well in small mixing bowl.

# Your Journal Entry

*Mikey, age 10*

# Raspberry Chocolate Fondue

1/2 cup raspberry jam
1 8 oz. cream cheese
1 cup semi-sweet real choc. chips
1 tbs. raspberry-flavored liqueur

Heat jam until softened in small saucepan, and then strain. Mix together jam with cream cheese in small mixing bowl. Melt choc. chips with liqueur in med. sauce pan over low heat, stirring until smooth. Gradually add cream cheese mixture beating with wire whisk until smooth and thoroughly heated. Serve warm with cake cubes, or banana slices.

# Your Journal Entry

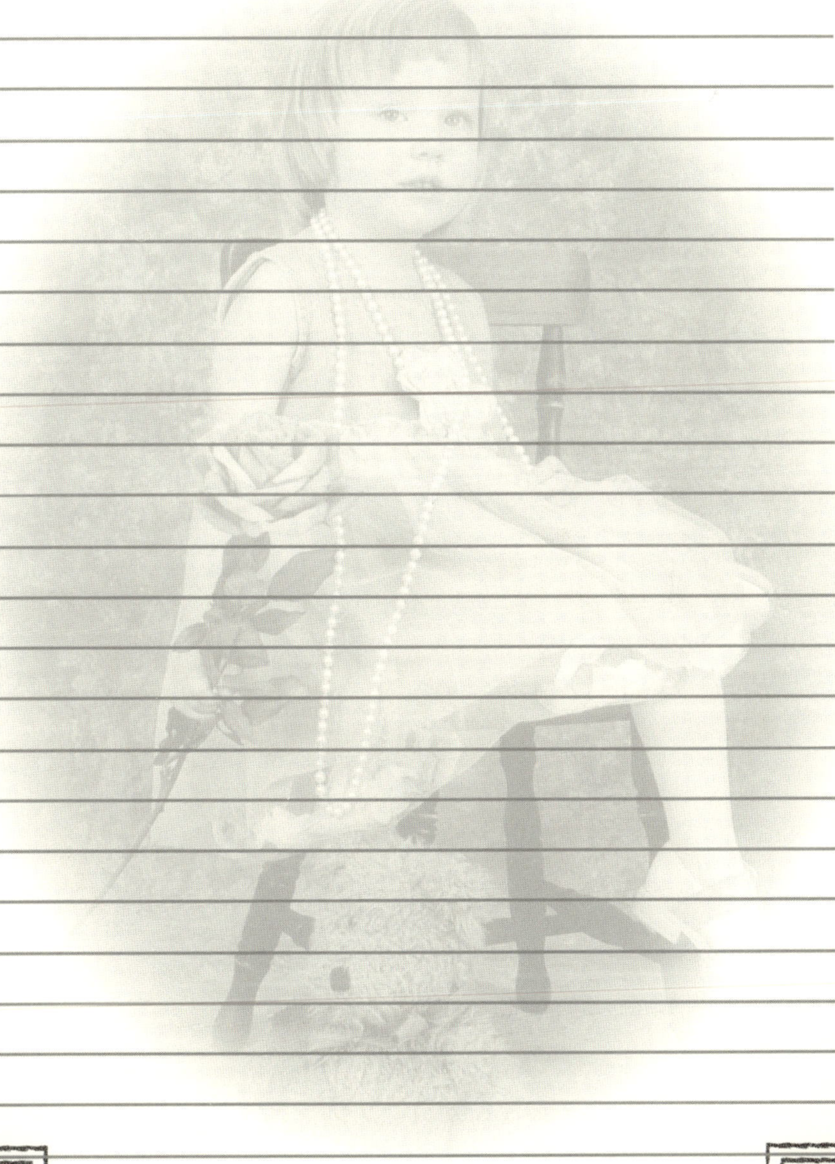

*Rachel*

# Raspberry Chocolate Sauce

2 pkgs. (6 oz. ea.) raspberries
1/4 cup milk
2 tbs. finely chopped semi-sweet chocolate
1/2 cup raspberry jam

In small saucepan, over low heat, combine milk and chocolate. Whisk until chocolate melts and mixture's smooth. Blend in jam with whisk. Heat and stir until smooth and shiny. Divide berries among steamed glasses or bowl and drizzle with warm sauce.

# Your Journal Entry

*Mandi York & daughter Nikole*

# Raspberry Sauce

BORDEN-PEKIN
Fruit Growers Association
PACKED AT
PEKIN, INDIANA
FANCY LATHAM RED RASPBERRIES

This Crate
Contains 24 Full Pints
Dry Measure

QUALITY FIRST

Thoughts...

When you were born,
you cried & the world
rejoiced. Live your life in
such a manner that
when you die, the world
cries & you rejoice.

1 8 oz. jar raspberry jam
2 tbs. orange-flavored liqueur

Blend ingredients together until smooth.

# Sweet - Sour Sauce

1 1/2 cup apricot pineapple jam
1 cup chicken broth
1/2 cup vinegar
2 tsp. soy sauce
1/2 green pepper, coarsely chopped

Take jam, chicken broth, vinegar, soy and smooth. Stirring twice, cook
on high 7-8 minutes until smooth and thickened.  Stir in green peppers.
Serve over meatballs.  Makes about 2 1/2 cups.

# Your Journal Entry

"Wander Baby"

Insert
your own...

...family favorites!

From the kitchen of: _____

# Grand Ole Opening

**M**ake it fancy!
Serve a starter
for a regular
family dinner.
Cut the tops of
fresh cut flowers
or greenery to
accent the
presentation.

Oh my gosh! Cher and I talked
Kim and Kendall into changing lockers
with us !! ☺ !! Now we locker
next to Craig and Bret !!!!! They are soooo
cute! ♥ Craig's mine and Cher ♥
Bret. We got to see them between third
and fourth for like 10 minutes!!
Now, if we can just get the guts to say
hi! EEEEKKKK!!!!

**H**ost an
"Appetizer Only"
progressive dinner
with your
neighbors or
extended family.

**S**tart a new garden
and involve your
children!
If you rent -
use containers;
if it is winter -
find a sunny window!

Preserving the fruits of time

# Apricot Chicken Pot Stickers

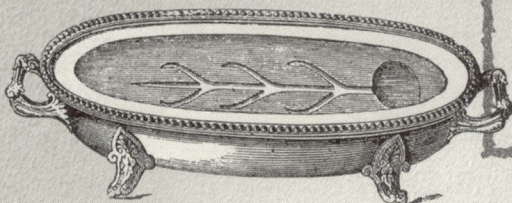

2 cups + 1 tbs. water, divided
2 small boneless skinless chicken breasts
2 cups chopped finely shredded cabbage
1/2 cup all fruit apricot jam
2 green onions with tops, finely chopped
2 tsp. soy sauce
1/2 tsp. grated fresh ginger
1/8 tsp. black pepper
30 wonton wrappers

Bring 2 cups water to boil in med. saucepan. Add chicken. Reduce heat to low; simmer, covered, 10 min. or until chicken is no longer pink in the middle. Remove from saucepan and drain. Add cabbage and remaining 1 tbs. water to saucepan. Cook over high heat 1-2 min. or until water evaporates, stirring occasionally. Remove from heat; cool slightly. Finely chop chicken. Add to saucepan along with jam, green onions, soy sauce, ginger and pepper. Mix well. Remove 3 wonton wrappers at a time from package. Spoon slightly rounded tablespoonful of chicken mixture onto center of wrapper; brush edges with water. Bring 4 corners together; press to seal. Repeat until wrappers and filling are gone. Spray steamer with nonstick cooking spray. Fill steamer basket without filling it too much so they do not stick. Cover; steam for 5 min. Serve onto plate with Sweet & Sour Sauce.

# Your Journal Entry

*Daddy Daughter Time*

# Chicken Fingers w / Marmalade Dip

1 cup chopped pecans
1 cup corn flake crumbs
1/2 cup sweetened flaked coconut
2 eggs, beaten
1 tbs. milk
1/2 cup flour

1/4 tsp. salt
4 boneless, skinless chicken breast
1/3 cup butter, melted
1/2 cup orange marmalade
2 tbs. chile sauce
1 tbs. cider vinegar
1/4 tsp. dry mustard

Heat oven to 400.° Process pecans in food processor until finely chopped; add corn flake crumbs and coconut. Pulse to blend. Place in shallow dish. Combine eggs and milk in separate shallow dish. Place flour and salt in separate shallow dish; mix well. Dip chicken strips into flour mixture until well coated. Dip flour coated chicken into egg mixture, then into pecan mixture. Press coating onto chicken. Grease 15x10 inch baking pan with 2 tbs. melted butter. Place coated chicken strips into buttered pan and sprinkle with remaining butter. Bake 10-15 minutes or until no longer pink inside. Combine all other ingredients for sauce. Mix well. Serve chicken fingers with sauce.

# Your Journal Entry

*Jessica & Rachel*
*at the piano*

# Just Peachy Bruschetta

**GEORGIA PEACHES**

CONTENTS SIX 4-QUART BASKETS
GROWN BY
**Americus Farm & Peach Co.**
AMERICUS, GEORGIA

Thoughts...

Bruschetta generally are savory, but this sweet fruit version deliciously breaks the rule.

1 - 8 oz. loaf of baguette bread
1 - 8 oz. cube of cream cheese
1 tbs. honey
2 cups peaches, sliced
1/4 cup peach jam

Preheat oven to 375°. Cut the Baguette in to 24 slices.
Slices should be about 1/4 inches thick. Place in a single layer on ungreased cookie sheet. Bake for 10 min. or until lightly brown.
Mix together cream cheese and honey; spread on one side of each slice of bread. Arrange peach slices on the cheese.
Heat jam in sauce pan over low heat until melted.
Brush jam over peaches.

# Your Journal Entry

*Liz's girls*

# Party Time
# Sweet and Sour Meatballs

1/2 cup finely chopped water chestnuts
1 tsp. fresh ginger root, divided
1/3 cup sliced green onions with tops
1 1/4 lb. lean ground beef
1 1/2 cups white bread crumbs (soft)
3 tbs. soy sauce
1 garlic clove, pressed
3/4 cup plum preserves
1/4 cup chili sauce

Preheat oven to 400°. Combine beef, bread crumbs, water chestnuts, 1/2 tsp. ginger root, green onions, soy sauce and garlic, mix gently. Shape into balls, place in a single layer in pan. Bake 15 min. Remove from oven. Remove juices from pan. Combine preserves, chili sauce and remaining 1/2 tsp. ginger root; pour over meatballs and mix gently to coat meatballs evenly. Return to oven, continue baking 15 min. Stir before serving. Makes about 40 meatballs.

*Marcia & Adam, 1988*

# Pineapple Jam Meatballs

## Meatballs

1 1/2 lb. meat loaf mixture or lean ground beef
1/2 cup bread crumbs
1/4 cup finely chopped onion
1 tsp. salt
1 tsp. dry mustard
2 tbs. chili sauce
1 egg

## Sauce

1 (12 oz.) jar pineapple jam
1/3 cup chili sauce
1/4 cup bourbon
1/4 tsp. hot pepper sauce

Heat oven to 400°. In large bowl, combine all meatball ingredients; mix well.
Shape into 1 1/4 inch meatballs. Place in ungreased 15 x 10 x 1 inch baking
pan. Bake for 15 to 20 min. Meanwhile, in large saucepan, combine all sauce
ingredients; mix well. Cook over low heat until mixture is bubbly, stirring
frequently. Add cooked meatballs to sauce; stir gently to coat.
48 meatballs; 24 servings
Sub with apricot or peach jam
Cut up large pieces of fruit in the jam.

# Your Journal Entry

Tevin Nuttall

# Quick Chicken Jubilee

1 - 3 1/2 lb. chicken, cut into serving size pieces
2 tbs. butter salt & pepper
1 jar plus 1/4 cup blackberry seedless jam
1 can pitted dark sweet cherries
1/4 cup lemon juice
2 tbs. cornstarch
1/4 cup water
2 tps. slivered lime peel

Brown chicken in butter at 350°. Season with salt and pepper. Blend in jam. Drain cherries and set fruit aside. Add liquid to sauce; stir in lemon juice. Reduce heat to 212°. Cover and simmer until chicken is tender; stir now and then. Blend cornstarch into water; stir into sauce and cook, stirring until sauce is thickened and smooth. Add cherries and lime peel. Heat and serve over hot cooked rice. Makes 4 servings.

# Your Journal Entry

*Boyce Family*

# Quick Fruit Dip

1 1/3 cup vanilla lowfat yogurt
1/4 cup jam
1/4 tsp. ground cinnamon

Combine all ingredients and chill for an hour.

*Chana & her daughters*

# Turkey - Cranberry Quesadillas

8 - (6 to 7) flour tortillas
1 (10 or 12 oz.) container cranberry-orange sauce,
    thawed if frozen
6 oz. thinly sliced smoked turkey
5 oz. harvarti cheese, thinly sliced
1 tbs. oil

Top each of 4 tortillas with 1 tbs. of the cranberry-orange sauce; spread to edges. Top each with turkey, cheese and second tortilla. Heat med. skillet over med. heat. Brush one side of 1 quesadilla with oil. Place, oiled side down, in med. skillet; press down with pancake turner. Cook 1 or 2 min. or until brown. Brush top side of quesadilla with oil, turn quesadilla. Cook and additional 1 or 2 min. or until browned and cheese is melted. Repeat with remaining quesadillas.
Cut each quesadilla into 6 wedges. Serve quesadillas with remaining cranberry-orange sauce.

# Your Journal Entry

*Picturetime at the Donaldson's*

Insert
your own...

...family favorites!

From the kitchen of: _____

# Dinner at Mom's Diner

*P*ut mom in "Time Out"!
*Alternate each family
member to choose the menu
for dinner and prepare
the meal!  Double up
if needed with the little ones!*

Joey called earlier and
put in his order for
dinner.
Michael wants  pumpkin pie,
Bob – green bean casserole,
his mother – sweet potatoes.
It doesn't matter what
occasion – each one has
a favorite. Must be the same
for everyone... If I could learn
to make my Grandma's
mustard pickles...

*T*oo busy for dinner
*together as a family!
Write a note to
everyone on the message
board about your day!
Give "atta boy's"
and stars to each
other as you read
their stories!*

*J*ust for fun!
*Have everyone
dress up in
"Sunday Best"
for dinner on
a regular occassion.
Or wear costumes!
Go silly and put
you clothes on
backwards.*

## Preserving the fruits of time

# Apricot Pineapple Chicken

1 bottle (16 oz.) creamy french dressing
2 pkgs dry onion mix
2 - 8 oz. jars apricot-pineapple jam
4-6 boneless chicken breasts
3 cups instant rice

Mix all ingredients together in a bowl.  Prepare chicken (saute, fry or bake).
Make about 3 cups instant rice.  Put rice in a 9 x 13 pan.
Put chicken on top of the rice and pour the sauce mixture on top
of the rice and chicken.
Bake for 25 min. at 350°.
You can add red sugared cherries on top for decoration.

# Your Journal Entry

*Grantsville Drug Store*

# Apricot Pork Chops

1 tbs. vegetable oil
4 boneless pork chops (1/2 to 1 inch thick)
1/2 cup apricot jam
1/4 cup apple cider
2 tbs. soy sauce
1 tsp. minced fresh ginger root
2 tbs. toasted walnuts

Heat oil in medium skillet; add pork.  Cook over medium-high heat
until browned, about 3 minutes.  Turn; brown second side.  Meanwhile,
combine jam, cider, soy sauce and ginger root.  Mix well.  Stir in toasted
walnuts.  Pour sauce over pork chops; reduce heat to low.
Cover; simmer about 10 mins. or until tender, turning once.
Romove pork; keep warm.  Boil sauce until it thickens slightly.
Serve sauce over pork.  Makes 4 servings.

# Your Journal Entry

*Art Higgins at the yard*

# Blackberry Glazed Pepper Steaks

Thoughts...

I'd rather say
"I'm fine"
with a grin
than tell'em
the shape I'm really in.

## Steaks
4 boneless steaks
1/2 cup fresh blackberries
3 tsp. ground pepper

## Glaze
1/4 cup red wine vinegar
1/2 cup blackberry jam

Heat glaze in small saucepan over medium heat. Stir well until jam is melted.
Remove from heat. Grill steaks over med. heat until done to your taste.
Spread with glaze topping and then put fresh berries on top.

# Your Journal Entry

The Pierce side of the family

# Butternut Squash Bisque

2 - 1/2 lbs. butternut squash
2 - sweet apples
3 - cups chicken broth
2 tbs. apricot jam
1/2 cup dry white wine
1/4 tsp. ground cinnamon
1/4 tsp. ground nutmeg

1/4 tsp. ground ginger
1/4 tsp. hot chili flakes
1/4 tsp. ground thyme
optional 1/4 cup butter
salt & pepper to taste

Rinse squash, cut in half and scoop out seeds. Place halves cut side down in a baking pan. Peel, halve, & core apples, add to pan, along with 1/4 cup water. Bake in a 400° regular or convection oven until squash and apples are tender when pierced (about 45 min.). Cool, scoop out flesh and discard peels. In a blender or food processor whirl squash and apples until smooth. Pour puree into 3 to 4 quart pan. Add wine, jam, and spices. Bring to a simmer over med. high heat; reduce heat and simmer, stirring occassionally, to blend flavors, about 15 min.
Add salt & pepper to taste.

# Your Journal Entry

When I was five my mom took me on my first trip to
Yellowstone, my big sister kissed a boy and I got to see a bear.

# Herb-Crusted
# Pork Roast w-Apricot

1 - 4 lb. pork roast, boneless
1 - (8 oz.) cream cheese with chives & onions
1 cup apricot jam
1/2 cup dried apricots chopped
1 garlic clove, minced
2 tsp. dried rosemary leaves

1 tsp. dried thyme leaves, crushed
3/4 tsp. pepper
1/2 tsp. salt
1 tbs. oil
gravy

Preheat oven to 325.° Remove string from meat. Cut 2 1/2 inch wide
pocket through meat. Stir together cream cheese, jam, & apricot in
small bowl until well mixed. Stuff it into the pocket of the meat. Coat
meat with combined garlic and seasonings; pat with oil. Place meat,
fat side up, on rack in baking pan. Roast 1 hour to 1 1/2 hrs. or until
meat temp. is at 165.° Let stand covered for 15 min. before slicing.
Remove meat from pan to platter.
Reserve dripping to make gravy, if desired

# Your Journal Entry

Rollin, Rollin, Rollin

*At the Homestead*

# Old Fashioned Jam Cake

1/2 cup butter
1 1/4 cup sugar
3 egg yolks
1 tsp. soda
1 cup buttermilk
2 1/4 cup flour

1/4 tsp. salt
1/4 tsp. cloves
1/2 tsp. cinnamon
1/2 tsp. allspice
1 cup strawberry jam
3 egg whites

Cream together butter, sugar, & egg yolks, Dissolve soda in buttermilk
separately.  Sift together flour, salt, cloves, cinnamon and allspice, and add to
creamed mixture.  Gently mix together and stir in jam.  Beat egg whites stiff
and fold in last.  Pour into loaf pans and bake at 375° for 35-40 min.
Frost with butter cream frosting.

# Your Journal Entry

*Pugh Family*

# Peach Cobbler

6 oz. peach jam
1 - 16 oz. canned peaches, save juice
1 tbs. flour
1 tbs. baking powder
1/3 cup milk
1 1/2 cup flour
1/4 cup butter

Place peaches into buttered 2 qt. baking dish. Combine 1 1/2 cup flour
& baking powder. Cut in with pastry blender 1/4 cup butter. Add milk
mixing lightly with fork. Turn on a well floured board and roll to fit the top
of the baking dish. Lay on top of jam making several incisions.
Add juice on top. Bake at 350° for 45 min.
Serve with cream, dairy topping, or ice cream.

# Your Journal Entry

*Grandpa Boyce in Holladay*

# Spice Rubbed Halibut

3/4 lb. halibut 1" thick; cut into pieces
1/2 tsp. corriander
1/2 tsp. ground cumin
1/2 tsp. curry powder
1/4 tsp. ground ginger
1/4 tsp. salt

1/8 tsp. cayenne
1/4 cup orange juice
3 tbs. rice vinegar
3 tbs. apricot jam
1 tbs. fresh ginger

Rinse fish and pat dry. In a small bowl mix spices. Rub mixture all over fish. Set pieces slightly apart in an 8" sq. pan. Broil 6" from heat for 3 min. With a wide spatula, turn fish over and broil until opaque but still moist looking in center of thickest part (3-5 min.). Meanwhile, in a 1 to 1 1/2 quart pan over med. heat, bring orange juice, vinegar, jam and fresh ginger to a boil. Stir often until reduced to about a 1/4 cup (about 10 min.). With a spatula, transfer fish to plates and spoon sauce over fish.

*Liz Ranes and fish @ Market Street Grill*

Insert
your own...

...family favorites!

From the kitchen of: _____

# Out with the In-laws

**B**uy a book and learn to fold napkins into animals and objects.

Jay's parents are coming to dinner next Sunday! My first for the in-laws. His mother is such a good cook – what can I make that will be special and a little different...

**A**t each place setting, put a card expressing your appreciation for each of your parents. Adults and children alike can participate here!

**T**o make your table special, scatter confetti or even objects from your own back yard.

Preserving the fruits of time

# Curry & Ginger
# Rubbed Lamb Chops

2 1/2 tbs. curry powder
1 1/2 tbs. minced peeled fresh ginger
1 1/2 tsp. olive oil
1/4 tsp. kosher salt
1/8 tsp. black pepper
8 6 oz. lamb chops
1/2 cup apricot-lime sauce

## Apricot-lime sauce

2/3 cup apricot jam            1/4 cup ketchup
1/2 cup fresh lime juice       1/4 cup worcestershire sauce
1/3 cup golden raisins         1 tsp. hot sauce
1/3 cup chopped fresh mint     1/4 tsp. kosher salt
1/4 cup balsamic vinegar       1/4 tsp. black pepper

Melt Jam in a saucepan over med.-low heat.
Stir in the remaining ingredients.
Remove from heat. Makes 2 cups.

Prepare grill. Combine the curry, ginger, oil, salt, and pepper; rub paste
evenly over lamb. Place lamb on grill rack, and cook 4 minutes.
Turn lamb; brush with 1/4 cup apricot-lime sauce. Cook for 4 minutes.
Turn lamb, and brush with 1/4 cup sauce. Cook 2 minutes, turning once.

# Your Journal Entry

*Lewis Hatch and friends celebrate the new Bamburger Line*

# Curry-Peach Glaze

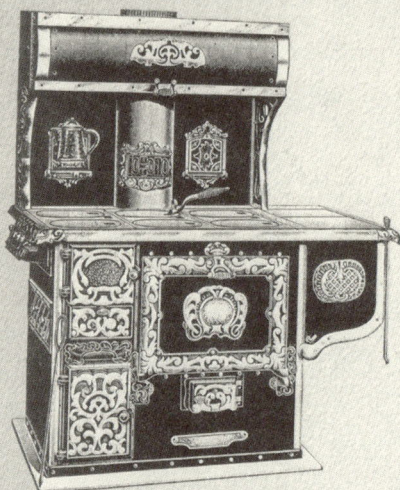

1/2 cup peach jam
1/4 cup margarine or butter
1 tsp. curry powder

In small saucepan, combine all ingredients: mix well. Cook over med. heat until melted and smooth, stirring constantly. Brush over poultry frequently during baking or grilling. If desired, heat any remaining sauce to a boil; serve with poultry.

# Your Journal Entry

*Madison Eckman, granddaughter*

# Glazed Peach Chicken with Pecan Dressing

## Glaze

1/2 cup peach jam
2 tbs. red wine vinegar
2 tbs. butter

## Stuffing

1/2 cup chopped celery
1/2 cup chopped onion
1/4 cup butter
3 cups herb seasoned stuffing
1/4 cup pecan halves, toasted
1/2 cup dried cranberries
1 1/4 cups chicken broth
4 boneless, skinless chicken breast

Combine jam, vinegar and butter in small saucepan. Bring to a boil over medium heat; boil 1 minute or until glaze thickens. Cool slightly. Heat oven to 375°. Cook celery and onion in butter in small skillet. Combine onion mixture with stuffing, pecans, cranberries and chicken broth. Stir until broth is absorbed. Place in lightly greased 3-quart casserole dish. Place chicken over stuffing. Brush with glaze. Cover. Bake 20 minutes. Remove cover, brush chicken generously with glaze. Bake 15 to 20 min. longer or until juices run clear. Basting once or twice. Makes 4 servings.

# Your Journal Entry

# Grape Dumplings

2 cups flour
4 tsp. baking powder
1/4 tsp. salt
1/3 cup sugar
1/2 cup butter
3/4 cup milk
4 cups grape juice
1 - 10 oz. jar grape jam
2 tbs. lemon juice

Sift flour, baking powder, salt and 1 tbs. sugar. Cut in butter using pastry blender or two kitchen knives until mixture resembles coarse meal. Stir in milk until mixture leaves sides of bowl. Roll out on lightly floured board and cut into 2 inch squares. In large heavy saucepan, heat juice and jam, remaining sugar, and lemon juice to boiling. Add dumplings. Cover and simmer 20 min. or until tender. Serve hot.

# Your Journal Entry

# Ham Grape Roll-ups

1 pkg. (3 oz.) cream cheese, softened
1/3 cup grape jam
1/4 cup crushed pineapple, well drained
1/4 cup chopped peanuts
8 slices ham
4 hot dog rolls
butter

Blend cream cheese, jam and pineapple. Stir in nuts. Overlap 2 slices of ham. Place about 1/4 cup pineapple mixture on one end and roll up. Repeat with remaining ham and spread. Spread rolls lightly with butter, place ham rolls inside.

# Your Journal Entry

*The family getting ready for a party*

# Peach Bars

YELLOW CRAWFORD PEACHES

4 1/2 cup flour
2 cup sugar
1/2 cup chopped nuts
2 cup butter
2 eggs
12 oz. peach jam
caramel topping

Preheat oven to 350°. In large mixer bowl combine all ingredients except peach jam and caramel topping. Beat at low speed until mixed well. Reserve 1/2 mixture; set aside. Press remaining mixture into the prepared 9 x 13 pan; spread jam to within 1/2" from edge. Spoon evenly the rest of the batter. Take the caramel topping and spread lightly for decoration. Bake for 45 minutes or until lightly brown.

# Your Journal Entry

*"No more training wheels"*

# Raspberry Ganache Fudge Cake

3 eggs
1 cup oil
1 cup buttermilk
1 1/2 cups hot water
2 tsp. vanilla
3 cups flour

3 cups sugar
1 cup cocoa
1 1/4 tsp. soda
1 tsp. baking powder
1 tsp. salt
1 3/4 cup heavy cream

Grease and flour 12 inch Dutch oven. Mix in bowl eggs, oil, buttermilk, water, vanilla, sugar, flour, cocoa, soda, baking powder, and salt. Mix on med. speed for 2 min. Bake on the bottom coals arranged on top for 50 min. or until done. Let cool for at least 15 min. then dump and cool completely on wire rack. When cool cut cake into two layers.

Ganache: In med. saucepan melt 1 1/2 lbs of choc. stir in 1 cup heavy cream. Stir will until smooth. Add raspberry jam until it looks about the same as frosting. You may need to add a little extra cream. Spread in between the two layers. Make the Glaze by melting 1 lb. choc. and stirring in 3/4 cup heavy cream. The glaze should be thinner than the Ganache. Spread over top of cake and top with some fresh raspberries.

Nancy Boyce

# Stuffed Veal Loin

2 (3/4 lb.) veal loins
8 oz. jar peach jam
2 tbs. honey
2 tbs. butter
1 onion finely chopped
1/3 lb. mushrooms finely chopped
1/2 tsp. tarragon
2 tbs. ricotta cheese
2 tbs. breadcrumbs
salt / pepper

Preheat grill. Trim fat from veal. Slice both loins open lengthwise. Take 6 oz. jam and put into small saucepan. Add honey and cook for 15 min. on high to thicken. Remove from heat and let cool. Heat butter in second saucepan. Cook onion 2 min. over med. heat. Add mushrooms and seasoning, cook 4 min. over high heat. Remove from stove. Stir in cheese and breadcrumbs. Spread stuffing on both sides of meat. Add peach jam and close, secure with kitchen string. Brush loins with peach mixture. Cook 30 minutes turning often. Baste before serving.

*Doris & Rags, age 3*

Insert
your own...

...family favorites!

From the kitchen of: _____

# Timeless Treasures

**T**ell a story! Tonight at dinner, or bedtime, share a story about your parents or grandparents with your children. Teach them to pass down the stories through generations.

I found some old love letters Grandma gave me. Grandpa wrote them to her while he in the war. I tried to imagine what life must have been like. Grandpa out defending our freedoms. Grandma here taking care of a little one. Grandpa didn't talk much about the war, but grandma always says how he was a hero and all...

**A**s a family go to a history museum or something to celebrate your pioneer heritage.

**H**ave one of the children record their version of the story in the jounal.

Preserving the Fruits of Time

APRICOT - PINEAPPLE JAM

## Preserving the fruits of time

# Cinnamon French Toast Bread Pudding

## Bread Pudding

1- 1 1/2 loaves of day old bread cut into pieces
Mix together the following:
2 qts. heavy whipping cream
1 cup sugar
1 tbs. vanilla
2 tbs. cinnamon
15 whole eggs

Pour this mixture over the bread. The cream mixture will soak into the bread and make sure all the bread is covered and well soaked. Bake at 325° for approximately 45 minutes to 1 hour. When cooked the mixture will "poof" up high and it should have a "set" look. Refrigerate overnight. Remove from refrigerator and cut into 12 pieces.

## French Toast Procedure

8 egg whites
3 cups peach slices in heavy syrup
6 oz. pure maple syrup

Separate egg whites and beat until frothy. Dip the cut pieces of bread in the egg whites. In 1 tbs. of butter saute the bread pieces in a hot skillet on both sides until golden brown and remove bread pieces and place on serving plates. To the skillet add the maple syrup, peach slices and syrup from the peaches. Reduce until glossy. Ladle over the french toast and top with Cinnamon Butter (8 oz. of butter and 1 tbs. of cinnamon).

# Your Journal Entry

# Crepes

Thoughts...

New table cloth - $40.
Chips and dip - $15.
Film - $5.
An afternoon of laughter
with friends and good food
- priceless.

3 eggs
1 1/2 cup milk
2/3 cup flour
1 tbs. sugar
1 tbs. melted butter or oil
1 tbs. brandy

Mix milk and eggs in blender. Blend until smooth. Cover and put in refrigerator for 2 hrs. Pour 2 tbs. batter for each crepe on to lightly buttered, 6-8 inch pan over medium heat. Cook on an old time skillet until brown on both sides.

# Your Journal Entry

*Jackie & her best friend (daughter)*

# Easel

1 cup shortening
3/4 cup sugar
1/2 cup brown sugar
2 eggs
1 1/2 cup seedless raspberry jam
1 tsp. vanilla
2 cups flour
1 tsp. baking soda
1 tsp. baking powder
1 1/2 tsp. cinnamon
2 cups oats

Preheat oven to 375°. Mix shortening, sugar, and brown sugar. Stir until creamy. Add eggs, jam, and vanilla. In separate bowl combine flour, soda, baking powder and cinnamon. Add to other mixture. Add oats.
Drop onto cookie sheet and bake for about 10 min.

# Your Journal Entry

*Chana & Andrew on their Wedding day*

# Ebleskivers

2 cups flour
4 eggs, separated
1/2 tsp. salt
1 tbs. sugar
1 tsp. baking powder
1/4 cup melted shortening
milk, scant 2 cups

*Serve with your favorite Jam.*

Beat egg yolks, add sugar.
Sift dry ingredients and add alternately with milk.
Fold in beaten egg whites. Bake in Ebelskiver pan
until brown on both sides.

_Great Aunt Lizzie_

# Lemon Curd

KING TUT BRAND
LEMONS

PACKED BY
JOHNSTON FRUIT CO., SANTA BARBARA, CAL.

Thoughts...

Now & then
everyone needs
a little
help from
a friend.

1 - 1/3 cups sugar
4 egg yolks
1 tsp. lemon zest
1/3 cup lemon juice
1/4 cup real butter

Combine all ingredients in a blender.  Put into a double boiler.  Heat over medium and stir continually.  Stir for about 40 min. or until thickened. Keep refrigerated.

# Your Journal Entry

*Reha Jacobs*

# Strawberry Cream Cheese Frosting

## THOUGHTS

*This flavorful topping adds a nice accent to plainer cookies. Try 1 teaspoon atop a Vanilla Wafer or 1/2 tablespoon spread on a sugar cookie.*

3 oz cream cheese,
at room temperature
1/3 cup ricotta cheese
1/3 cup strawberry jam
1/4 teaspoon orange extract
1/4 cup confectioners sugar

Combine the cream cheese and ricotta cheese in a bowl and beat with an electric mixer at medium speed until creamy and smooth. Beat in the jam and orange extract. Sift in the confectioner's sugar and beat at medium speed until the mixture is well combined and thick.

# Your Journal Entry

*This cake is mine --- all mine!*

# Strawberry - Rhubarb Pie

1 baked pie shell
21 oz. strawberry-rhubarb jam

**Topping**
1/4 cup flour
1/2 cup brown sugar, well packed
1/3 cup butter softened

Prepare shell. Spoon jam into shell. Blend flour, brown sugar & cut in
softened butter. Sprinkle topping over strawberry- rhubarb mixture.
Bake at 425 for 10 min. Reduce heat to 350 and bake for 40 min.
or until done.

# Your Journal Entry

*Grandma's 85th Birthday*

# Thumbprints

1 - 8 oz. pkg. cream cheese, softened
3/4 cup butter
1 cup powdered sugar
2 1/4 cup flour
1/2 tsp. baking soda
1 cup pecan nuts
1 tsp. vanilla
your favorite jam

Preheat oven to 325°. Beat cream cheese, butter and sugar in a large mixing bowl at med. speed. Add flour and baking soda, mix well. Add chopped pecans and vanilla to dough and chill for 30 min. Shape dough into 1-inch balls. Place on engrossed cookie sheet. Indent centers and fill each with 1 tsp. of jam. Bake 14-16 min. or until edges begin to brown. Cool on wire rack.

# Your Journal Entry

_Eleisa, 8_

Insert
your own...

...family favorites!

From the kitchen of: _____

# Home on the Range

**W**ho is your hero?
Tell a story about
someone in your
family who has done
something you think
is heroic!

When I was twelve my dad
took me hunting. Just us!
I felt like the big man.
We left when it was
still dark and carried
the decoys out about
500 miles - well it felt
like it. Then set up
to wait for the ducks.
We got skunked. I still
look forward to hunting
with him.

**W**rite a special
message to your
wife between the
pages of this book.
She'll see how much
you love her every
time she uses her
favorite cookbook!

**P**aste a
favorite
photo with
a favorite
recipe
from grandma
in the journal!

*Preserving the fruits of time*

# Apple Red Current Bread

1 cup canola oil
2 cups sugar
4 tsp. soda
1 tsp. salt
2 cups raisins or cut-up dates
2 tsp. nutmeg
1 cup nuts, chopped

4 cups flour
3 cups applesauce
2 eggs
4 tsp. cinnamon
2 tsp. allspice
1 tsp. cloves
1/2 cup red current jelly

Mix sugar, oil, applesauce and eggs together. Add sifted dty ingredients.
Mix well; then add raisins and nut. Bake at 350° for 50 min.
Makes 3 big bread loaves, or 6 small loaves.

# Your Journal Entry

# Apricot - Pineapple Bread

3/4 cup water
2 1/2 cups flour
1/2 tsp. baking soda
1/2 cup chopped walnuts
1/3 cup shortening
3 tbs. orange juice

16 oz. apricot-pineapple jam
1 tsp. baking powder
1/2 tsp. salt
2/3 cup sugar
2 eggs
1/2 cup raisins

Preheat oven to 350.° Cover and simmer water and Apricot/Pineapple
jam in small sauce pan. Sift together flour, baking powder, baking soda,
and salt. Mix in nuts. Mix together sugar and shortening bowl; beat in
orange juice and Apricot-Pineapple jam. Add flour nut mixture and
mix well. Pour batter into 9x5x3 greased bread loaf pan. Bake for
40-50 mins. or until done. Cool 10 minutes remove from pans
and cool on racks.

# Your Journal Entry

*Smile Joanie Smile*

# Cranberry Bread

2 cups whole wheat flour
2 cups white flour
1 tsp. baking powder
1 tsp. baking soda
1 tsp. salt
1/2 tsp. cinnamon
1/4 tsp. nutmeg
1 cup brown sugar
1 cup white sugar

1/2 cup butter
1 tbs. grated orange rind
1/2 cup orange juice
1 cup orange marmalade
2 eggs
2 cups fresh cranberries - coursely chopped
1 cup chopped nuts
2/3 cup raisins

Sift dry ingredients. Cut butter until mixture is like coarse meal. In another bowl, combine orange rind, orange juice, orange marmalade, and eggs. Add to dry, mix to moisten. Fold in berries, nuts and raisins. Bake at 350° in floured 9"x5" loaf pans for 40-45 min.

Thoughts...

The shell must break before the bird can fly.

Tennyson

# Your Journal Entry

*Learning proper dental hygiene at an early age is a very important thing*

# Cranberry Scones

3 1/2 cups old fashioned heavy whipping cream
1/2 cup sugar
1 cup dried cranberries
1 tbs. baking powder
1 tsp. salt
5 1/2 cups flour

Use dough hook attachment on mixer. Add 3 cups of the heavy whipping cream (reserving 1/2 cup of the heavy whipping cream for the top of the scones). Hook until mixture pulls away from the sides of the mixing bowl, but don't over mix. Remove dough to a lightly floured surface and with a rolling pin roll to an inch and 1/2 thickness. Cut with the 3" circle cookie cutter and dip the top of the scone into the reserved heavy whipping cream and place on the lightly greased baking sheet or baking sheet with parchment paper. Generously sprinkle the top of each scone with sugar after you have dipped the scone.
Bake at 325° for approx. 20-25 min., or until golden brown.

*Homestead Recipe*

# Your Journal Entry

# Lemony Chicken Puff

## Popover Puff

3 tbs. butter
1 cup milk
6 eggs
1 cup flour
1/2 tsp. salt

## Chicken & Veggie filling

2 med. carrots, peeled and cut
1 cup sugar snap peas, cut in half
1/2 cup chopped onion
1 tbs. butter
1 lemon (juice of a lemon to make 2 tbs.)
1 can condensed cream of chicken soup
1/2 cup peach jam
1 cup diced red bell pepper
1 1/2 cup dill mix
1/2 cup shredded cheddar cheese
2 cups diced white meat chicken

Preheat oven to 450°. Brush 1 tbs. butter into baking dish. Combine milk, eggs and remaining butter with a whisk. Stir together flour and salt in a separate bowl. Add flour mixture to egg mixture. Whisk 1 min. or until smooth. Pour batter into baking pan. Bake 20 min. Reduce oven temp. to 350°. Continue to bake 10-15 min. or until golden brown.
Prepare chicken and veggie filling. Cook in microwave carrots, snap peas, onions and butter for 2-3 on high; set aside. Combine lemon juice, soup, chicken, bell pepper and dill mix. Microwave on high 4-5 min. Add cheese and half of the veggie mixture into filling. Remove puffs from oven, cool. Spoon filling into puff to the edges. Pull the edges from the sides of pan.

# Your Journal Entry

*Halloween favorites*

# Peanut Butter Yummies

Thoughts...

A year from now
don't wish you
had started today.

2 cups peanut butter
1 lb. powdered sugar
2/3 cup butter
1 pkg. graham crackers
1/3 cup butter
12 oz. chocolate chips
1 cup jam

Combine graham crackers (finely crushed), butter, powdered sugar and peanut butter until blended by hand. Pack down into an 8 x 8 inch square pan. Spread jam onto mixture. In small sauce pan, melt 1/3 cup butter and chocolate chips until melted. Spread over jam. Refrigerate for one hour and serve in small pieces.

# Your Journal Entry

*Art in the Garden*
*Allan Lipman & John Lemke*

# Old Jam Cookies

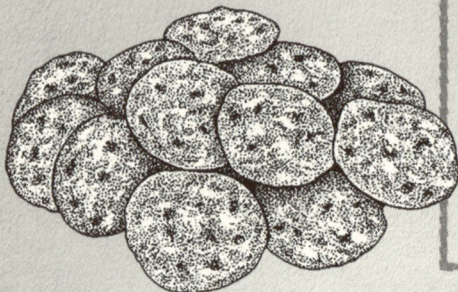

1 1/2 cups jam
2 eggs
1/2 cup shortening
2 cups flour
1 tsp. baking soda

1 tsp. baking powder
1/2 tsp. cinnamon
1/2 tsp. nutmeg and cloves
1 cup nuts

Mix all ingredients until well blended.
Bake at 350° for 10 to 20 minutes.

# Your Journal Entry

*This is my "Cool" hair doo!*

# Pineapple Zucchini Bread

1 cup vegatable oil
3 eggs
1/2 cup sugar
1 tsp. vanilla
2 cups shredded zucchini
1 cup pineapple jam

3 cups flour
1 1/2 tsp. ground cinnamon
1 tsp. baking soda
3/4 tsp. salt
3/4 tsp. ground nutmeg
1 cup raisins
1/2 cup chopped walnuts

Mix oil, eggs, sugar, and vanilla in large bowl; stir in zucchini and pineapple jam. Combine flour, cinnamon, baking soda, salt, and nutmeg in med. mixing bowl; stir into oil mixture. Stir in raisins and walnuts if desired. Spread batter evenly in 2 greased and floured 8 1/2 x 4 1/2 x 2 1/2 inch loaf pans. Bake in preheated 350° oven, until breads are golden and toothpick comes out clean, 50-60 minutes.
Remove from pans and cool completely.

# Your Journal Entry

Grantsville Drug Store

Insert
your own...

...family favorites!

From the kitchen of:

# Home for the Holidays

*T*he little ones can participate in holiday occasions by coloring place mats or name cards for each of the family members.

Three more days... I can make it. No more stress of finals. A long drive to paradise. Mom's cooking and Dad's big bear hugs. I talked to Joey last night. He'll be there in time for the blessing on the turkey. Said he'd asked mom to make extra mashed potatoes and jam cookies - said I better get my order in now...

*C*reate a special center piece from favorite family pictures of holiday's past.

*S*tart a genealogy scrapbook. Begin with your own family. Let the children pick the photos!

APRICOT - PINEAPPLE JAM

*Preserving the fruits of time*

# Apricot Marmalade Bars

1 1/2 cup matzo meal
3/4 cup potato starch
1 tsp. ground cinnamon
1 tsp. salt
6 large eggs
1 1/2 cups sugar

1 cup canola oil
2 large peaches peeled/sliced/stoned
7 apricots peeled/sliced/stoned
1/2 cup apricot-peach jam

Preheat oven 350°. Lightly grease 9x13 baking pan. Put the matzo meal in food processor. Process for 1 minute. Add the potato starch, cinnamon, and salt and process for another 15 seconds. Mix eggs and 1 1/2 cup sugar in large mixing bowl. Beat at med. speed until light and frothy. At low speed, beat in the oil, mixing until well combined. Add the matzo mixture and stir with wooden spoon. Pour 2/3 of the batter into the prepared baking pan. Layer the peaches and apricots on top of the batter. Dollop the jam over the fruit by the tbs. Pour the remaining batter on top. Bake for 55-60 minutes or until cake is golden. Remove to a wire rack, dust top with remaining tbs. of sugar. Cool in the pan.

# Your Journal Entry

"Sisters"

Ruth      Luana      Irene

# Black Forest Pie

15 oz. pkg. refrigerated pie crusts
1 tsp. flour

### Filling
2/3 cup sugar
1/2 cup unsweetened cocoa
2 tbs. flour
1/4 cup margarine or butter
1/4 cup milk
2 eggs, beaten
21 oz. can cherry fruit pie filling
1/3 cup cherry preserves

### Topping
9 oz. container frozen whipped topping, thawed
1 oz. (1 square) unsweetened chocolate, coarsely grated

In med. saucepan, combine sugar, coca, preserves and flour. Stir in margarine and milk. Cook over medium heat until mixture begins to boil, stirring constantly. Remove from heat. Blend small amount of hot mixture into eggs. Return to saucepan; blend well. Fold half of cherry pie filling into chocolate mixture; reserve remaining pie filling for topping. Pour chocolate mixture into pie crust-lined pan. Bake at 350° for 35 to 45 min. or until center is set but still shiny. Cool. Refrigerate 1 hour. Combine 2 cups of the whipped topping and grated chocolate; spread over cooled pie. Top with reserved pie filling and remaining whipped topping. Decorate with chocolate curls or as desired. Refrigerate at least 30 min. before serving time.

# Your Journal Entry

# Blackberry Linzer Squares

1 cup almonds
1 1/4 cup flour
1/2 cup sugar
1/2 tsp. baking powder
1/8 tsp. salt
1 tsp. ground cinnamon

1/2 tbs. finely grated lemon zest
1/4 tsp. ground cloves
1/2 cup butter, melted
2 large eggs
10 oz. seedless blackberry jam
1 tsp. powdered sugar

Preheat oven to 350°. Finely chop almonds. Put them in large mixing bowl. Add flour, sugar, salt, baking powder, cinnamon, cloves, and lemon zest. Whisk thoroughly. Add butter and eggs. Stir with wooden spoon. Form into ball and cut in half. Wrap one half in wax paper, put in fridge for 15 minutes. Put the other half in 9 x 9 ungreased pan. Pat it down to cover bottom of pan. Coat the top evenly with blackberry jam leaving a 1/2 inch outer border. Divide the chilled dough into 14 pieces. Work each into a thin rope about 9 inches long. In each direction, lay 5 ropes of dough over the top at 1 1/2 inch intervals, forming a lattice pattern. Place 4 ropes around outer border. Bake for 35-40 minutes or until golden brown. Cool in the pan on wire rack for 1 hour. Sprinkle with powdered sugar.

# Your Journal Entry

*Sisters by fate,*
*friends by choice*

# Blintzes with Raspberry Sauce

1 16 oz. cottage cheese
3 tbs. egg beaters
1/2 tsp. sugar
10 prepared crepes (see crepe recipe pg. 112)

## Raspberry Sauce
8 oz. raspberry jam
1 package frozen raspberries thawed

In small bowl, combine cottage cheese, egg beaters, and sugar; spread 2 tbs. mixture down center of each crepe. Fold two opposite ends of each crepe over filling, then fold in sides like an envelope. In lightly greased large nonstick skillet, over med. heat, place blintzes seam-side down.
Cook for 4 minutes on each side or until golden brown. Serve hot with raspberry sauce.
Raspberry sauce: In blender puree pkg. of raspberries, strain, stir in jam. Serve over hot blintzes.

# Your Journal Entry

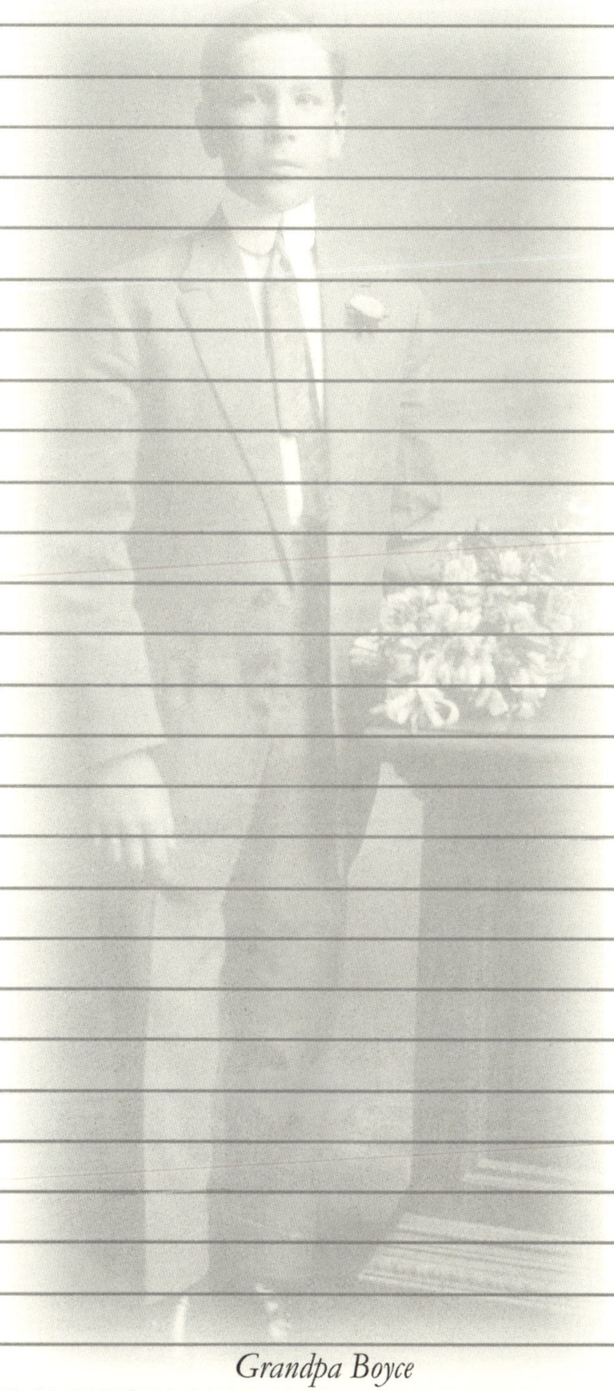

*Grandpa Boyce*

# Fresno Fruit Sauce

FRUIT.

1/2 cup raisins
1/2 cup water
1/4 cup peach jam
1/2 cup orange juice
1/4 cup packed brown sugar
1 tbs. cornstarch
1/8 tsp. ground allspice

In a 4 cup saucepan, combine raisins, water, jam, and orange juice.
Cover with waxed paper. Stirring once, heat on high 3-4 minutes or until
jam is melted. Set aside. In small bowl, combine brown sugar, cornstarch,
and allspice. Stir into raisin mixture. Stirring every 30 seconds, cook on
high 1 1/2-3 minutes. Serve with baked ham, pork chops, or duck.
Makes 1 1/2 cups.

# Your Journal Entry

*Kathy and the kids*

# Holiday Fruit Salad

2 apples, chopped
1 ripe pear, peeled and chopped
1/2 cup shelled walnuts, broken and toasted
1/4 cup dried cranberries
1/2 cup sour cream
1/4 cup orange marmalade

1 tbs. lemon juice
2 tsp. orange rind
1 banana, sliced
lettuce for garnish

Combine all ingredients except banana and lettuce; mix well. Cover and refridgerate until serving. Salad may be prepared up to 4 hours prior to serving. Add bananas before serving. Place lettuce leaf on individual serving plates. Spoon salad onto lettuce leaves.

# Your Journal Entry

_Grandma Hollee & Tevin_

# Rio Grande Pork Roast

Thoughts...

Even if you're on the right track, you'll get run over if you just sit there.

Rogers

1/2 cup apple jam
1/2 cup ketchup
1 tbs. vinegar
1/2 tsp. chili powder
1/4 tsp. liquid smoke
3-4 lb. boneless pork loin roast

1/2 tsp. salt
1/2 garlic salt
1/2 tsp. chili powder
1 tbs. flour
1 cup crushed corn chips

Preheat oven to 350°.
Combine jam, ketchup, vinegar, and 1/2 tsp. chili powder in a 2 cup measure. Heat on high 3 1/2 min. or until mixture comes to a boil. Stir and set aside. Rub liquid smoke over roast. Combine salt, garlic salt & 1/2 tsp. chili powder, sprinkle over roast. Shield ends of roast by covering with small, smooth piece of foil. Place roast fat-side down in a 10 x 16 oven cooking bag that has been sprinkled with 1 tbs. flour. Place bag with roast in a 12 x 17 inch baking dish. Cook on low 16-20 min. per pound for 1/2 time required. Remove foil; turn roast fat-side up. Brush with jam and cook on low remaining time. Meat should temp at 160 F. Remove from bag. Brush generously with glaze. Sprinkle with corn chips. Brown 10 minutes.

# Your Journal Entry

*Handsome & out-doorsy,*
*What more could a girl want?*

# Split Seconds

2/3 cup sugar
3/4 cup margarine or butter, softened
2 tsp. vanilla
1 egg
2 cups flour
1/2 tsp. baking powder
1/2 cup jam

Preheat oven to 350.° In large bowl, beat sugar and margarine until light and fluffy. Add vanilla and egg, beat well. Lightly spoon flour into measuring cup, level off. Stir in flour and baking powder, blend well. On lightly floured surface, divide dough into 4 equal parts. Shape each into a roll 12 x 3/4 inches, place on engrossed cookie sheets. Using handle of wooden spoon or finger, make a depression lengthwise down center of each roll about 1/2 inch wide and 1/4 inch deep. Fill each with 2 tbs. of the jam. Bake for 15-20 min. until golden brown. Cool slightly, cut diagonally into bar.

_Tersadie, Granddaughter_

Insert
your own...

...family favorites!

From the kitchen of:_____

# Slice of Life

**M**ake a basket with your favorite flavors of jam and write a couple of recipes from the cookbook to give as a gift! Or buy an extra copy for a friend!

My wedding day!! Allison stayed over the night before, we talked and talked! The next morning Jana and Chrissy came to the house! It was make up, hair, and nails a go-go! My mom and dad kept coming in the room, but we'd all start crying and have to fix my make up, so Allie shooed everyone out!...

**C**elebrate each child with their own day! Have the whole family participate. End the day with their favorite cake decorated in their honor!

**T**ake a "slice" of your life and record a journal entry today! Have each person in the family write one on the same day!

Preserving the fruits of time

# Amazin' Raisin Cake

3 cups flour
1 cup mayonnaise
2 eggs
1 1/2 tsp. cinnamon
1/2 tsp. salt
2 3/4 cups apples, peeled and chopped
1/2 cup walnuts, coarsely chopped
1 cup apple jelly

2 cups sugar
1/4 cup milk
2 tsp. baking soda
1/2 tsp. nutmeg
1/4 tsp. cloves
1 cup raisins
2 cups whipped cream

Grease and 2 - 9" round baking pans. Beat first 10 ingredients 2 min., scraping bowl frequently. Stir in apples, raisins and nuts. Pour into pans; bake at 350° for 45 min. Cool in pans 10 min.; remove from pans. Fill and frost with whipped cream. This is great cooked in loaf pans with a powdered sugar glaze too!

# Your Journal Entry

*Two things we give our children -- roots and wings !!*

# Anytime Oatmeal Cake

1 1/2 cups quick-cooking rolled oats
1 cup boiling water
3/4 cup sugar
1/2 cup brown sugar
1 cup margarine or butter, softened
1 tsp. vanilla
3 eggs
1 1/2 cups all purpose flour

1 tsp. baking soda
1/2 tsp. baking powder
1/2 tsp. salt
1 1/2 tsp. cinnamon
1/2 tsp. nutmeg
1/2 cup apricot jam

Heat oven to 350°. Grease and flour 13x9-inch pan. In small bowl, combine rolled oats and boiling water; let stand 20 min. In large bowl, beat sugar, brown sugar, margarine, and add vanilla, apricot jam and eggs. Bake for 30 minutes.

# Your Journal Entry

*Potential Plumber*

167

# Awesome Chocolate Cake

Thoughts...

Go as far as
you can see,
and when you
get there,
you will see farther.

2 cups sugar
1 3/4 cup flour
3/4 cup cocoa
1 1/2 tsp. baking powder
1 1/2 tsp. baking soda
2 eggs
1 cup milk
1/2 cup oil
2 tsp. vanilla extract
1 cup boiling water
1 cup seedless raspberry jam

## Frosting

1 stick butter
2/3 cup cocoa
3 cups powdered sugar
1/3 cup milk
1 tsp. vanilla

Heat oven to 350.° Combine dry ingredients in large bowl. Add eggs,
milk, oil and vanilla. Beat for 2 min. on medium speed. Stir in boiling
water. Pour into two 9" round greased and floured pans.
Bake 30-35 min. Cool 10 min. Remove pans to wire rack .
Cool completely. Put jam between layers, then frost.

## Frosting

Melt butter. Stir in cocoa. Alternately add powdered sugar and milk,
beating on med. speed to spreading consistency.
Add more milk if needed. Add vanilla.

168

# Your Journal Entry

*Fred's adopted folks*

# Blackberry - Lemon Pudding Cake

1 1/2 cups blackberries
3/4 tsp. powdered sugar
3/4 cup sugar
3 large egg whites
2 large egg yolks
1/4 cup flour
1/8 tsp. salt
1/8 ground nutmeg
1 cup buttermilk
1 tsp. grated lemon rind
1/4 cup lemon curd (see recipe)
2 tsp. butter

Preheat oven to 350°. Combine flour, 2/3 cup sugar, salt, and nutmeg
in large bowl. Add buttermilk, lemon rind, lemon curd, butter & egg yolks.
Stir well until smooth. Beat egg whites until foamy. Add 1/4 cup sugar,
1 tbs. at a time. Gently stir 1/4 of egg white mixture into the buttermilk
mixture. Gently stir in remaining egg whites. Add in blackberries.
Pour the batter into 8 in. square pan greased. Place 8 in. pan into larger
pan filled 1 deep of hot water. Bake for 35 minutes or until cake springs
back. Sprinkle cake with powdered sugar.

# Your Journal Entry

*Hollee Eckman (Author) & "greatest supportive" husband Fred*

# Blueberry Pie Supreme

Thoughts...

Choice,
not chance,
determines destiny.

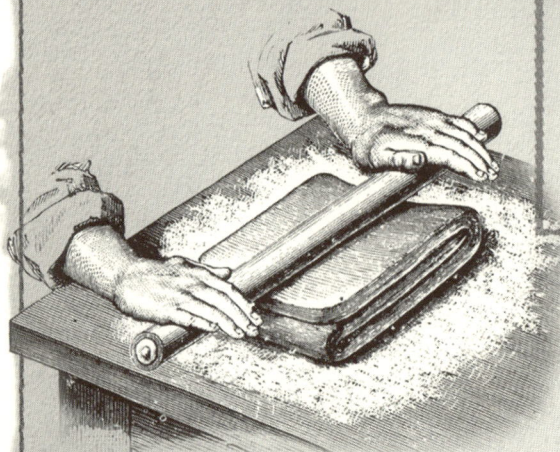

9 inch unbaked pie shell
21 oz. blueberry jam
12 oz. soft cream cheese
2 eggs
1 cup dairy sour cream
1/2 cup sugar
1/2 tsp. vanilla

Preheat oven to 425°. Prepare pie shell. Spread half blueberry jam in bottom; set rest of jam inside. Bake shell for 15 minutes, or just until crust is golden brown. Remove from oven. Reduce oven temp to 350.
In small bowl beat cream cheese, sugar, eggs and vanilla until smooth. Pour over hot blueberry jam, bake for 25 minutes (filling will be slightly soft in the center). Cool completely on wire rack. To serve, spoon sour cream around edges of pie. Fill with remaining jam.

# Your Journal Entry

*Big Brothers Big Sisters river trip*

# Easy Apricot - Pineapple Pie

Thoughts...

Here all mankind
is equal;
rich or poor alike;
they love
their children.

9" prepared graham cracker pie shell
1 pint sour cream
12 oz. apricot/pineapple jam
1 pkg. instant vanilla pudding (powdered)

Place in 9 inch pie shell.
Chill and serve.
Top with whipped cream if desired

# Your Journal Entry

Madison Eckman

# Raspberry Lemon-Mousse Cake

1pkg french vanilla cake
1 cup sour cream
3 eggs
1/4 cup oil
1tbs. grated lemon zest
3 cups heavy cream

3 tbs. sugar
1 1/4 cup lemon curd
1 cup seedless raspberry jam
1 cup fresh raspberries
1/4 cup water

Preheat oven to 350.° Grease and flour 2 9-in-round cake pans. Mix well on low speed, Cake mix sour cream, eggs, oil, 1/4 cup water and zest for 30 seconds. On med. speed mixer 2 minutes. Divide batter between pans. Bake for 25 minutes or until done. Cool on racks for 10 minutes. Remove from pans and cool completely. On med.-high speed beat cream and sugar. Reserve 3/4 cup. Cover and chill remaining whipped cream. For lemon mousse, fold in reserved 3/4 cup whipped cream the lemon curd and chill. Cut each layer in half horizontally. Place one layer on serving plate. Spread with 1/3 cup jam, leaving 1/2 in border. Speed 1/2 cup lemon curd over jam. Top with another cake layer and repeat until remaining stuff is gone. Spread top and side of cake with left-over whipping cream. Top with raspberries. Refrigerate until ready to serve.

# Your Journal Entry

*Reba & Marg Boyce*

# Swiss Almond Apple Cake

## Cake

2/3 cup sugar
1/2 cup butter or margarine, softened
2 eggs
2 tbs. lemon juice
2 cups all purpose flour
2 tsp. baking powder
1/4 tsp. salt
1/4 cup blackberry preserves
4 (3 1/2 cups) apples, peeled, thinly sliced

## Topping

1 cup ground almonds
1/2 cup sugar
1/2 cup dairy sour cream
2 eggs, beaten
2 tbs. flour
1 tsp. grated lemon peel

## Glaze

1/4 cup powderd sugar
1 to 2 tsp. lemon juice

Grease and flour 9 or 10-inch springform pan. In large bowl, combine 2/3 cup sugar and butter; beat until light and fluffy. Add 2 eggs and tbs. lemon juice; beat until well blended. In small bowl, combine 2 cups flour, baking powder and salt; blend well. Add to egg mixture; beat at low speed until well blended. Spread in prepared pan. Spoon preserves over batter; carefully spread to cover. Top with apple slices; slightly press into batter. In med. bowl, combine all topping ingredients; blend well. Pour over apples. Bake at 350°for 55 to 65 min. or until apples are tender, edges are light golden brown and toothpick inserted in center comes out clean. Cool 10 min. Carefully remove sides of pan. In small bowl, blend all glaze ingredients until smooth; drizzle over cake. Serve warm or cool.

# Your Journal Entry

*When you get in a jam, who better than friends?*

Insert
your own...

...family favorites!

From the kitchen of:_____

# Encore

*T*ake a minute
to send in your
favorite recipe,
photo or story
to Holleeberry's
for our encore
performance!

Even before the
Jam Journal was
finished we were
contemplating our
next adventure.
We are looking
forward to the
stories and flavors
from your lives
as we prepare
The Holiday Journal.

*A*pplause only!
Go around the
table and have
each person sing
their favorite
cowboy song!
When they finsh
yell ENCORE!!

*L*ife is short!

*Serve dessert first!*

Preserving the fruits of time

# Blueberry Pear Cream Cheese Crisp

2 cups quick oats uncooked
1 cup flour
1/3 cup sugar
1/3 cup packed brown sugar
1/2 cup margarine melted
2 8 oz. cream cheese

1/2 cup sugar
2 eggs 2 tbs. lemon juice
1 tbs. grated lemon peel
2 pears, peeled, cored, sliced, halved
8 oz. jar blueberry jam

Preheat oven to 325°. Mix together oats, flour, 1/3 cup sugar, and brown
sugar in med. mixing bowl. Stir in margarine. Reserve 1 cup oat mixture
for topping. Put remaining in bottom of 13x9 inch pan and press firmly.
Bake for 10 minutes. Beat cream cheese and 1/2 cup sugar in
large mixing bowl on med. speed until well mixed. Add eggs, one at a time,
mixing well in between each egg. Blend in lemon juice and peel;
pour over crust. Layer pears evenly over cream cheese mixture; top
with blueberry jam. Sprinkle with oat mixture. Bake for 45 minutes.
Serve warm with ice cream.

# Your Journal Entry

# Blueberry Pizza

## Filling

2 cup cool whip
1 cup powdered sugar
1 8 oz. cream cheese
1 8 oz. jar blueberry jam

## Crust

1/2 cup margarine
1/4 cup powdered sugar
1 cup flour

Mix crust ingredients and pat well into a greased round pizza pan. Bake for 15 min. at 325°. Let cool for two hours. Beat powdered sugar and cream cheese; fold into cool whip and spread over crust. Top with jam and chill.

# Your Journal Entry

# Danish Raspberry Ribbons

1 cup butter
1/2 cup sugar
1 large egg
2 tbs. milk
2 tbs vanilla
1/4 tsp. almond extract
2 2/3 cups flour
6 tbs. seedless raspberry jam

**Glaze**
1/2 cup powdered sugar
1 tsp. milk
1 tsp. vanilla

Beat together butter and sugar in large bowl on med. speed. Beat in egg, milk, vanilla, and almond extract. Gradually add 1 1/2 cups flour. Beat at low speed until well blended. Stir in enough remaining flour to form stiff dough. Form dough into disc: wrap in plastic wrap and refrigerate until firm, about 30 minutes. Preheat oven to 375°. Cut dough into 6 equal pieces. Rewrap 3 dough pieces and return to fridge. With floured hands, shape into 12 in. long 3/4 inch thick ropes. Place ropes 2 inches apart on cookie sheets. Make lengthwise groove down center of each rope with handle of wooden spoon or finger. Bake for 12 minutes. Remove from oven; spoon 1 tbs. jam into each groove. Return to oven; bake 5 to 7 minutes longer or until strips are golden. Cool for 15 minutes on cookie sheet. Prepare Glaze. Drizzle over each strip.

# Your Journal Entry

# Dessert Quesadillas

6-6 inch flour tortillas
2 ozs. swiss cheese, shredded
1-3 oz. package cream cheese
1/4 cup apricot jam
1 1.5 oz. bars milk chocolate, broken
cooking oil, or nonstick spray

Brush one side of tortilla with cooking oil, or spray with nonstick cooking spray. Stir together swiss cheese and cream cheese; spread evenly over un-oiled side of 3 tortillas. Top with jam and chocolate pieces. Top with remaining tortillas oiled side up. Heat a heavy skillet or griddle over med. heat. Cook quesadillas, one at a time, about 1-2 minutes per side until chocolate is melted. Cut each quesadilla into four wedges.

# Your Journal Entry

*Nancy Boyce*

# Raspberry Triangles

1 cup flour
1/8 tsp. baking powder
1/2 cup unsalted butter
1/2 cup nonfat ricotta cheese
1/4 cup + 2 tbs. seedless raspberry jam
1 large egg, beaten

Whisk together the flour and baking powder in a small mixing bowl. In another bowl, cream the butter with mixer at low speed. Add the ricotta cheese and mix until well blended. Add the flour mixture and stir with wooden spoon to form a dough. Wrap the dough in wax paper and refrigerate for 1 hour. Preheat oven to 425°. Divide the dough in half. Rewrap half and return it to fridge. On work surface that has been lined with wax paper and lightly floured, roll out the other half to a thickness of 1/8 inch, shaping it into a 10 x 7 1/2 inch rectangle. Cut it into 12, 2 1/2 inch squares. Put 3/4 tsp. jam in the bottom left-hand corner of each square. Moisten the edges with water. Fold the top right-hand corner over the filling to create a triangle and crimp the edges closed. Make a deep 3/4 inch long slit in top of each one. Repeat with other half of dough. Brush cookies with the beaten egg and bake for 10 minutes until lightly browned.

# Your Journal Entry

*Our son Kyle*

# Strawberry Heavenly Hash

Thoughts...

What did one Strawberry say to the other?

How did we end up in this Jam?

1 pkg. (3 oz.) vanilla pudding
1 1/2 cups milk
1/2 cup strawberry jam
1 cup heavy cream, whipped
3/4 cup pineapple tidbits
1/2 cup miniature marshmallows
1/4 cup diced maraschino cherries, well drained

Prepare pudding according to pkg. directions using 1 1/2 cups milk. Pour into a bowl; place plastic wrap directly on pudding. Chill. Blend strawberry jam into chilled pudding. Gently fold in remaining ingredients. Spoon into dessert dishes. Chill, garnish with additional whipped cream and a whole maraschino cherry. Makes 6 servings.

# Your Journal Entry

*Glenn "3"*

# Strawberry Rhubarb Swirls

3/4 cup unsalted butter
4 ozs. nonfat cream cheese
1/4 cup non-fat liquid egg substitute
1 3/4 cup flour
3/4 cup strawberry rhubarb jam

Cream butter and cream cheese in bowl on low speed. Add the liquid egg and beat at med. speed until mixture is smooth. Beat in flour at low speed to form dough. Gather the dough into a ball, wrap it in wax paper, and refrigerate for at least 2 hours. Preheat oven to 350.° Lightly coat cookie sheets with light vegatable oil cooking spray, spreading the oil evenly over the surface. Cover a work surface with a sheet of wax paper and lightly flour. Divide dough in half. Roll half into 1/8 inch thick rectangle measuring about 9 x 12 inches. Spread 6 tbs. of jam over dough. Starting at a long end, roll the dough up like a jelly roll. Trim the ragged ends and cut the roll into 1/2 inch slices. Transfer the slices to prepared cookie sheets. Repeat with remaining dough. Bake for 18 - 20 minutes, until lightly browned. Any jam could work with this.

*Greg & Jay*
*owners of "Curtells Bakery"*

# Wild Blueberry Gelato

2 cups blueberries
1/4 cup blueberry jam
1/4 cup water
1/4 tsp. salt
2/3 cup sugar
3 large egg yolks
2 cups milk
2 tsp. lemon juice

In med. saucepan, mix together blueberries, jam, water, & salt. Bring to a boil and reduce heat to med. Cook for 10 min. Put in blender, process until smooth. Beat sugar and egg yolk in a large bowl with a whisk until thick and pale. Heat milk over med.-high heat in small saucepan until slightly boiling around edges. Don't let it come to a full boil. Add 1/3 hot milk to sugar mixture stirring with whisk. Slowly add remaining hot milk stirring constantly. Cook over med. heat until mixture coats back of spoon. Remove from heat. Stir in blueberry mixture and cool completely. Stir in juice. Pour mixture into freezer can of an ice cream freezer.

# Your Journal Entry

*Craig "7"*

Insert
your own...

...family favorites!

From the kitchen of: _____

*Be part of the new and exciting*

# Holiday Journal

### *The next in our captivating and tasty series of cookbook journals.*

### *The Holiday Journal will be a collection of holiday traditions, stories and flavors to be shared with friends, new and old.*

Do you have a recurring story told 'round the table at Thanksgiving, or maybe a special place your family goes to celebrate Independence Day, maybe it's a recipe that just says Happy St. Patricks Day?

Join us in celebrating the holidays by sending in your favorite holiday story or tradition along with any time tested recipe or picture representing your story or tradition to:

### Holleeberry's
### P.O. Box 701963
### West Valley City, UT 84170-1963

*\*Please make sure to include all necessary information in the recipe!*

Visit us at
www.holleeberrys.com